Sanskrit Studies

Vol. 3, Saṁvat 2069-70

(CE 2013-14)

Sanskrit Studies

Vol. 3, Saṁvat 2069-70

(CE 2013-14)

Edited by

Shashiprabha Kumar

Special Centre for Sanskrit Studies
Jawaharlal Nehru University
New Delhi

in association with

D.K. Printworld (P) Ltd.
New Delhi

Cataloging in Publication Data – DK
[Courtesy: D.K. Agencies (P) Ltd. <docinfo@dkagencies.com>]

Sanskrit studies, vol. 3, Saṁvat 2069-70 (CE 2013-14) /
edited by Shashiprabha Kumar.
p. cm.
Includes bibliographical references.
ISBN 13: 978-81-246-0741-1

1. Sanskrit philology – Study and teaching. I. Kumāra, Śaśiprabhā, 1951- II. Jawaharlal Nehru University. Special Centre for Sanskrit Studies.

DDC 491.2071 23

ISBN 13: 978-81-246-0741-1
First published in India in 2014

Published by:
Special Centre for Sanskrit Studies
Jawaharlal Nehru University
New Delhi - 110 067

in association with

D.K. Printworld (P) Ltd.
Regd. Office : *Vedaśrī*, F-395, Sudarshan Park
(Metro Station: Ramesh Nagar), New Delhi - 110 015
Phones : (011) 2545 3975; 2546 6019; *Fax* : (011) 2546 5926
e-mail : indology@dkprintworld.com
Web : www.dkprintworld.com

Printed by: D.K. Printworld (P) Ltd., New Delhi

Key to Transliteration

VOWELS

अ *a* (but)	आ *ā* (palm)	इ *i* (it)	ई *ī* (beet)	उ *u* (put)	ऊ *ū* (pool)
ऋ *ṛ* (rhythm)	ए *e* (play)	ऐ *ai* (air)	ओ *o* (toe)	औ *au* (loud)	

CONSONANTS

Guttural	क *ka* (skate)	ख* *kha* (blockhead)	ग *ga* (gate)	घ *gha* (ghost)	ङ *ṅa* (sing)
Palatal	च *ca* (chunk)	छ* *cha* (catch him)	ज *ja* (john)	झ *jha* (hedgehog)	ञ *ña* (bunch)
Lingual	ट *ṅa* (start)	ठ* *ṭha* (anthill)	ड *ḍa* (dart)	ढ* *ḍha* (godhead)	ण* *ṇa* (under)
Dental	त *ta* (path)	थ *tha* (thunder)	द *da* (that)	ध* *dha* (breathe)	न *na* (numb)
Labial	प *pa* (spin)	फ* *pha* (philosophy)	ब *ba* (bin)	भ *bha* (abhor)	म *ma* (much)
Others	य *ya* (young)	र *ra* (drama)	ल *la* (luck)	व *va* (vile)	
	श *śa* (shove)	ष *ṣa* (bushel)	य *sa* (so)	ह *ha* (hum)	
	क्ष *kṣa* (*kṣatriya*)	त्र *tra* (*trishūl*)	ज्ञ *jña* (*jñāni*)	ळ* ḷ (*play*)	ॠ* *ṝ*

अं (–̇) *ṁ anusvāra* (nasalization of preceding vowel) like *saṁskṛti*
अः *ḥ* (*prātaḥ*) *ḥ visarga* (aspiration of preceding vowel)
ऽ 'Avagraha' = consonant #'consonant (like:- *ime 'vasthitā*)
ँ (*guṁ*) = ँ
Anusvàra at the end of line is presented by म् = m (not ṁ)

* No exact English equivalents for these letters.

Editorial

It is with a sense of joy and gratification that the third volume of *Sanskrit Studies* is being presented to the readers after a gap of almost six years, which was mainly caused due to the non-availability of funds for publication during the XIth Plan.

The first two volumes of *Sanskrit Studies* published in the guidance of two great scholars as guest editors have charted a roadmap before us and it is hoped that the present volume will be able to follow the path shown by them.

Sanskrit Studies is a vast and variegated discipline which covers language and literature, grammar and historical linguistics, sources of history and systems of philosophy, principles of poetics and details of dramaturgy, lexicography, palaeography and manuscriptology, subtleties of Indian social thought and prudence of legal provisions, medical wisdom, environmental consciousness and scientific awareness in Sanskrit literature, vision of Vedic texts and varieties of Vedic traditions besides Buddhist canon, including Pāli texts as also different versions of Prākr̥t language and the emerging field of computational linguistics. The Special Centre for Sanskrit Studies at Jawaharlal Nehru University (JNU) is dealing with all these diverse areas so as to foster the multi-disciplinary approach in Sanskrit studies.

The volume in hand has been prepared to cover as many areas of Sanskrit studies as possible. This has been made possible as a result of generous co-operation by several scholars: young and old, as also from within the country and abroad. Accordingly the first article by Miquel Peralta, a young scholar from Spain discusses "The Theory of Oral Composition and the Veda" in general while the next paper by Prof. Madhav Deshpande, an eminent grammarian, deals with a specific topic, namely "The Yājuṣa Hautra Dispute in Early Modern Maharashtra". In the next paper Prof. R. Balasubramanian, a very senior philosopher, has explained "Hermeneutics of the Upaniṣads" and Dr M.K. Byrski, a renowned Indologist from Poland, has dwelt upon the concept of "Dharma: Integrating Factor of Consciousness and Science" in his paper.

Besides the above-mentioned articles on Veda and Vedic ideas, there are contributions on various other aspects of Sanskrit learning. Prof. Radhavallabh Tripathi has depicted the "Aesthetic Universe of Bharta's Nāṭyaśāstra" and Prof. C. Rajendran has expounded "Kālidāsa's Cultural Geography of India" through his narration of the nation. "History and Background of the Sanskrit Commentary-tradition" has been discussed in detail by Prof. Uma C. Vaidya in her paper while Prof. Subhash Kak, the acclaimed mathematician, has written at length on "Archaeoastronomy in India".

Next four papers of this volume focus mainly on Indian Logic – Prof. Kisor K. Chakrabarti enunciates the "Universal Premise in Early Nyāya", Prof. Stephen H. Phillips in his paper titled "Gaṅgeśa on Showing Inference Failure" has translated with comments the "Asādhakatā-Sādhakatva-Prakaraṇam from the Tattvacintāmaṇi" of Gaṅgeśa Upādhyāya; Prof. Toshihiro Wada's paper represents the fourth and final part of his translation with annotation of "Ākhyātavāda" from the same text; Dr Katsunori Hirano has written "On the Concept of Ayutasiddha in the Definition of Inherence". In the next article, Prof. Purushottama Bilimoria has elaborated on "Mantric Effect, Effervescent Devatās, Noetic Supplications and Apūrva in the Mīmāṁsā".

In addition to these, there is an invaluable paper of Dr

Lokesh Chandra on "Translation as the Cultural Space of Tibetan". Prof. S. Revathy has discussed "Sanskrit and Tamil Interrelation".

In short, the fifteen articles collected herein represent the richness and rigour of Sanskrit studies in contemporary times across the world. It is hoped that the volume will provide an enlightening as well as enjoyable reading to all those who are interested in Sanskrit studies.

Shashiprabha Kumar

Acknowledgement

First of all, I am indebted to Prof. S.K. Sopory, Vice-Chancellor and other officials at JNU for sanctioning a grant and facilitating publication of this volume.

I am obliged to all the scholars for their learned contributions without which the task would have remained unfulfilled.

I express my sincere gratitude to Prof. Kapil Kapoor and Dr. Wagish Shukla for their accomplished editorship of the first and second volumes of *Sanskrit Studies*.

I must acknowledge the positive support extended by all my colleagues and students at the Special Centre for Sanskrit Studies, JNU.

Dr. Devendra Singh, currently guest faculty at SCSS, deserves due credit for helping in proofreading and preparing the press copy.

Finally, I must thank Shri Susheel K. Mittal of D.K. Printworld for his keen interest and unfailing effort in ensuring quality of production and timely publication of this volume.

Contents

1

The Theory of Oral Composition and the Veda

Miquel Peralta

AROUND the beginning of the 1930s, the American scholar Milman Parry, then just a doctoral candidate, wrote a dissertation that revolutionized the field of classical studies with a radically new analysis of the Greek epics. In Parry's view, the works of Homer contained enough internal evidence to firmly establish the fact that they were the works of an oral poet. In other words, he sustained that Homer did not know how to write. Needless to say that in a society that equates the possession of the technique of writing with the implementation of rational processes, Parry's hypothesis provoked quite an uproar. Nevertheless, since Parry's bold theorizing, many academic authors – and even non-scholarly figures such as the German writer Hans Magnus Enzensberger[1] – have shown that literacy does not *per se* imply rationality and, conversely, that orality does not have to be equated by any means with simple or undeveloped thought.

Besides the fact that they engaged the whole field of

---

1 See his harsh criticism of alphabetization in the essay "Lob des Analphabetentums", belonging to the collection *Mittelmass und Wahn*, Suhrkamp: Frankfurt am Main, 1988. See also the article by the late UCLA professor William Bright "Le virtù dell'analfabetismo", in La Ricerca Folklorica (Milan) 5.15-19.

classical studies in a radically new development, Parry's ideas elicited the appearance of a vast amount of papers and monographs that tried to apply his insights to other traditions. In the words of John Miles Foley, a leading scholar in the field of the oral tradition in literature:

> Thanks to that research . . . we recognize that stories and histories as vital to our civilization as the biblical gospels, Old Testament Scriptures, . . . and most of the early literary works of the European nations have their roots in oral tradition.[2]

Indeed, a plethora of studies encompassing as many as ninety national literatures showed the relevance of Parry's new conceptual framework beyond the bounded area of classical studies.

Which were then Parry's ideas, to which developments did they lead, and what relevance may they have in the field of Vedic studies? The late Walter J. Ong who elaborated in his works what he calls "the psychodynamics of orality", an enormously fruitful concept to which we shall return later, summarizes Parry's main idea saying that "the fundamental axiom governing his thought [points to] the dependence of the choice of words and word-forms on the shape of the (orally composed) verse line".[3] In other words, that "virtually every distinctive feature of [this] poetry is due to the economy enforced on it by oral methods of composition".[4] This point of view introduces a whole new way of considering matters in any tradition either totally oral or with roots in orality. It is an approach which implies, for instance, that "the use of a given epithet is determined not by its precise meaning so much as by the metrical needs of the passage in which it turned

[2] *Oral Tradition in Literature*, p. 1.

[3] *Orality and Literacy*, p. 20.

[4] Ibid., p. 21.

up".[5] In this sense, Parry coins the concept of "ornamental adjective". He contends against "the modern notion that epithets are summoned only or chiefly for their situation-specific applicability and contends in favour of the view that they serve in the role of a metrical convenience".[6] The needs of the metrical structure, then, impose a "selection process" on words that favours, precisely, the alternatives that will give a satisfactory rendition of the verse over other possibilities perhaps more adequate to the ideal semantic value in a given passage. This fact has consequences on the characteristics of vocabulary – to cite now just a relevant point – since old words or out of use expressions will tend to be kept in the language if they are – or have been – of any help in easing the verbal discourse into the required verse structure.

Parry's approach led to what has been called "the formulaic system", which he defined as "a group of phrases which have the same metrical value and which are enough alike in thought and words to leave no doubt that the poet who used them . . . knew them as formulas of a certain type".[7] Foley warns us that Parry was not advocating "a memorized list of expressions as the elements that comprise a formulaic system", a criticism that Parry's detractors have often put forward. On the contrary, he was actually postulating "a category of related phrases which the poet 'knows', in the same way that one 'knows' a language and is, therefore, able to use it fluently".[8] A last quote by Parry will further clarify the concept. In his *Studies in the Epic Technique of Oral Verse-Making*, he asserts:

> Without writing, the poet can make his verses only if he has a formulaic [style] which will give him his verses all made,

5 *Orality and Literacy*, p. 21.

6 *The Theory of Oral Composition*, p. 22.

7 *The Making of Homeric Verse*, p. 257.

8 *Oral Tradition in Literature*, p. 118.

> and made in such a way that, at the slightest bidding of the poet, they will link themselves in an unbroken pattern that will fill his verses and make his sentences.[9]

One could then summarize Parry's insights in the following points: First, a new appraisal of the limitations that form imposes on the expression of thought; second, the presence of the ornamental adjective; third, the conservation of fossilized expressions over time; fourth, the role of metrical convenience; and last, the "economy" of a given phraseology.

Could Parry's approach be of use in the analysis of the Vedic hymns? Parry's ideas implied that, in one sense or another, the verses were composed *in performance*. In fact, Parry's untimely death in 1935 left for his close collaborator Alfred Lord to check the appropriateness of Parry's ideas in the still surviving world of south-Slavic oral poets. Lord's results were first published in his book *The Singer of Tales*, a work which is considered the bible of Oral Theory. Lord's study corroborated in a still-living tradition the results arrived at by Parry with a strictly theoretical methodology.

Therefore, Parry's approach is definitely one of the possible scenarios that one can come across when working with oral or oral-related materials. But is it the only possible alternative? We could pose, with Lord, the following question:

> We know that oral poetries exist elsewhere. Do they follow the same laws of composition and transmission?[10]

The British anthropologist Ruth Finnegan, who has developed an important part of her work in Africa, states clearly:

> It is just not true empirically that oral literary forms are always composed-in-performance. There are a number of

[9] *The Making of Homeric Verse*, p. 317.

[10] "Perspectives on Recent Work on Oral Literature", p. 190, in *Forum for Modern Language Studies*, vol. X, no. 3, July 1974.

> known cases of composition *before* performance and of instances where, . . . memorization rather than improvization is in fact involved.[11]

It is clear that the case of the Vedic hymns would fall in the memorization instances that Finnegan refers to. In this sense, the process of Vedic transmission, as we know it, would plainly deny Parry's hypothesis, corroborated by Lord in the Slavic tradition. On close inspection, though, the question offers many nuances that seem worth exploring.

For one, the complex system devised in order to guarantee verbatim transmission in the case of Vedic hymns is in itself a proof that when creative materials are involved, if one wants stability through the centuries, plain memorization will just not do: verbatim transmission needs a special technique. The converse, then, will also hold true: unless one wants verbatim transmission, it is more efficient to devise a different technique which allows the *oral* poet to present his verses in a fluid way. This technique could very well be the technique described by Parry and Lord or, at least, it could incorporate many of the technical resources that they describe. Could it be possible to find traces of these techniques in the Vedic hymns? There is certainly nothing against it, since the fact that from a certain point onwards the hymns were transmitted verbatim does not preclude the possibility that their authors went through a certain amount of experimentation – possibly in performance, or in an improvisatory milieu – until they found a final satisfactory version of their works.

A possible instance of the approach that this kind of analysis has to offer could be sketched concerning the always thorny matter of semantic precision. In her detailed study of the linguistic features of the Vedic hymns *The Language and*

---

[11] *The Oral and Beyond*, p. 107.

Style of the Vedic Rsis, the late Russian scholar Tatyana Elizarenkova asserts:

> The vocabulary of *R̥gveda* is characterized by both polysemy and synonymy.[12]

In other words, a single concept can be expressed by many terms and, conversely, a single term can express many concepts. Further ahead she adds: "The metaphorical transfer of meanings occurs so frequently that the borderline between polysemy and homonymy almost disappears",[13] and at a later point she acknowledges that in some extreme cases "polysemy borders . . . even on enantiosemy",[14] that is to say on instances where one sense of a word is in some respect the opposite of another of its senses. Could this situation concerning R̥gvedic vocabulary be related – if not caused – by what Parry calls "the role of metrical convenience"? If a sufficient amount of these occurrences where the categories of polysemy, homonymy and enantiosemy seem somewhat blurred in the case of a given term could be shown to happen at metrically relevant spots, then it would become clear that at those points, "the limitations that form imposes", have the upper hand "on the expression of thought" and therefore it would become also clear that – in those cases – trying to find an absolutely precise semantic contour of the term discussed is not an adequate philological strategy.

This is but one example of the kind of approach with which the ideas of the Oral Composition Theory can contribute to open new paths of interpretation in the field of Vedic studies. Other possibilities include the description of the possible formulas and repeated epithets, or the analysis of metrical

---

12 *The Language and Style of the Vedic R̥ṣis*, p. 29.

13 Ibid., p. 31.

14 Ibid., p. 40.

faults as a side effect to the "joining of formulas which do not fit".[15]

At any rate, the developments of the Theory of Oral Composition offer a set of ideas that put into value the priorities of the oral poet – in our case the Vedic poet – which could broadly differ from our own expectations, fashioned in an age where the written word has gained an almost absolute pre-eminence over the spoken word.

There is still another area where the new interest in orality shown by Western scholars in the last forty to fifty years can be of interest for the adequate appraisal of the Vedic literature. The general line of reasoning would go as follows: since any work created under the conditions of a primarily oral culture will be generated in a milieu determined by the psychodynamics of orality, "the circumstances of performance, the composition, and the transmission of oral versus written materials are sufficiently distinct *so as to postulate separate hermeneutics*", as we are reminded by Werner Kelber, an American scholar whose work centres on the impact of oral tradition in the Christian Gospels. Which are, then, these "psychodynamics of orality"? In his work *Orality and Literacy*, published in 1982, Walter Ong elaborates on the characteristics of orally-based thought and expression and finds that in an oral culture, thought and expression tend to be of the following sorts: additive rather than subordinative; aggregative rather than analytic; redundant or "copious"; conservative or traditionalist; close to the human lifeworld; agonistically toned; empathetic rather than objectively distanced, tending to equilibrium in the present; and situational rather than abstract. Although Ong does not work on the implications of his list in the hermeneutical sense, everyone of these characteristics points to an aspect of what can be termed as "poetics of

[15] *The Making of Homeric Verse*, p. 342.

orality", taking the term "poetics" as defined in the following manner by Tzvetan Todorov:

> In contradistinction to the interpretation of particular works, the discipline of *poetics* does not seek to name meaning, but aims at a knowledge of the general laws that preside over the birth of each work.[16]

In this sense and in correlation with the characteristics of oral psychodynamics enumerated by Walter Ong, a tentative body of "general laws", as Todorov puts it, that could help delineate a "poetics of orality", can be summarized as follows:

1. The use of aggregative structures instead of subordinative is not a demerit. As Ong puts it:

   > Written discourse develops more elaborate and fixed grammar than oral discourse does because to provide meaning it is more dependent simply upon linguistic structure, since it lacks the normal full existential contexts which surround oral discourse and help determine meaning in oral discourse somewhat independently of grammar.[17]

2. In orality, the mode of expression tends to clusters of items, such as parallel terms, antithetical terms and epithets. These aggregations tend to be the standard, "once a formulary expression has crystallized, it had best be kept intact".[18] In an oral milieu, the amount of originality has to be kept in check:

   > Traditional expressions must not be dismantled: it has been hard work getting them together over the generations, and there is nowhere outside the mind to store them.[19]

---

[16] *Introduction to Poetics*, p. 6.

[17] *Orality and Literacy*, p. 38.

[18] Ibid., p. 39.

[19] Ibid.

In an oral aesthetics, originality is definitely not a desideratum.

3. Any modern author would shun repetition as boring or cumbersome (unless it is aimed at a particular aesthetic effect). In orality, though, repetition is a must for several reasons. In oral discourse, "the mind must move ahead more slowly, keeping close to the focus of attention much of what it has already dealt with. Redundancy, . . . keeps both speaker and hearer surely on the track".[20] A listener cannot "turn back the page" if he or she has lost track. They need to be constantly reminded of what is being dealt with. Repetition is a natural process of oral noetic processes, of oral processes of intellectual apprehension.
4. The conservative trend of oral societies generates less individually marked styles. The oral poet gathers traditional elements and in its milieu will never be accused of lack of novelty. Parry illustrated this point saying that the poet has "less freedom of choice". Of course, oral cultures "do not lack originality of their own kind", but "formulas and themes are reshuffled rather than supplanted with new materials".[21] Authorship as we know it in the modern era does not exist in oral tradition. Poets composing in an oral tradition owe a great deal to the generations of poets that preceded them.[22] Lord stresses this point in a way which can be directly related to the Vedic materials:

> The tenacity of tradition does not spring . . . from an abstract principle of absolute art, but from a compelling conviction that what the tradition is

---

20 *Orality and Literacy*, p. 40.

21 Ibid., p. 41.

22 *Oral Tradition in Literature*, p. 8.

> preserving is the very means of attaining life and happiness. The traditional . . . oral singer is not an artist, he is a seer.[23]

This idea has a strong connection with the following point.

5. Writing can elaborate analytic categories to structure knowledge that will be distanced from the living experience. Oral cultures must conceptualize all their knowledge with close reference to the human lifeworld, assimilating the objective world to the more familiar interaction of human beings.[24] In an oral medium poetry has a utilitarian aspect, the aesthetic elements will not be found isolated in a "pure artistic experience". As Ong reminds us: "an oral culture has no vehicle so neutral as a list".[25] When a list is needed, it will be presented as a part of the poetic discourse.
6. "Orality situates knowledge within a context of struggle." It tends to "engage others in verbal and intellectual combat".[26] Vituperation and praise-poems belong to this tenet of orality. Once again, aesthetic elements will amalgamate with structures that tend to reflect everyday life.
7. In one of his works devoted to the rise of Greek literacy, the British classicist Eric Havelock notes:

> For an oral culture, learning or knowing means achieving close, empathetic, communal identification with the known.[27]

---

23 Cited in *The Theory of Oral Composition*, p. 44.

24 *Orality and Literacy*, p. 42.

25 Ibid.

26 Ibid., p. 44.

27 *Preface to Plato*, p. 145.

In an oral culture, one does not approach a work with a sense of personal disengagement or distancing. Any aesthetic consideration based on this attitude, then, will fail to address the work in its own terms.

8. Oral societies live in a present which keeps itself in equilibrium or homeostasis by abandoning memories which no longer have present relevance.[28] In an oral culture, the meaning of each word is controlled by what Jack Woody in his essay "The Consequences of Literacy"[29] calls "direct semantic ratification". The consequence for a characterization of oral poetics is clear: meaning is not decided by definitions in a dictionary but by a complex interplay of "gestures, vocal inflections, facial expression and the entire human, existential setting in which the real, spoken word always occurs".[30] Aesthetic appraisal based on a text will fall short of the true nature of the work.

9. "Oral cultures tend to use concepts in situational, operational frames of reference that are minimally abstract, in the sense that they remain close to the living human lifeworld."[31] The meaning of many terms, then, is regulated not by abstract concepts but rather by situational experiences which the listeners share. Meaning is attached to a situation rather than a concept. This last point makes clear the extent to which we are helpless in trying to determine meanings through chains of comparative abstractions, the standard method of Western philology.

---

[28] *Orality and Literacy*, p. 46.

[29] Ibid., p. 29.

[30] Ibid., p. 47.

[31] Ibid., p. 49.

In the short span of this paper we have been able to ascertain that the Theory of Oral Composition can furnish new ideas to tackle many technical questions posed by the Vedic hymns. In a second area, related to the aesthetic appraisal of these works, the vast corpus of studies which centres on the psychodynamics of orality and the consequences of literacy have been shown to be of great help when trying to establish the basic trends of an aesthetic appraisal which strives to free itself from the prejudices of the chyrographic and typographic culture in which we are immersed.

References

Bright, William, *Le virtù dell'analfabetismo,* La ricerca folklorica (Milan), **5**: 15-19.

Elizarenkova, Tatyana, *The Language and Style of the Vedic R̥ṣis,* Chicago: University of Chicago Press, 2007.

Enzensberger, Hans Magnus, *Mittlemass und Wahn,* Suhrkamp: Frankfurt am Main, 1988.

Finnegan, Ruth, *The Oral and Beyond,* Chicago: University of Chicago Press, 2007.

Foley, John Miles, *Oral Tradition in Literature,* Columbia: University of Missouri Press, 1986.

———, *The Theory of Oral Composition,* Bloomington: Indiana University Press, 1988.

Havelock, Eric, *Preface to Plato,* Cambridge: Belknap Press, 1963.

Lord, Albert, "Perspectives on Recent Work on Oral Literature", *Forum for Modern Language Studies,* vol. **X**(3), July 1974.

Ong, Walter J., *Orality and Literacy,* London and New York: Routledge, 2002.

Parry, Milman, *The Making of Homeric Verse,* Oxford: Clarendon Press, 1971.

Todorov, Tzvetan, *Introduction to Poetics,* Minneapolis: University of Minnesota Press, 1981.

2

The Yājuṣa Hautra Dispute in Early Modern Maharashtra

Madhav M. Deshpande

Abstract

During the eighteenth and nineteenth centuries, a particular dispute occupied the Brāhmanical community in Maharashtra. This dispute is generally labeled Yājuṣa Hautra Dispute in the available literature. The dispute hinges on the fact that *Taittirīya Saṁhitā* (*TS*) contains the Hautra *mantras* for sacrifices up to, but not including the Soma sacrifice. The Vaidika priests who were trained in the Taittirīya branch were naturally capable of themselves performing the function of Hotṛ for some sacrifices, but not for others. This created a situation where the Ṛgvedins of Maharashtra claimed that they alone should be entitled to the office of Hotṛ for all sacrifices, while the Taittirīyas claimed that they needed the Ṛgvedins only where the Taittirīya texts did not provide the *mantras* for the Hotṛ. This dispute was discussed, debated, and variously resolved by different authors of the period. There were also eye-witness reports of actual local conflicts and news reports from various parts of Maharashtra. There was obviously more than ritual function at stake. The dispute also had economic consequences that were noted by some contemporary reports. This paper surveys the available information on this dispute and analyses this dispute for its wider implications for the construction of the Śākhā texts and the goals of the Śākhā communities.

WHILE editing and interpreting an eighteenth/nineteenth-century text titled *Vedavicāra* ascribed to Śāmaśāstri Draviḍa Dvivedī, I came across the following discussion:

यजुर्भिन्नेतरशाखिनामेव यजुर्वेदापेक्षत्वात्। ननु वाजसनेयिनां मैत्रायणीयानां वा तैत्तिरीयापेक्षा तैत्तिरीयाणां वा तयोरपेक्षेति। अत्रोच्यते। भवतु तैत्तिरीयाणां सोमयागादर्वागितरानपेक्षा। तेषां स्वशाखायामेव सर्वश्रौतस्मार्तमन्त्राणां विद्यमानत्वात्। तैत्तिरीयभिन्नानां वाजसनेयिनां मैत्रायणीयाणां च ऋक्सामाथर्ववेदिनामिव तैत्तिरीयापेक्षाऽस्त्येव। तयोरपि शाखयोर्यावदपेक्षित-श्रौतस्मार्तमन्त्राभावात्। ननु तयोः शाखयोर्यजुर्वेदत्वाद्दर्शपूर्णमासादयः सर्वे क्रतव आम्नाता एव। कुतस्तयोरपि शाखयोस्तैत्तिरीयापेक्षेति। न चैवमुचितम्। यद्यपि निरुभा दर्शपूर्णमासादयोऽश्वमेधान्तास्तयोः शाखयोराम्नातास्तथापि तद्विकृतयः स्वर्गसत्रनक्षत्रसत्रादयोऽन्ये च बहवः काम्याः पशवो बह्वचः काम्येष्टयश्च नाम्नाताः किं च प्रकृतिभूता अपि सावित्रनाचिकेतादयश्चितयोऽपि। निरुभानुष्ठानसिद्ध्यर्थं तयोरपि शाखयोस्तैत्तिरीयापेक्षा। किं चाद्यापि शिष्टा आहिताग्नयो वाजसनेयिनो मैत्रायणीयाश्च तैत्तिरीयशाखोभं स्वर्गसत्रादिकमनुतिष्ठन्ति तथा स्मार्तमपि सन्ध्यावन्दनादिकं कूश्माण्डगणहोमोदकशान्त्यादिकं सर्वेऽप्यनुतिष्ठन्त्येव। किं बहुना सर्वैरपेक्षणीयां तैत्तिरीयशाखामनादृत्य ब्राह्मणत्वावच्छेदेनाकरणे प्रत्यवायजनकानि नित्यानि प्रतिदिनं विहितानि षट्कर्माण्यपि न सिध्यन्ति।

Only the Vedic traditions other than *Yajurveda* are dependent upon *Yajurveda* [for the completion of their ritual, while *Yajurveda* does not depend upon others]. Now [among the branches of *Yajurveda*], do the Vājasaneyins and Maitrāyaṇīyas depend upon the Taittirīyas, or do the Taittirīyas depend upon these two? Here we say the following. The Taittirīyas do not depend upon other [Vedic branches] up to the [prescriptions for] the Soma sacrifice, because all the required Śrauta and Smārta *mantra*s are found in their own [Taittirīya] branch. But, like [the dependence of] the Ṛgvedins and the Atharvavedins [upon the Taittirīyas], the other schools of *Yajurveda*, namely the Vājasaneyins and the Maitrāyaṇīyas, do depend upon the Taittirīyas.

> But those two branches [of *Yajurveda*] do have prescriptions for all sacrifices like Darśa and Paurṇamāsa. Then why do they need to depend upon the Taittirīyas?
>
> This is not correct. Even though sacrifices ranging from Darśapaurṇamāsa to Aśvamedha are described in these two branches, they do not describe the modified sacrifices like the Svargasattra and the Nakṣatrasattra, nor many *kāmya* animal sacrifices and *kāmya iṣṭi*s, nor do they describe even the basic [*prakṛti*] sacrificial rites like the Sāvitraciti and Nāciketaciti. For the performance of these sacrificial rites, these two branches do depend upon the Taittirīyas. Moreover, to this day, learned Āhitāgnis from the Vājasaneyī and the Maitrāyaṇīya branches carry out rites like the Svargasattra as prescribed by the Taittirīya branch. Similarly, everyone carries out the Smārta rites [prescribed in the Taittirīya texts] like the evening offering [*sandhyāvandana*] as well as rites like the Kūṣmāṇḍa, Gaṇahoma, and Udakaśānti. Ultimately, by disregarding the Taittirīya branch that everyone needs to depend upon, and [consequently] by not performing [many rites] required of all brāhmaṇas, one cannot carry out even the basic six prescribed obligatory functions, whose non-performance results in sin.

This passage from Śāmaśāstri's *Vedavicāra*, like many other discussions in this text, point to self-perceptions of members of various Vedic traditions about their particular Vedic branch being more complete and independent, and about other branches being less complete and dependent. Such perceptions and consequent measures taken by the various Vedic branches to achieve a degree of completion and independence from others are not new, and may be the background for wholesale incorporations of portions of other traditions into the texts of one's own tradition. Incorporation of a very large number of Ṛgvedic *mantra*s in the twentieth *kāṇḍa* of the *Śaunakīya Atharvaveda* may be an instance of this kind of activity.

In the introduction to his book, *The Vedic Sacrifice in Transition*, Frederick M. Smith (1987: 25, n. 95) briefly refers to this situation:

> Traditionally, ritualists of the Hiraṇyakeśi school have insisted on performing all the [ritual] roles themselves, without requesting the assistance of members of other schools, including the *R̥V* and *SV*, even if they were available. This forced them to learn the ritual of the other schools, and contributed to their sense of community as a *śākhā*. Āp and Hir contain a *yājuṣa hautra* for the Darśapaurṇamāsa (Āp 24.11-24; Hir 21.1-2). These are based on *TB* 3.5, which early on adopted the parts prescribed for the *R̥V* (*hautra* into the *YV*). Much later the Kātyāyana school adopted its own Hautrapariśiṣṭa. In the contemporary performance of Soma sacrifices, which require detailed and highly specialized knowledge of the *R̥V*, *SV*, and *YV*, certain *śākhās* train their own members to recite the necessary texts and perform the rites prescribed in other texts, e.g., the Āpastambins of A.P. perform all the duties of the *R̥V* and *SV*. This is a convenient arrangement because it frees one community from the vacillating fortunes of another. . . . An Āhitāgni in Sangli, Maharashtra, Shankara Vasudeva Natu, a follower of the *Hiraṇyakeśi-Sūtra*, performed a Sarvatomukha Soma sacrifice in 1943. This sacrifice requires sixty-five officiants. He employed other Hiraṇyakeśins, many of them young boys, in order to teach them the ritual, including the *hautra* and *audgātra*, as preserved in the Hiraṇyakeśi tradition.

While Smith's account is informative and seems to assume such practices as a sort of wholesome effort on the part of certain *śākhās*, I want to focus my attention on a number of other sources that indicate that such practices were a result of and creations of a whole world of social and economic rivalry between various *śākhā* communities that led to social strife from time to time, as well as encouraged protagonists of various positions to argue out their ideological stances in published and unpublished booklets of various kind.

TS and *Taittirīya Brāhmaṇa* contain explicit listings of *hautra mantras* for various sacrificial rites. The *Vedavidyā* volume of S.V. Ketkar's *Mahārāṣṭrīya Jñānakośa* (1921: 75ff) contains detailed cataloging of various sacrificial rites and their *hautra* as provided in *Taittirīya Saṁhitā*, under the following headings:

- Kāmya Iṣṭis and their Hautra
- Abhicāraka Iṣṭis and their Hautra
- Cāturmāsya and its Hautra
- Darśapaurṇamāsa and its Hautra
- Nitya and Kāmya Paśu Sacrifices and their Hautra.

This pattern is discontinued with the listing of Soma sacrifices like Agniṣṭoma. So, to sum up the situation, the *hautra* for some sacrifices is directly contained in the Taittirīya texts, while for others it is not. In a preliminary understanding of the Vedic sacrificial performances, one assumes that the roles of Hotṛ, Adhvaryu, Udgātṛ, and Brahmā are to be carried out by priests belonging respectively to *Ṛgveda*, *Yajurveda*, *Sāmaveda*, and *Atharvaveda*. Texts like *Vedavicāra* of Śāmaśāstrī attempt to formalize associations between the various sub-schools of the four Vedas, saying in general that the Gauḍa branches to associate with each other, and the Draviḍa branches should associate with each other. Thus for the region of Maharashtra, we are told that there is a co-operative relationship between the branches of *Śākala Ṛgveda*, *Taittirīya Yajurveda*, *Rāṇāyanīya Sāmaveda*, and *Paippalāda Atharvaveda*. Thus, one would assume that in the region of Maharashtra, the Hotṛ would belong to *Śākala Ṛgveda*, the Adhvaryu to *Taittirīya Yajurveda*, the Udgātṛ to *Rāṇāyanīya Sāmaveda*, and the Brahmā to *Paippalāda Atharvaveda*. Now, given the fact that *TS* explicitly contains *mantras* for the Hotṛ for a number of sacrifices, but not for all, how is the role of the Hotṛ to be determined for a Taittirīya *yajamāna*. Theoretically, we see the following possibilities:

1. One always employs a Śākala Hotṛ, even for a Taittirīya *yajamāna*.
2. One always employs a Taittirīya Hotṛ, offering him additional *ṚV* training where necessary.
3. One employs a Taittirīya Hotṛ for the *hautra* portions contained in *TS*, but then switches to a Śākala Hotṛ for the *hautra* portions not contained in *TS*.
4. One follows one of the above choices admitting a free choice.

These four alternatives help us flush out various aspects of historical narratives of what happened at particular instances of sacrifices, as well as aspects of particular ideological positions. Kashikar (1977: 160ff) provides some useful information regarding the history of opinions relating to the question of *yājuṣa hautra*. He says (1977: 160) that in most of India, the *yājuṣa hautra* is carried out optionally, but in certain parts of Tamil Nadu and Maharashtra, particularly in the localities of Pune, Wai and Sangli, the Taittirīyas carried out the *yājuṣa hautra* without option. However, it was customary in most places that the *hautra* was carried out by a Ṛgvedin beginning with the Soma sacrifices. However, Kashikar refers to some of the differing views. The eighteenth-century commentary *Jyotsnā* by Gopīnātha Oka (CE 1733-83) on the Agniṣṭoma section of *Satyāṣāḍhasūtra* insists on the performance of *yājuṣa hautra*, but it also insists that only a Ṛgvedin Hotṛ must recite the *hautra* in the Soma sacrifice. This view was supported by the Banaras *paṇḍit* Bālaśāstrī Rānaḍe in the nineteenth century. However, the Ṛgvedins held an opposite view. They interpreted the statement of the *Āśvalāyana-Śrauta-Sūtra* 8.13.34:

tad ye kecana chāndogye vādhvaryave vā hautrāmarśāḥ samāmnātā na tān kuryād akṛtsnatvād hautrasya

This was interpreted to mean that the Taittirīyas must not carry out the *hautra* explicitly provided in their own tradition, because it is incomplete, and hence they must employ a Ṛgvedin Hotṛ for the entire function of *hautra*.

The Hiraṇyakeśins argued that this rule of Āśvalāyana refers only to the *hautra* in a *sattra*, and has no general application to all the *hautra* given in *TS*. It is clear that the Ṛgvedins and the Taittirīyas were interpreting different texts to suit their own claims. The incorporation of the Ṛgvedic *hautra mantra*s into the very text of *TS* indicates an attempt on the part of the Taittirīya school to at least partially obviate the need to employ an outside Hotṛ. The economic side of the issue is not talked about in the texts, but clearly it is an attempt to keep a certain portion of the ritual fee (*dakṣiṇā*) within the community. The Ṛgvedins obviously stood to lose a portion of their income and were not happy with this behaviour of the Taittirīyas. The situation clearly got worse in those instances where, as discussed by Frederick Smith, the Taittirīyas attempted to completely cut off the Ṛgvedins from the function of Hotṛ even in Soma sacrifices, where traditionally the Taittirīyas ceded the role of Hotṛ to Ṛgvedins.

In the remaining part of my paper, I want to draw attention to two sources of information regarding the dispute of *yājuṣa hautra*. The first source consists of a rich set of eighteenth and nineteenth century reports from Maharashtra. Such reports appeared in the local newspapers and magazines like *Dharma* (edited and published by Bhāuśāstrī *alias* K.V. Lele from Wai). In the issue of the magazine *Dharma*, dated 6 August 1905, we have the following report on pp. 543-44:

हौत्र संबंधी वादविवाद

सांप्रत कोणत्याही जातीच्या मनुष्याला कोणत्याही प्रकारचा धंदा करण्यास राजाची

आडकाठी नाही. हे पाहून पुण्यातील काही लोकांनी तेथे होणाऱ्या एका यज्ञात हौत्र प्रयोग कोणत्या धर्माने करावा या विषयी वाटाघाट सुरू केलेली आहे.... अध्वर्यूने जे कर्म करावयाचे ते यजुर्वेदाने करावयाचे आणि होत्याने जे कर्म करावयाचे ते ऋग्वेदाने करावयाचे असेही ठरलेले आहे. परंतु ऋग्वेद कोणाला म्हणावयाचे व यजुर्वेद कोणाला म्हणावयाचे हाच अलीकडे लोकांना भ्रम पडत चाललेला आहे.... दहा हजार ऋचा एवढाच ऋग्वेद ही समजूत चुकीची आहे. यजुर्वेद म्हणून प्रसिद्ध असलेल्या ग्रंथात शेकडो ऋचा आहेत. परंतु तो ऋक्शेष म्हणून प्रसिद्ध आहे. ऋग्वेद नावाने प्रसिद्ध असलेला ग्रंथ ऋग्वेद व यजुर्वेद नावाने प्रसिद्ध असलेला ग्रंथ यजुर्वेद हे सर्वस्वी खरे असते तर पूर्वमीमांसा शास्त्रामध्ये महर्षि जैमिनींना ऋग्लक्षण व यजुर्लक्षण सांगण्याचे प्रयोजनच नव्हते गायत्री, त्रिष्टुप, जगती इत्यादी छंदांनी युभ असलेले मंत्र त्या ऋचा आणि अशा छंदांनी युभ असलेले मंत्र यजुर्मंत्र असा पूर्वमीमांसेचा सिद्धांत आहे. हा सिद्धांत लक्ष्यात घेतला असतां यजुर्वेदात आढळणाऱ्या ऋचा ऋग्वेदातील भाग नव्हे असा भलतेच गृहीत धरून कलह करण्यास तयार होणे योग्य नव्हे.

At the present time [during the rule of the British], the king does not prevent any person from doing any profession. Considering this [freedom] some folks in Pune have started a discussion regarding the manner in which one should perform the *hautra* at a sacrifice taking place there. It has been traditionally settled that the task of the Adhvaryu is to be carried out with *Yajurveda* and the task of the Hotṛ is to be carried out with *Ṛgveda*. However, lately people are confused about what exactly is *Yajurveda* and what exactly is *Ṛgveda*. The belief that only the collection that has ten thousand *ṛk*s is to be considered to be *Ṛgveda* is incorrect. There are hundreds of *ṛk*s in [*Taittirīya*] *Yajurveda*, and that portion is well known as an appendix to *Ṛgveda*. If the term *Ṛgveda* were limited to the popularly known Saṁhitā of *Ṛgveda*, and if the term *Yajurveda* were limited to the popularly known Saṁhitā of the *Yajurveda*, then it would not have been necessary for the Sage Jaimini to provide explicit definitions of a *ṛk* and a *yajus*. He defines *ṛk*s as *mantra*s composed in meters like Gāyatrī, Triṣṭubh, and Jagatī, and *yajus* as those *mantra*s that are not so metrically composed. Such is the final determination of the Pūrva-Mīmāṁsā. Once this determination is taken into

> consideration, it is inappropriate to fight arguing that *ṛks* found in *Yajurveda* are not [part of] *Ṛgveda*.

This report highlights one of the arguments used by the debaters. The Ṛgvedins obviously believed that the term *Ṛgveda* applies exclusively to the Saṁhitās like the one attributed to Śākalya. If the task of the Hotṛ is to be accomplished by using the *Ṛgveda*, then clearly the Hotṛ must be a Ṛgvedin. On the other hand, the Yajurvedin argument expanded the scope of the term *Ṛgveda* to include *ṛk*s given in *Yajurveda*, and hence created an occasion for a trained Yajurvedin priest to carry out the role of a Hotṛ, at least in some of the rites. The second report I want to point to is also from the same magazine dated 31 August 1905 (p. 635):

> याजुष हौत्र निर्णय
>
> वेदमूर्ति राजश्री रामदीक्षित बापट अग्निहोत्री यांनी पुणे मुक्कामी गेल्या ज्येष्ठमासी यज्ञ केला व त्यात याजुष हौत्र केले .... पुणे मुक्कामी जो यज्ञ झाला तो करणारा यजमान हिरण्यकेशी म्हणजे अर्थात् यजुर्वेदी असल्यामुळे ज्या यजुर्वेदात पठित असल्याप्रमाणे हौत्र कर्मांत म्हणणे आवश्यक आहेत तया तशाच म्हटल्या गेल्या। म्हणजे स्वशाखेमध्ये जो पाठ झाला नाही तो पाठ स्वीकारून सदोष हौत्र कर्म केले गेले नाही. अर्थात् त्या यज्ञात जे हौत्र कर्म झाले ते विधियुभच झाले. परंतु या विधियुभ झालेल्या हौत्र कर्मामुळे पुण्यातील काही गृहस्थ मंडळींचे पित्त विनाकारण खवळून गेले. रा० रा० बाककृष्ण रामचंद्र उर्फ आप्पासाहेब वैद्य वकील. रा० रा० वामन बाळाजी नाईक केळकर इत्यादी गृहस्थ यापैकी होत. हे दोन्ही गृहस्थ आश्वलायन शाखेचे आहेत.
>
> The honourable Veda expert Rāma Dīkṣita Bāpaṭ Agnihotrī performed a sacrifice at Pune during the last month of Jyeṣṭha, and during that sacrifice, he performed the *yājuṣa hautra*. Since the *yajamāna* carrying out this sacrifice at Pune was a Hiraṇyakeśī Yajurvedı, the *hautra mantra*s were recited exactly as they are provided in *Yajurveda*. That means the *hautra* performance did not involve the fault of accepting readings of the *mantra*s as they are not given in one's own *śākhā*. Thus, the performance of the *hautra* was ritually quite appropriate. However, because of this appropriately carried

> out *hautra*, the temper of certain people in Pune flared for no good reason. Among these are Bāḷakṛṣṇa Rāmacandra *alias* Appāsāheb Vaidya, Pleader, and Vāman Bāḷājī Nāīk Keḷkar. Both of these gentlemen belong to the Āśvalāyana Śākhā [of *Ṛgveda*].

This report while providing the dates and places of the actual disputes with names of participants makes it clear that the Taittirīyas were happy in carrying out the *yājuṣa hautra*, while the Ṛgvedins were unhappy with this practice, as they clearly stood to lose some income to the Yajurvedins. This also hints at the likelihood that this behaviour of the Yajurvedins, at least locally, marked a shift from the previous practice. Had the Yajurvedins been performing the *yājuṣa hautra* in this fashion for a long time, there would be no reason for the eruption of this dispute at this time.

This conclusion is fully supported by a consolidated narrative of reports of this dispute presented by S.V. Ketkar in his Marathi encyclopaedia, *Mahārāṣṭrīya Jñānakośa, Vedavidyā* volume, Appendix, 1921, pp. 5-7. Ketkar reports that this dispute erupted in Maharashtra about fifty years prior to the publication of his *Vedavidyā* volume, namely around 1870s. Until then the Taittirīya Kṛṣṇa Yajurvedins of Maharashtra followed one of the two patterns. They either employed a Ṛgvedin Hotṛ right from the beginning of Agnyādhāna, thus setting aside the *hautra* contained in their own Saṁhitā, or they accepted the Taittirīya Hotṛ where the *hautra* was fully specified in the Taittirīya texts, and then employed a Ṛgvedin Hotṛ for Soma sacrifices, etc. Ṛgvedins were happy with both of these patterns. However, around 1870, Kāśīnātha Dīkṣita Karandikar, a Taittirīya Hiraṇyakeśi brāhmaṇa, performed the Agniṣṭoma sacrifice in the village of Pachwad, near the town of Wai, on the banks of Kṛṣṇā River. But one of the attendees, Merushastri Godbole, suggested that the *yajamāna* need not employ a Ṛgvedin Hotṛ even for the Agniṣṭoma, but that a Taittirīya Hotṛ could recite *mantras* from *TS* instead, using the indications (*liṅga*) in these *mantras*, and not worrying about the explicit prescriptions of the Ṛgvedic *hautra*. This view was opposed by the Ṛgvedin priest, Shaligram Shastri, who was present there. Finally, the Agniṣṭoma sacrifice took place with Yajurvedic *hautra*.

This dispute again erupted at the Dīkṣaṇīya Iṣṭi that was being performed at Wai around CE 1900, and again here the Taitttirīya Yajamāna insisted that the Hotṛ should recite Yajurvedic *hautra* during this *iṣṭi*. These practices were perceived by the Ṛgvedins as Yajurvedic encroachments upon their rights and they were clearly unhappy. Ketkar reports that this lead the Ṛgvedins of Pune to build an argument that any version, even a limited version of *yājuṣa hautra* was improper and against the tradition (*aśāstra*). This extreme view was of course unacceptable to the Hiraṇyakeśins. Ketkar narrates that at a Pune sacrifice where the Hiraṇyakeśins were going to use the extended *yājuṣa hautra*, disregarding the sentiments of the Ṛgvedins, the Ṛgvedins tried to steal away the sacrificial animal and pelted the Yajurvedins with rocks. Finally the sacrifice concluded only with the help of the police officers. The Ṛgvedins imposed excommunication on the Hiraṇyakeśins for two years, and under their pressure, the Śaṅkarācārya of the Saṅkeśvara Maṭha issued a proclamation that the Yajurvedins are not entitled to perform *hautra*, without undergoing a separate Ṛgvedic *upanayana*. Ketkar finally says that in spite of all the ideological and textual evidence that was cited in this dispute, it was finally rooted in the economic loss and gain among the participating priestly brāhmaṇas.

There are relatively few older sources on the issue of the *yājuṣa hautra* dispute. As pointed out by Kashikar (1977: 160-62), *Āpastamba-Śrauta-Sūtra* (*ĀŚS*) (24.14.21: *ādhvaryava evāto 'nyāni karmāṇi hotur āmnātāni bhavanti/upadeśād itarāṇīti*) tells us that apart from the *hautra* for the Darśapaurṇamāsa Iṣṭi provided in *ĀŚS*, the other *hautra* is specified in the Adhvarya of *TS*, and the remaining *hautra* should be understood from the R̥gvedic tradition. Commenting on this *sūtra*, Dhūrtasvāmin remarks that the *hautra* contained in the Taittirīya texts is an appendix to the R̥gvedic tradition (*bahvr̥caśeṣatvād asmadīyahautrasya*). The commentators Dhūrtasvāmin, Rāmāgnicit, Kapardisvāmin, Rudradatta, Cauḍapācārya and Haradatta all take a position that the *r̥k hautra* and *yājuṣa hautra* are to be treated optional (Kashikar 1977: 160-61). As I have noted earlier, the Hiraṇyakeśin Gopinātha Oka (CE 1733-83) was evidently the first one (Kashikar 1977: 160) to argue that the entire *hautra* for rites for a Hiraṇyakeśin *yajamāna* must come from the Taittirīya texts, and one must not allow the *r̥k hautra* even optionally. This clearly seems to be the beginning of the dispute that came to boil in the nineteenth and twentieth centuries.

Besides *Vedavicāra* of Śāmaśāstrī Draviḍa Dvivedī that I cited at the beginning, there are a few nineteenth/twentieth-century texts that have come down to us that deal with the question of *yājuṣa hautra*. All such texts that I have seen seem to be composed by Taittirīyas, particularly those belonging to the Citpāvana Hiraṇyakeśin Śākhā in Maharashtra. Among the published texts, *Sūtrāntaraparigrahavicāra* of Vāsudeva Shastri Abhyankar, published in 1922, is marginally concerned with this particular debate. However, it brings up other interesting efforts on the part of the Hiraṇyakeśin tradition. In this text, Abhyankar argues that even though there are very many *Yajurveda* branches in existence, a Citpāvana R̥gvedin must employ a Hiraṇyakeśin Taittirīya as his Adhvaryu, because through traditional intermarriage between the Citpāvana R̥gvedins and the Citpāvana Hiraṇyakeśins, this choice is the most suited one.

cittapāvanabahvr̥cānāṁ hiraṇyakeśīyaiḥ saha sūtrajñātikulo-

citayonisambandhasattvena taiḥ satyāṣāḍhasūtramevānu-sartavyaṁ bhavati – p. 1.

The discussion by Abhyankar points out how the social relations within a community also governed economic and ritual relations, creating networks of proximity. One would, under normal natural circumstances, employ a ritualist from outside one's community only as a last resort.

The other published source that directly focuses on the *yājuṣa hautra* dispute is a booklet titled *Sarvārtvijayaprayogasāra* composed by Kaśīnātha Viśvanātha Sāṭhe, a Hiraṇyakeśi Citpāvana brāhmaṇa from Wai published in Śaka 1837 = CE 1915. This booklet deals with most of the issues involved in the *yājuṣa hautra* disputes. In the preface of the booklet, Kāśīnātha Sāṭhe says that great scholars like Vidyāvācaspati Tryambaka Shastri has already composed works like *Hautramīmāṁsā* and *Yājuṣahautravicārasaṁkṣepa*; these works are too advanced (*prauḍha*), and hence he felt the need to compose a simpler treatise that not only dealt with the question of *yājuṣa hautra*, but also with other related issues, especially pointing to occasions where a R̥gvedin can carry out the function of Adhvaryu (*bāhvr̥cyam ādhvaryavam*, p. 24, referring to *Sāṁkhyāyana-Śrauta-Sūtra* 1.1.15, 17):

āsīnanyāyaṁ bāhvr̥cyaṁ, hotā ca kuryād anādiṣṭam,

and *Āśvalāyana-Śrauta-Sūtra* 1.1.14:

karmacodanāyāṁ hotāram.

He also argues that a single *upanayana* allows a brāhmaṇa to study and practise all the Vedas, thus, in effect, allowing the Yajurvedins to carry out the function of Hotr̥.

Besides these few published materials, there are a number of short works, all composed by Hiraṇyakeśins, that are available only in the form of manuscripts. I have photocopied five such manuscripts from the library of the Vaidika

Samshodhana Mandala in Pune, and here I just list these titles:

1. *Yājuṣahautravicāra* by Vāsudeva Shastri Abhyankar. Śaka 1827 = CE 1915 (VSM: 3445)
2. *Yājuṣahautraprayoga* (VSM: 3587)
3. *Yājuṣahautrajyotsnā* (VSM: 3588)
4. *Yājuṣahautraprayogavicāra* (VSM: 3589)
5. *Yājuṣahautropodghāta* (VSM: 3843).

These works, all composed by Hiraṇyakeśins, seem to argue in favour of the practice of *yājuṣa hautra*, some extending its scope a little bit, but not completely removing the *ṛk hautra*, where there is no explicit provision of *hautra* in the Taittirīya tradition. But they uniformly seem to be against the older view that the *yājuṣa hautra* can be treated to be optional, and that a Taittirīya *yajamāna* can employ Ṛgvedic *hautra* for all ritual contexts.

References

Abhyankar, Vasudeva Shastri, 1922, *Sūtrāntaraparigrahavicāra*, Pune: Anandashrama Publication.

Kashikar, C.G., 1977, *Śrauta Dharmācī Svarūpacikitsā*, Pune: University of Pune.

Ketkar, S.V., 1921, *Mahārāṣṭrīya Jñānakośa, Prastāvanākhaṇḍa*, part 2, *Vedavidyā*, Pune: Mahārāṣṭrīya Jñānakośa Maṇḍaḷa.

Smith, Frederick M., 1987, *The Vedic Sacrifice in Transition: A Translation and Study of the Trikāṇḍamaṇḍana of Bhāskaramiśra*, Pune: Bhandarkar Oriental Research Institute.

Vedavicāra, attributed to Śāmaśāstrī Draviḍa Dvivedi, ed. K.V. Lele, published in *Dharma*, 1912, Wai.

3

Hermeneutics of the Upaniṣads

R. Balasubramanian

THE work of interpretations is not new. It is said that Jesus interpreted himself to the Jews in terms of scriptural prophecy. Also, the Gospel writers interpreted Jesus to their audiences. However, hermeneutics as a systematic, rigorous method of biblical interpretation came into prominence in the West in the context of European Protestant theology during the seventeenth century. But in India the Mīmāṁsakas and the Vedāntins, to whom the Vedic texts are important, used this method for textual interpretation for a long time, probably from the first century BCE. Hermeneutics is a system of understanding. It is the interpreter's system for finding the "hidden" meaning of the text.

Like a trustworthy conductor who ably guides the traveller to the destination, the Upaniṣadic seers safely guide the spiritual aspirant to the goal of Self-realization stage by stage. Implicit in their utterances is the well-known method of *adhyāropa* (superimposition) and *apavāda* (subsequent denial). Since they proceed from the known to the unknown, restating the given, exposing the difficulties in the accepted position, and then moving on to the next, their utterances are contextual or "horizonal". Their statements are very often suggestive and symbolic; sometimes, they are puzzling and paradoxical. One should, therefore, apply the principles or canons of interpretation carefully in order to understand their purport (*tātparya*). Consider, for example, the *Īśāvāsya* text (5) which says:

> *That moves; That does not move; That is far off; That is very near; That is inside all this; and That is also outside all this.*

To a casual reader, the above text which is paradoxical does not make any sense. How is it possible, one may ask, for one and the same entity to move and to be stationary, to be near and far off, to be inside everything and also to be outside everything? It is difficult for a novice who does not know the background to comprehend the purport of the text which conveys the idea that the Supreme Being is beyond the categories of thought. The reader should have a "pre-understanding" of the text and also should pay attention to the context in which it occurs. It is here that we require the help and guidance of the commentator. Commenting on this text, Śaṅkara observes:

> The meaning of the text is that, though in itself the Supreme Reality is motionless, it seems to move. Moreover, it is far off, because it is unattainable by the ignorant even in hundreds of millions of years. It is very near indeed to the men of knowledge. The reason for this is as follows. Being their very Self, . . . it is also near. It is inside everything as stated in the Vedic text, "The Self that is within all" (*Bṛhadāraṇyaka Upaniṣad*, 3.4.1) is inside this world consisting of name, form, and activity. It is outside all this, because it is all-pervasive like ether; and it is inside, because it is extremely subtle.

Texts which are paradoxical occur not only in the Upaniṣads, but also in *Bhagavad-Gītā*. For example, *Bhagavad-Gītā*, 13.13, describes Brahman–Ātman as possessing hands and feet, eyes, heads, and mouths everywhere in order to convey that it is infinite and that it exists everywhere. The text reads:

> With hands and feet everywhere, with eyes, heads, and mouths everywhere, with hearing everywhere, That [*Brahman*, which is to be known] exists enveloping all.

Hands, feet, and other organs are not-Self; they are material; they constitute, in the language of *Bhagavad-Gītā*, *kṣetra* (the body). In his commentary on this text, Śaṅkara says that the Self, which is devoid of organs, is spoken of as possessing organs only for the purpose of indicating its existence through them; and whatever is attributed to the Self is denied in the next verse (13.14) which reads:

> Shining by the functions of all the organs, yet without the organs; unattached, yet supporting all; devoid of qualities, but is the enjoyer of qualities.

In the words of Śaṅkara:

> There is the saying of those who know the right traditional method of teaching, "that which is devoid of the world of duality is described by superimposition and denial". Hands, feet, and the like, constituting the limbs of all bodies in all places, derive their activity from the energy inherent in the knowable (*Brahman*), and as such they are mere marks of its existence, and are spoken of as belonging to it only by a figure of speech.

A careful study of Śaṅkara's hermeneutics reveals three important points for our consideration. The first one is that, though a superficial reading of the Upaniṣads may suggest to us that they do not speak with one voice, they contradict one another; a deeper study will reveal that they have only one message to convey, viz. that the primal Reality which is called *Brahman*, *Ātman*, *Sat*, and so on is one without a second and that, due to our ignorance, we view it in multiple forms. Second, the method followed by Śaṅkara for reconciling the different texts is not his invention. Third, the method itself is an old one embedded in the tradition, and Śaṅkara scrupulously follows this method in his hermeneutics. What Śaṅkara says in his commentary on *Brahma-Sūtra*, 3.2.17, summing up the purport of the teaching of both Śruti and Smṛti texts, is worth quoting here:

> That *Brahman* is *nirviśeṣa* is proved by Śruti texts also which expressly deny characteristics attributed to it; e.g. there are texts like, "then follows the teaching 'not this, not this'"; "it is different from the known; it is also above the unknown"; "from which all speech, along with the mind, turns away unable to reach it". Also, this idea is conveyed by the Śruti text which relates how Bādhva, being questioned about *Brahman* by Bāṣkali, explained it to him by silence. When Bāṣkali approached Bādhva with the request, "please teach me *Brahman*, Sir", the latter was silent. When the request was repeated a second and a third time, he said: "I am teaching you indeed; but you do not understand. Silent is that Self." The same teaching is conveyed by Smṛti texts such as: "I will proclaim that which is the object of knowledge, knowing which one attains immortality; beginningless is the Supreme *Brahman*. It cannot be said to be *sat* or *asat*." Of a similar purport is another Smṛti text, according to which Nārāyaṇa in his cosmic form instructed Nārada: "O Nārada, you see me endowed with the qualities of all beings because of *māyā* projected by me; do not understand me in this form (as the reality)."

Though Advaita accepts more than one *pramāṇa*, Śruti alone, strictly speaking, is "the *pramāṇa*" according to it. What remains concealed and therefore what is to be known is *Brahman–Ātman*, and nothing else. Since Śruti alone conveys the knowledge of *Brahman–Ātman*, Advaita holds that it alone is the *pramāṇa*. From the standpoint of the empirical realm (*vyāvahārika*), perception, inference, etc. are admitted to be *pramāṇa*s; and here we proceed on the assumption that material objects due to concealment remain unknown. This assumption is not, in the final analysis, justified, because there can be concealment only for *Brahman–Ātman*, which is consciousness. So long as we think, due to ignorance, that there are insentient objects which remain unknown to us – and this is what we ordinarily do – we can, according to Advaita, speak of perception, inference, etc. as *pramāṇa*s. There is yet another point to be noted here about Śruti. Śruti as a *pramāṇa* is just informative, i.e. it only reveals *Brahman–Ātman* which is already there, but which remains concealed and unknown due to *avidyā*. The work of Śruti as a *pramāṇa* is needed only so long as *Brahman–Ātman* is not known; and once it is known, there is no need for Śruti. One who is ignorant of the truth needs *pramāṇa*, and not one who has known the truth. It means that Advaita accepts perception and other *pramāṇa*s including Śruti only in the state of bondage and that Śruti, though indispensable for attaining *parā-vidyā*, ceases to be a *pramāṇa* once the highest truth is known. Śaṅkara conveys this idea of the contrast between the state of ignorance and that of knowledge and all that it implies with regard to *pramāṇa*s including Śruti by citing the authority of Śruti itself as follows:

> Prior to enlightenment, there is transmigratory existence for the *jīva*; and in this state alone, there is scope for the work of perception and other *pramāṇa*s, because Śruti texts such as, "but when to the knower of *Brahman* everything has become the Self, then what should one see and through what?" point out the absence of perception, etc. in the state of enlightenment. If it be said that the absence of perception, etc. would also mean the absence of Śruti, this conclusion is quite acceptable to us. For, following the texts starting with, "in this state the father is no father", and ending with, "the Vedas are no Vedas", we do admit the absence of Śruti itself in the state of enlightenment.

Thus, Śruti is viewed as the only *pramāṇa* from one perspective, and the final *pramāṇa* (*antyaṁ pramāṇa*) from another perspective for attaining *parā-vidyā*, as there is no work for any *pramāṇa* thereafter.

The Upaniṣadic texts, which give an account of creation employing the category of cause–effect relation, presuppose duality; but they purport to teach the non-duality of *Brahman* which is the source, support, and end of the world. To take the well-known case of clay and pot, which are related as cause and effect, it may appear that the effect (pot) is different from the cause (clay), but the truth is that it is non-different from the latter (*kārya-kāraṇayoḥ ananyatvam*). For example, the *Taittirīya* text, 3.1.1: "That, verily, from which these beings are born, that by which, when born, they leave, that into which, when departing, they enter. That, seek to know. That is *Brahman*", defines *Brahman* as the cause of the world. But how can *Brahman*, which is one only without a second and also immutable, be the cause of the world? There is the world of day-to-day experience, which calls for an explanation, and Śruti is the *pramāṇa* which tells us that *Brahman* who is omniscient, omnipotent, and so on is the cause of it. However, the description of *Brahman* as the cause of the world is for the purpose of establishing the non-duality of *Brahman* even though it operates at the level of duality. It is only provisional, and so the Upaniṣad withdraws it. Its final position is that *Brahman* is neither the cause nor the effect of anything. Śaṅkara knew the contradictions involved in the causal explanation. Cause–effect relation involves a series with an indefinite number of terms before and after any given number of the series. Since we assume that the causal series has no beginning, to postulate a first cause is arbitrary. Either the first cause has a previous cause, or else the whole causal design is illogical. But the fact remains that the causal explanation cannot be given without assuming a first cause. Hence the difficulty in the causal explanation. In the course of his commentary on *Brahma-Sūtra*, 2.1.14, Śaṅkara observes:

> The effect is this manifold world consisting of ether, etc.; and the cause is the Supreme *Brahman*. So far as the effect is

> concerned, it is understood that in reality it is non different from the cause, i.e. it has no existence apart from the cause. . . . There are texts which purport to convey the unity or oneness of the Self: "In that all this has its Self; it is the true; it is the Self; you are that" (*Chāndogya Upaniṣad*, 6.8.7); "*Brahman* alone is all this" (*Muṇḍaka Upaniṣad*); "there is in it no diversity" (*Bṛhadāraṇyaka*, 4.4.25). On any other assumption it would not be possible to maintain that, by the knowledge of one thing, everything becomes known. . . . So this manifold world with its objects of enjoyment, enjoyers, and so on has no existence apart from *Brahman*.

Let us now consider the negative texts which purport to convey that *Brahman* is *nirguṇa*. There is the *Bṛhadāraṇyaka* text, 2.3.6, which says:

> Now therefore the description of *Brahman*: "Not this, not this". There is no other and more appropriate description than this "not this, not this".

It is first of all necessary to bear in mind the context in which this negative description occurs. The Upaniṣad first describes *Brahman* as having two forms – the gross (*mūrtta*) consisting of earth, water, and fire, and the subtle (*amūrtta*) consisting of air and ether. After explaining the two forms of *Brahman*, it proceeds to describe it as "not this, not this" with a view to show that *Brahman* is really free from these two forms. The two negative particles are used by Scripture in an all-inclusive sense to deny every possible specification or attribute that one may think of with regard to *Brahman*. The procedure that is adopted here is based on the well-known technique of superimposition (*adhyāropa*) and subsequent denial (*apavāda*). Śaṅkara's commentary on this text brings out the significance of the twofold negation, and also highlights why it is the most appropriate description. First, Śaṅkara refers to a possible objection to this mode of description and then gives his reply.

Objection: How can the two negations, "not this, not this", bring out the nature of the Reality spoken of as the Truth of Truth?

Reply: By the elimination of all differences due to limiting adjuncts, the two expressions refer to something that has no distinguishing mark such as name, or form, or action, or genus, or species, or qualities. Words denote objects through one or other of these. But *Brahman* has none of these distinguishing marks. Consequently, it cannot be described as "it is such-and-such" in the same way as we describe a cow by saying, "there moves a white cow with horns". It is possible to describe *Brahman* by superimposing on it name, form, and action. For example, there are texts which speak of *Brahman* as "knowledge and bliss" (3.9.28) and as "pure consciousness" (2.4.12) and so on. When, however, we wish to describe its true nature, free from all differences due to limiting adjuncts, then it is an utter impossibility. Then there is only one way left, viz. to describe it as "not this, not this" by eliminating all possible specifications of it that have been known.

Śaṅkara points out that *Brahman–Ātman,* which is other-than-the-empirical, cannot be described by means of words in the same way in which we describe empirical objects. In his commentary on *Bhagavad-Gītā*, 13.12, Śaṅkara says:

> It stands to reason to say that *Brahman* cannot be expressed in words such as *sat*; for, every word employed to denote a thing denotes that thing – when heard by another – as associated with a certain *genus*, or a certain *act*, or a certain *quality*, or a certain mode of *relation*. Thus: *cow* and *horse* imply genera, *cook* and *teacher* imply acts, *white* and *black* imply qualities, *wealthy* and *cattle-owner* imply possession. But *Brahman* belongs to no genus wherefore it cannot be denoted by such words as "*sat* (existent)". Being devoid of attributes, it possesses no qualities. If it were possessed of qualities, then it could be denoted by a word implying a

> quality. Being actionless, it cannot be indicated by a word implying an act. The Śruti says: "It is without parts, actionless and tranquil" (*Śvetāśvatara Upaniṣad*, 6.19). It is not related to anything else; for it is one, it is without a second, it is no object (of any sense), it is the very Self. Wherefore, it is but right to say that it can be denoted by no word at all; and the passages of the Śruti like the following point to the same thing: "Whence (i.e. away from *Brahman*, unable to approach *Brahman*) all words return" (*Taittirīya Upaniṣad*, 2.4.1).

It must be borne in mind that every text, be it affirmative or negative, occurs in a context, and so we must take into consideration the meaning which the text purports to convey in the context. It is true that the Upaniṣads declare that *Brahman*, which is not an empirical entity like a tree or table, cannot be signified by speech and comprehended by the mind. But it does not follow from this that the Supreme Being is really beyond the reach of words and mind. If that were the case, the Upaniṣadic texts serve no purpose and would be useless. Both the affirmative and the negative texts have a specific and important role to play: they are intended to help us understand the principal texts (*mahāvākyas*). It means that these texts, which are called *avāntara-vākyas*, must be construed along with the principal texts such as *tat tvam asi* and *aham brahmāsmi*. It is true that the negative texts, which say that the immutable *Brahman* is "neither gross nor minute, neither short nor long . . ." (*Bṛhadāraṇyaka Upaniṣad*, 3.8.8), are intended to bring out the nature of *Brahman* as *nirguṇa*. *Brahman* which is devoid of attributes, specifications, and relations is not an objective entity. But at the same time it is not a void or nothingness even though it has been emptied of all categories. Being of the nature of consciousness, it is identical with the Self of everyone of us. It is, therefore, something positive, and also spiritual in nature. Though it is beyond the reach of conceptual and representative thinking, it is not beyond or outside our experience. That is why Śaṅkara says that there is no one to whom the Self remains unknown. Since negation is only a preliminary to affirmation, the negative texts have a positive import. What Rudolf Otto says about negative theology is relevant in this context:

> A conception, negative in form, may often become the symbol for a content of meaning which, if absolutely unutterable, is none the less in the highest degree positive. . . . A negative theology can and indeed must arise . . . from purely and genuinely religious roots, the experience of the luminous.
>
> — *The Idea of the Holy*, p. 189

Brahman, which is no other than *Ātman,* is self-luminous *svaprakāśa*. It shows itself all the time while revealing other things. We should, therefore, construe the negative texts along with the *mahāvākya*s which have a positive import.

4

Dharma
An Integrating Factor of Consciousness and Science

M.K. Byrski

Modern cosmogonical scientific theories seemingly ignore the fact that the ultimate consequence of the creative Big Bang is the very perception of its consequences. How comes that out of the hubbub of emergence of the physical universe eventually emerged also consciousness, which in all beings, but in human beings also vocally, manifests itself in the form of the faculty of perception? Our contention is that *dharma* rooted in the Vedic thought takes note of this problem and taking recourse to the metaphor of the self-sacrifice of Puruṣa-Prajāpati, i.e. his *yajña* comes to grips with that stupendous challenge. The present paper is only a preliminary reconnaissance regarding this problem and its author is well aware of his limitations in this respect.

In one of my previous contributions I delved upon the problem of what exactly is the import of the notion of *dharma*? Is it just religion or more properly, is it science dealing with the nature of reality albeit couched in terms of a myth? My answer unmistakably was in favour of science. Limited size of that paper did not allow me to elucidate properly my point of view. Obviously if I call *dharma* a science, the very first question to be asked is whether it can withstand comparison with the tenets of modern science? Can we consider the basic premises of *dharma* scientific? First of all we have to answer the question what are these premises and can they be considered scientific, since in formulating them the scholars of yore (*ṛṣis*) did not have at their disposal anything close to modern technological means such as computers, labs, telescopes, cyclotrons and such other nowadays indispensable contraptions? Can intuition alone and keen faculty of observation suffice?

My contention is that if we accept as valid the presupposition that Ultimate Reality, not unlike in mathematics[1] is one – *ekam sat,* then honest enquiry of whatever sort will have to bring similar results. The problem is whether we are able to read and properly decode texts that were composed in a style totally different from the one we have been used to employ in current scientific discourse.

There can be no difference of opinion that the Vedas are the mainstay of *dharma.* There is also nothing new, especially in the context of indigenous Indian scholarship, in saying that Vedas should be treated as science. There is also no dearth of studies of that sort. It is therefore very difficult to be original in this respect. Yet, I shall risk presentation of my views with the hope that the particular context of my enquiry may throw some additional light upon the interpretation of relevant Vedic texts.

No doubt the Nāsadīya hymn has to be considered first for the simple reason that it takes the state of pre-creation as the point of departure. The state when even "when" is irrelevant because neither being (*sat*), nor non-being (*asat*) are yet in existence. So, consequently time had not yet become operative. The description of pre-creative state, which we find in this hymn tallies well with the opinion of modern

[1] See my paper entitled "The Arithmetic of Hinduism", in *Dialogue and Universalism*, Center for Universalism, Warsaw University, nos. 11-12/1997, pp. 125-39.

cosmologists. This may be illustrated by an anecdote connected with the meetings of Pope John Paul II with scholars at his Castel Gandolfo summer residence in Italy. In one of those meetings – as the story goes – Stephen William Hawking took part and the Big Bang theory of creation was on the agenda. The famous astrophysicist presented his views on what might have happened just after the Big Bang and the Pope asked him whether he could say what had preceded the Big Bang. Hawking answered that this question cannot be addressed to scholars. It is the prerogative of such people like Pope himself. I would add – it is a prerogative of inspired poets and this is exactly what such poets did in the Nāsadīya hymn. This text demonstrates well how far human speech can go in describing the reality that preceded creation. To my mind it is optimal description and its assumption that "the one breathed with its own will"[2] is as I have already indicated, justified by the universal language of mathematics. "One" is the cornerstone of mathematics, so if it is true that mathematics is the queen of sciences, we may safely accept this contention of the Vedic *r̥ṣis* that it was the One from which creation started.

That One had in itself some latent energy, which obviously detonated the Big Bang. This energy was called *svadhā* and the etymology of the term is revealing – "deposited in itself". The inspired author of the text at this stage of his enquiry obviously steered clear of the danger of "anthropomorphization" or even deification of the idea. The formula used strikes with its scientific restrain, mathematical precision and elegance. The sort of "apophatic" attitude, which Hawking shares, evident from the very beginning also characterizes following passages, where *tamas* and *salila* appear as the only suitable terms for description of the then state of reality. This was that far that the author dared to move, being obviously

---

2 *ānīd avātam svadhayā tad ekam.* – *R̥V* X.129.2

aware that if more definite terms were used, the argument would become unscientific. Now comes the crucial point. "And what was to become, surrounded by the void, that One got born through the power of heat."[3] No one will convince me that the term Big Bang is more scientific than the term – Power of Heat.[4] After all for everyone it is as clear as that the sun shines in heaven (NB!) that our existence is possible thanks to the heat precisely of the same sun!

Now, let us take up the most controversial opinion, which in the eyes of modern physicists and more so astrophysicists and cosmologists will sound as totally unscientific. "At the beginning love enveloped the primary seed of mind."[5] Let me first clarify one important point. The term *kāma* here is usually understood as denoting desire or even lust. I submit that the "One without the Second"[6] whose primary seed of mind is concerned here – is an absolute plenitude, so it cannot have any wishes or desires and the least – lusts! Thus obviously it has to have much broader meaning. Extremely interesting is in this context the order in which three terms appear in the hymn: first, it is *tapas;* next, it is *kāma;* and finally, it is *manas.* It strikes one that we have here as if a reverted order of three *puruṣārthas. Tapas* or *Agni,* heat or fire are tantamount to material dimension of reality (*artha*). Without this energy discursive reality could not emerge. But reality to become manifest and to acquire its proper name needs the Second

---

[3] *tucchyenābhvapihitam yad āsīt tapasas tan mahinājāyataikam.* – *R̥V* X.129.3

[4] *tapasas mahin.* For *mahin* see Monier-Williams *Sanskrit-English Dictionary,* Oxford: The Clarendon Press, 1899, p. 803 and Macdonell, *Practical Sanskrit Dictionary,* Oxford University Press, 1958, p. 222.

[5] *kāmas tadagre samavartatādhi manaso retaḥ prathamam yad āsīt.* – *R̥V* X.129.4

[6] *ekamevādvitījam.* – *Chāndogya Upaniṣad* 6.2.1

(*dvitīya*). This is the name of *Vāc* (Speech).[7] Speech is the manifestation of "consciousness" (*cit*), i.e. perceiving capability – the same consciousness personified as Prajāpati, which according to the Vedic exegesis generates the *tapas* of the Big Bang.[8] Consciousness, in turn, in the context of reality manifests itself as psyche (*kāma*) and rationality (*dharma*). This is the common experience of each and every sentient being. Whatever can be said about this line of thought, no one can deny its perfect logic. Without consciousness universe would become – NB! – meaningless! So including this aspect in the discourse on cosmogony is very much justified. After all, the character of the creative Big Bang must have had somehow anticipated "the primary seed of mind". Otherwise consciousness would not have appeared within the scheme of the universe! Now, *manas* is the residue of both psyche and rationality. Looking for proper equivalent among Western terms one is tempted to call it either "thinking heart" or "feeling intellect". The division of these two faculties in Western thought is totally unfounded. Now, the hymn summarizes it, saying that "thus the inspired poets searching their heart with the help of a hymn[9] discovered the bond between Being and

---

[7] "Prajāpati was alone and Speech was his second. He emitted Speech and Speech made all this manifest." (*prajāpatir vā idam eka āsīt tasya vāg eva svam āsīd vāg dvitīyā sa aikṣatemām eva vācam visṛjā iyam vā idam sarvam vibhavanty. . . .* – *Tāṇḍyamahābrāhmaṇa* XX.12.2. Also see: S. Lèvi, *La Doctrine du sacrifice dans les Brāhmaṇas*, Paris: Ernest Leroux, 1898, str. 23.

[8] *prājapatiḥ prajātikāmas tapo 'tapyata tasmāt taptāt pañcājāyantāgnir vāyur ādityaś candramā uṣāḥ pañcamī tān abravīd yūyam api tapyadhvam iti. . . .* – *Kauṣītaki Brāhmaṇa* VI.1. Also see: Lèvi, op. cit., p. 21.

[9] Manīṣā – wise utterance, hymn, prayer. The word of Śruti precedes meaning and generates it. Bhavabhūti (*c.* 700 CE) in his play *Uttararāmacaritam* writes: "The speech of the wise men of the world follows the sense. But the sense follows the speech of →

Non-Being",[10] for the two are Siamese twins and they cannot exist without each other as indeed zero cannot exist without "one". Eventually spreading of space and its measuring, which is mentioned next was a simple consequence of the emergence of Being that – as we mentioned – implicates its negative *alter ego*, but itself is characterized by time and space and since it is measurable, therefore it is called *māyā*.[11] Thus the "up" and "down" of space emerge and *svadhā* is located down while the offering gift (*prayāti*) is placed up. The offering gift mentioned here anticipates the notion, which is going to dominate later exegesis, namely that of the Man–Lord of Creatures (Puruṣa–Prajāpati), who precisely while becoming the original *prayāti* generates fire and since there is no fuel for that fire, He offers himself as fuel. Yet, physical fire is not enough to generate consciousness. It was necessary that fire turns into the eater of food and fuel into food. Only after the exothermic fire turned into endothermic digestive "fire" consciousness could manifest itself!

The Nāsadīya hymn simply considers reality as *par excellence* perceptive one, so most naturally it integrates in its description the physical aspect of creation, which is the consequence of Big Bang with its perceptiveness, which implies consciousness as the integral element of the process and consequently this justifies "anthropomorphization" in the form of Puruṣa–Prajāpati, i.e. in the form of a Person (= *Puruṣa*) tantamount to "I" (= *Aham*).

But before we tackle in detail this aspect of Vedic

→ the ancient sages" (*laukikānām hi sādhunām artham vāg anuvartate* | *ṛṣinām punar ādyānām vācam artho 'nudhavati* – Act I, verse 10)

10 *sato bamdhum asati niravindan hṛdi pratīṣyā kavayo manīṣā.* – *ṚV* X.129.4

11 The mystical etymology derives it from the root √*mā*.

cosmogony, let us remain for a while within the physical context of the act of creation when the Big Bang of Western cosmologists, is called *tapas*. We trust that to assume the identity of *tapas* and Agni is not a *tour de force*. After all in the opening hymn of *Ṛgveda*, Agni is called *purohita*, i.e. "the one who comes first". So, in order to travesty the name Western scholars have given to the original eruption of energy, we could call it the "Foremost Bang" (*Purohitavisphoṭa*). The import of this pivotal hymn is obvious. Nothing could become, was it not for the creative power of Fire – today we would rather use the term energy here. This is how we should understand the phrase: "Agni, only this sacrificial liturgy reaches divine beings, which you envelope from all sides".[12] Nothing indeed there exists, which is not prompted by that original eruption of energy. This energy manifests itself for us as Fire, as Agni. But it is the same energy that makes the sunshine and that makes volcanoes erupt,[13] as well as keeps our bodies warm. Yet, the poet of yore must have felt that it is not simply the blind, purely physical force, since, it also bestows upon him and upon all living creatures the faculty of perception.[14] Therefore at the end he prays: "Be accessible to us the way father is accessible to his son and lead us unto propitiousness".[15] The father–son relationship in this context indicates rapport in the sphere of consciousness. The poet was aware that his conscious power of perception as the result of Big Bang cannot be solely defined in terms of physical cause and effect, therefore he

---

12 *agne yam yajñamadhvaram viśvataḥ paribhūrasi sa id deveṣu gacchati.* – *ṚV* I.1.4.

13 "The Gods used the fire as the base of creation of the heaven and earth." – *ṚV* II.2.3. Also see: K.D. Dvivedi, *The Essence of the Vedas*, Varanasi: Vishva Bharati Research Institute, 1990, p. 273.

14 After all, it is thanks to our body temperature that our senses are capable of perception.

15 *sa naḥ piteva sūnave 'gne sūpayano bhava sa ca svā naḥ svastaye.* – *ṚV* I.1.7

expresses hope that consciousness must have been begotten in creatures (NB!), so he prays that the physical manifestation of the power that obviously stands behind all acts of perception may reveal its fatherly nature.

The second stanza of the Puruṣa-Sūkta hymn sounds like an answer to this pleading. "All this that was and that is to become is the Person."[16] For sure, the term *puruṣa* has to be taken to mean Person, because He is thousand-headed, thousand-eyed and having thousand feet. Only "I" (*aham*), i.e. person *par excellence* meets such description. So the import of this hymn boils down to a straightforward response to the request found in *"agnimīḷe . . ."* hymn. Further on Puruṣa-Sūkta seems to imply that the Big Bang of cosmologists was indeed preceded by consciousness (*cit* – tantamount to a Person = *aham*), which to be true to its very nature (*vastusvabhāva* = *dharma*)[17] had to accomplish an act of self – perception precisely as "I" (*Aham* = *Puruṣa*). Since time and space are the condition *sine qua non* of perception, they had to emerge as well and the only way to bring them about was for *Puruṣa* to submit its "I" to death,[18] which is tantamount to the emergence of time and space. This decision triggers the self-sacrificial (*ātmayājin*) process of creation, which results in sovereignty (*svarājya*)[19] a state that, to my mind, is tantamount to the self-perception. Next step is to create forces, which would enable *Puruṣa* to achieve its "I"s aim. Thus deities, i.e. natural forces like fire (Agni) emerge, who are already a product of that emanation.[20]

---

16 *puruṣa eve 'dam sarvam yad bhūtam yac ca bhavyam.* – *R̥V* X.90.2

17 Svāmi-Kumāra, *Kārttikeyānuprekṣā*, Agās: Śrī Parama-Śruta Prabhāvaka Mandal, 1997, p. 364. XII.478.

18 *Kāla* means "time of death" also! See Monier-Williams *Sanskrit–English Dictionary*, Oxford: The Clarendon Press, 1899, p. 278.

19 *Manu-Smr̥ti* XII.91.

20 *arvāg devā asya visarjanena.* – *R̥V* X.129.6

Although, since it all happens in a speck of time — the point modern cosmologists also make – it may appear to us as if almost simultaneous. Only after that the Person (*Puruṣa*) as the sacrificial animal lets its "I" be bound and offered as victim and thus the creative activity is continued. How come that while dying its "I" never dies indeed!? One [1] of the arithmetic, divided by three, never disappears and while remaining always one, it accounts for the emergence of countless "ones" always in triads; perceiving "one" ("I" as "I"), perceived "one" ("I" as "you") and third "one" as the witness ("I" as "he", "she" or "it"). The One "I" that was in the beginning, had to become its own object of perception. That "I" split into two. Its one half became man and another half became woman[21] and thus that "I" multiplied. In that way the Person's "I" (*Puruṣa's Aham*) never perishes[22] while becoming countless[23] *ahams* in all beings.

It seems to me that in the modern scientific discourse the so-called West concentrates on the reality as an object of perception, while apparently ignoring the very perception itself and the subject of perception – the perceiving "I", which by the way cannot be properly grasped without considering the phenomenon of consciousness. In the context of this dilemma, let us refer to Francis Crick, the famous Nobel Prize winner. According to him we now know what consciousness is. It is the activity of neurons.[24] But one is tempted to ask wherefrom neurons have come and what makes them active in this particular way? The same scholar earlier declares:

---

21 *Manu-Smṛti* I.32.

22 See *Bhagavad-Gītā* II.20.

23 *Sahasra* stands for countless.

24 The interview by Bozena Kastory published in the Polish language in the weekly *Wprost*, 9 June 2002, p. 99.

> Many people find it unacceptable that what we are seeing, it is only a symbolic interpretation of the world but not real objects. . . . Although the world does exist but we do not have direct knowledge of it. World consists only of pictures created by our consciousness.[25]

If so we, then we find it perfectly legitimate to ask the following question: what is the primary Big Bang of which this activity of neurons is a product or consciousness as a triggering factor of the Big Bang and in consequence the root cause of emergence of time and space within which neurons could become active and in that way could give satisfaction (*ānanda*) to the urge of consciousness (*cit*) to perceive its own being (*sat*). The argument to my mind boils down to the perennial dispute between *āstika*s and *nāstika*s. My encounter with the Vedic thought, i.e. with *sanātana dharma* made out of me a very determined *āstika*.

---

25 *Wprost*, 9 June 2002, p. 98.

5

Aesthetic Universe of Bharata's Naṭyaśāstra

Radhavallabh Tripathi

BHARATAMUNI stands as a Vyāsa in the Indian theatric universe and like Vyāsa's *Mahābhārata*, his *Nāṭyaśāstra* (*NŚ*) is a Saṁhitā (compendium) that presents a systematized view of the concepts having evolved during a few millenniums in our country before Common Era. We can find the foundations of these concepts in Vedic literature. The corpus of Vedic literature had been growing in oral traditions a few millenniums before the compilation of *NŚ*. The hymns of Vedas were being seen or composed,[1] and were constantly being preserved in oral traditions a few millenniums before the common era. These hymns not only reveal a world-view that formed the foundations of Indian culture, they also envisage certain aesthetic concepts that have percolated down in the whole tradition of art and literature in Sanskrit and many other Indian languages. The seers of Veda viewed the world as an everlasting vivacious piece of art created by the Supreme Being.[2] The words like *kāvya* (lit. meaning the work of a *kavi* or a poet) and *śilpa* (art) have been used by them in this context. They have viewed the world as a *kāvya* or a *śilpa* created by the

1 *stoman dadarśa iti aupamanyavaḥ.* – *Nirukta* II.11

2 *devasya paśya kāvyam na mamāra na jīryati.* – *Atharvaveda* X.8.32

Supreme Being out of his desire to manifest in multifarious forms. This desire is *kāma* (creative urge).[3] It is through *kāma* that *sat* (existent) could be created out of *asat* (non-existent). The one who could visualize the existent out of the non-existent is termed *kavi* and the word *kavi* has been used for a poet also in Sanskrit.

The creative urge leads the *Puruṣa* or the Primordial Being to reproduce Himself in multifarious forms.[4] The hymns of Veda reflect the experiences that the seers had at beginnings of our civilization; they comprise initial outburst of wonder and mystic feelings experienced by these seers. As soon as these hymns were compiled in the form of Saṁhitās or collections of hymns, the Brāhmaṇa texts were composed for exposition of various concepts in the hymns. In fact the *mantras* (psalms) or hymns as collected in the Vedic Saṁhitās and the Brāhmaṇa texts composed after them, taken together are called as the Veda.[5]

There are two terms used in Vedic literature for the form — *rūpa* (form, beauty) and *pratirūpa* (parallel form). *Rūpa* forms the base and *pratirūpa* is created out of it.[6] This *pratirūpa* is art or craft.[7] It is possible to create numerous forms out of one *rūpa*.[8]

The concept of *śilpa* as given in *Yajurveda, Śatapatha, Aitareya, Kauṣītaki* and other Brāhmaṇa texts is reflected in *Nāṭyaśāstra*. *Yajurveda* holds *ṛk* and *sāman* as *śilpas*.[9]

---

3 *Ṛgveda* X.129.

4 *so 'kāmayadeko 'ham bahu syam.* – *Bṛhadāraṇyaka Upaniṣad*

5 *mantrabrāhmaṇayor vedanāmadehyam* – *Yanjñapavibhāṣā*. Quoted in *Saṁskṛta Sāhitya kā Bṛhad Itihāsa*, ed. Baldev Upadhyaya and B.B. Chaube, vol. I, 1996, p. 376.

6 *rūpam rūpam pratirūpo bhabhūva.* – *Ṛgveda* VI.47.18

7 *yad vai pratirūpam tat śilpam.* – *Śataptha Brāhmaṇa* I.5.8

8 *indro māyābhiḥ pururūpa īyate.* – *Ṛgveda* I.47.18

9 *ṛksāmayoḥ śilpe sthite.* – *Śukla Yajurveda* IV.9, *Taittirīya Saṁhitā* II.2.1, *Maitrāyaṇī Saṁhitā* I.2.2, *Kāṭhaka Saṁhitā* II.5

Aitareya Mahīdāsa, the first great aesthetician in Indian tradition, who flourished around 1000 BCE, discussed the concepts of *śilpa, rasa, gīta,* and their effect or experience on *ātmasaṁskṛti* (purification or refinement of the self).

Aitareya says that there are two types of *śilpa*s – *daiva* and *mānuṣa*. The world as created by the God is *daivaśilpa* and a piece of art produced by *anukṛti* (making once again) of this *daivaśilpa* is *mānuṣaśilpa*. Extending the applicability of this concept of twofold art to music, Aitareya says that there are two types of *gīta* (song) – *daivagīta* (the divine song) and *mānuṣagīta* (the human song). *Ṛk* (verse in the *Ṛgveda*) is *daivagīta*; *gāthā* (popular song) is *mānuṣagīta*.[10]

Aitareya also defines *śilpa* as a continuous process of *ātmasaṁskṛti*.[11] *Stotra*s (hymns) are also said to be the cause of *ātmasaṁskṛti*.[12] *Ātmavistṛti* (self-expansion) and *ātmasaṁskṛti* are the two purposes of creative activity.

There is a correlation between *daivaśilpa* (divine art) and *mānuṣaśilpa* (human art). The art activity by the human beings functions for the betterment of the world as created by the Supreme Being. The latter is the *anukṛti* (an artefact created by re-making or re-doing) of the former. Aitareya cites numerous examples of *mānuṣaśilpa* (human art) that can be created by the process of *anukṛti* (re-making or re-doing) – they may be toys, sculptures or paintings of animals or forms created out of gold or earth.[13] *Kauṣītaki Brāhmaṇa* holds *nṛtta, gīta,* and *vāditra* as the three types of *śilpa*.[14]

Like the concepts of *śilpa* and *anukṛti*, the idea of *chandas*

10 *Aitareya Brāhmaṇa* XXX.1, part III, p. 131, Delhi, 2006.

11 Ibid.

12 Ibid.

13 Ibid.

14 *trivṛd vai śilpaṁ – nṛttaṁ, gītaṁ vāditraṁ iti. – Kau. Br.* IXX.5

(a metre or a *mantra* in metrical form), involves the fundamental principles of Indian aesthetics as envisaged by the Vedic seers. The Brāhmaṇas and Upaniṣads say that *chanda*s is termed so, because it functions as a cover or shield to protect the man from sins.[15] It also serves as a cover to protect from the heat of fire in the performance of *yajña*, and ultimately, it dispels the fear of death.

*Chanda*s in fact, reflects the cosmic order. This order has correspondences and rhythmic patterns and cycles. It is a manifestation of the Universal Being. Every thing in this world is therefore enveloped in *chanda*s, and this *chanda*s is said to be abounding in *rasa* (taste, relish, aesthetic experience). Aitareya says that *rasa* was oozing out of *chanda*s. Prajāpati became afraid that if *rasa* goes on flowing out of the *chanda*s this way there will be no *rasa* left for the people. Then he made an attempt to fasten the gushing flows of *rasa* in the periphery of forms of popular poetic metres. The *rasa* coming out from Gāyatrī was collected in Nārāsaṁśī, the *rasa* emanating from Triṣṭubh was collected in Raibhī, and *rasa* of Jagatī in Pārikṣitī, the *rasa* of Anuṣṭubh in Kāravī.[16] After collecting this *rasa* of different metres in diverse forms of *kāvya*, Prajāpati then replaced that *rasa* again in those metres. So that one can perform the *yajña* with metres that are filled with *rasa*.[17]

Alaṁkāra is a vital concept. It incorporates the means of décor, the process of décor and aesthetic structure that is built

---

15 *Aitareya Āraṇyaka* II.5; *Tiattirīya Saṁhitā* V.6.6; *Ṛgveda Sāyaṇabhāṣya*, VSM, part I, p. 32.

16 Gāyatrī, Triṣṭubh, Jagatī and Anuṣṭubh are Vedic metres, Nārāśaṁsī, Raibhī, Pārikṣitī and Kāravī are popular forms of songs that were being practised during the Vedic age. This myth of Prajāpati collecting the *rasa* of the *mantra*s of Veda in popular forms of poetry also suggests the process of interaction between the Vedic hymns of popular literature.

17 *Aitareya Brāhmaṇa* XXX.6.

through these means. The hymns are supposed to become *alaṁkāras* for the gods.[18]

There is a Sūrya-Sūkta (hymn for Sūrya) both in *Ṛgveda* and *Atharvaveda*. It describes the marriage of Sūryā, a virgin. The *gāthā* (songs) being sung on the occasion of her marriage became *alaṁkāras* to décor her.

Alaṁkāras invest *śilpa* – including all arts and poetry – with divinity. Sāyaṇa has interpreted *mantra* in the following way – *dīvyate iti devaḥ, mantreṇa dyotyate* – *deva* (god) is the one who shines through the *mantras*.[19] *Mantras* are issued forth through the Supreme Being and He resides in *mantras*.[20]

The cosmos is a *śilpa*, replenished with *alaṁkāras*. This *śilpa* is said to be *chandomaya* – created out of *chandas*.[21] This metrical composition has rhythm, pauses, and movements. The universe therefore has its own rhythmic patterns, movements, and pauses. The movement of time has rhythm, the coming of days and nights appears to be a divine dance to Aitareya.[22] This cosmic movement is also defined as *yajña*. The different metres become offerings in the *yajña*. Various metrical compositions become offerings in this cosmic *yajña* or sacrifice.[23]

There is a correlation between *śilpa, chandas* and *yajña*. Basically they denote a cosmic view. This cosmic view is reflected in the aesthetics of *NŚ*. *Śilpa* is the core of cosmic *yajña*, *mantras* or *chandas* its offerings and *alaṁkāra* its beauty.

These postulations of Vedic seers have been adopted by

---

18 *indra kā te asti araṅkṛtiḥ sūktaiḥ kadā nu te maghavan dāśema.*
– *Ṛgveda* VII.29.3

19 *Ṛgveda* with *Sāyaṇabhaṣya*, Pune: Vedic Samshodhana Mandala, 1933, part I, p. 32.

20 *Aitareya Brāhmaṇa* VII.8.

21 Ibid., V.15.

22 Ibid., XVIII.7.

23 Ibid.

Bharata to build the conceptual framework of *NŚ*. Bharata uses the terms *kāma, krīḍā, chandas, anukṛti, alaṁkāra kāvya, kavi,* and *rasa;* with their connotations as given in the Veda (Saṁhitās and Brāhmaṇa texts).

The concept of *kāma* in *NŚ* has its roots in the hymn of *Ṛgveda* referred above. All beings have come out from *kāma* – Bharata says – and this *kāma* consists of a particular quality of desire.[24]

It is in this background that *kāma* has been correlated with *puruṣārtha* (the aspirations of a man). From this point of view it is of three types – in accordance with the three *puruṣārthas*[25] – *dharma, artha,* and *mokṣa* embracing the psychic, empirical, and the spiritual levels of human life. Manu, Vātsyāyana (the author of *Kāmasūtra*) and Bharata all these three authors, belonging almost to the same period in BCE, have defined *kāma*. In two ways – at one level they emphasize over its cosmic view, as a creative urge forming the roots of all activities. Manu says:

> *Kāma* has roots in *saṁkalpa* (resolve) for any action, the *yajñas* are also performed by *saṁkalpa* (resolve). Without *kāma* no function is possible by any being. Whatever (any being) does here, proceeds from *kāma* only.[26]

---

24 प्रायेण सर्वभावनां कामान्निष्पत्तिरिष्यते।
स चेच्छागुणसम्पन्नो बहुधा परिकल्पितः॥ – *NŚ* XXII.95

25 धर्मकामोऽर्थकामश्च मोक्षकामस्तथैव च। – *NŚ* XXII.96
धर्मकामोऽर्थकामश्च मोक्षकामस्तथैव च।
स्त्रीपुंसयोस्तु योगो यः स तु काम इति स्मृतः॥
सर्वस्यैव हि लोकस्य सुखदुःखनिबर्हणः।
भूयिष्ठं दृश्यते कामः स सुखव्यसनेष्वपि॥ – *NŚ* XXII.95.98

26 सङ्कल्पमूलः कामो वै यज्ञाः सङ्कल्पसम्भवाः।
व्रतानि यज्ञधर्माश्च सर्वे सङ्कल्पजाः स्मृताः॥
अकामस्य क्रिया काचित् दृश्यते नेह कर्हिचित्।
यद्यद्धि कुरुते किञ्चित् तत् तत् कामस्य चेष्टितम्॥
– *Manu-Smṛti* II.3.4

Vātsyāyana says:

> When the five sense-organs – the ear, the skin, the eyes, the tongue and the nose – presided over by the mind, which is enjoined with the soul, are inclined towards the objects suited to each; this *pravṛtti* (inclination) is called *kāma*. The experience of joy by touch (of the beloved) which bears fruit is mainly *kāma*.[27]

At another level, *kāma* consists of sensuous form of love, born out of physical attraction between persons of opposite sex.

The word *krīḍā* (sport) has been used to define the form and function of *nāṭya* (theatre) in *NŚ*. Describing the myth of the origin of *nāṭya* it is said that when people became desperate with worldly grievances, the gods approached Brahmā – the creator and told him that they want a sport that could be seen and heard.[28]

After this, there is a long description of the qualities of *nāṭya* created by Brahmā, and there also it is said that *nāṭya* included *krīḍā* also.[29] Vedic seers as referred above, found this universe created as a sport by the Supreme Being and theatre is shaped the same way. In fact, the correspondence between the philosophical tradition and the aesthetic thought in India has continued for centuries in the later period as well. In Vedānta, the term *līlā* was used to define the creativity of the Supreme Being,[30] and in the Śaiva philosophy Śiva is described as *krīḍāpaṇḍita* (a master of sport).[31]

---

27 श्रोत्रत्वक्चक्षुर्जिह्वाघ्रानामात्मसंयुभेन मनसाऽधिष्ठितानां स्वेषु स्वेषु विषयेष्वानुकूल्यतः प्रवृतिः कामः ॥११॥ स्पर्शविशेषविषयात्त्वस्याभिमानिकसुखानुविद्धा फलवत्यर्थप्रतीतिः प्राधान्यात् कामः ॥१२॥ तं कामसूत्रान्नागरिकजनसमवायाच्च प्रतिपद्येत ॥ – *कामसूत्रम्* १. २

28 क्रीडनीयकमिच्छामो द्रश्यं श्रव्यं च यद् भवेत् ॥ – ना. शा. १.११

29 क्वचिद् धर्मः क्वचित् क्रीडा क्वचिदर्थः क्वचिच्छमः ॥ – ना. शा. १. १०८

30 *lokavattu līlā kaivalyam.* – *Brahmasūtra*

31 किन्तु दुर्घटकारित्वात् स्वाच्छन्द्यान्निर्मलादसौ।
स्वात्मप्रच्छादनक्रीडायण्डित परमेश्वरः ॥ – *Tantrāloka* IV.10

→

In the sixth chapter of *NŚ* (named as Rasādhyāya or chapter on *rasa*) Bharata names *kāvyasevā* (remaining devoted to *belles lettress*) as one of the causes of *śr̥ṅgāra rasa*. *Rasa*s are named as *kāvyarasa*s and *nāṭyarasa*s, and they expressed through forty-nine *bhāvas*.[32] Even though Bharata is dealing with drama and theatre, he is conscious of the wide connotation of the term *kāvya* – incorporating all forms that have literary beauty. The concept of *kāvya* in his *NŚ* therefore incorporates qualities of the poetic universe. He terms them as *lakṣaṇa*s. There are thirty-six *lakṣaṇa*s of *kāvya*. Interestingly, in the Āgama tradition of Śaivaśāstra, there are thirty-six fundamental elements that form this cosmos. Just as this universe is formed by thirty-six elements, the poetic universe is formed by thirty-six *lakṣaṇa*s.[33] Bharatamuni also discusses the interrelationship of *kāvya* and *rasa* which Aitareya Mahīdāsa had elaborated upon through mythological narration. Accepting the postulation that there is *rasa* in the *kāvya*, and in different metres, he gives a scientific treatment. Different metres or types of *chanda*s are correlated with *rasa*s.[34]

→ क्रीडा ते लोकरचना सखा ते चिन्मयः शिवः।
आहारस्ते सदानन्दो वासस्ते हृदयं सताम्॥ – *Lalitāstavarājaḥ*

32 ऋतुमाल्यालंकारैः प्रियजनगान्धर्वकाव्यसेवाभिः।
उपवनगमनविहारैः शङ्गाररसः समुद्भवति॥ – *नाट्यशास्त्रम्* ६.४८
एवमेते काव्यरसाभिव्यभिहेतव एकोनपञ्चाशद्भावाः प्रत्यवगन्तयाः। एभ्यश्च सामान्यगुणयोगेन रसा निष्पद्यन्ते। – *नाट्यशास्त्रम्* ७. ७ इत्यतः पूर्वम्

33 षट्त्रिंशललक्षणान्येवं काव्यबन्धेषु निर्दिशेत॥ – *नाट्यशास्त्रम्* १६. ५
एतानि वा काव्यविभूषणानि
षट्त्रिंशदुद्देश्यनिदर्शनानि।
काव्येषु सोदाहरणानि तज्ज्ञैः
सम्यक् प्रयोज्यानि बलानुरुपम्॥

34 लघ्वक्षरप्रायकृतमुपमारूपकाश्रयम्।
काव्यं कार्यं तु नाट्यज्ञैवीररौद्राद्भुताश्रयम्॥
गुर्वक्षरप्रायकृतं बीभत्से करुणे तथा।
कदाचिद्वीररौद्रभ्यां यदा धर्षणजं भवेत्॥ →

Following Aitareya, Bharata also says – there is no word without *chandas* and there is no *chanda*s without the word.[35] The world is created out of speech and speech generates the aesthetic universe as well.[36]

The *vṛtta*s (metres) of Piṅgalaśāstra are also termed as *chanda*s. In fact, they are expressions of *chanda*s in poetry or language. Bharatamuni establishes this linkage of *chanda*s, *vṛtta*s and literary structure when he says that the *vṛtta*s are generated by *chanda*s and they form *kāvyabandha.*[37] A *vṛtta* is formed by specific rhythmic movement (*gati*) patterns and pause (*laya*). It reflects cosmic rhythm. *Viṣṇudharmottara Puraṇa* therefore rightly identifies the seven Vedic metres as the seven horses of the Sun.[38]

→ रूपदीपकसंयुभमार्यावृत्तसमाश्रयम्।
शृङ्गारे तु रसे कार्यं काव्यं स्यान्नाटकाश्रयम्॥
उत्तरोत्तरसंयुभं वीरे काव्यं तु यद्भवेत्।
जगत्यातिजगत्या वा संकृत्यां (त्या?)वापि तद्भवेत् ॥
तथैव युद्धसम्फेटौ प्रकृत्यां सम्प्रयोजितौ।
करुणे शक्करी चैव तथा चातिधृतिः स्मृता॥
यद्वीरे कीर्त्यते छन्दस्तद्रौद्रे सम्प्रयोजयेत्।
शेषाणामर्थयोगेन छन्दः कार्यं तथा रसः॥
त्रिविधं ह्यक्षरं काव्ये विज्ञेयं नाटकाश्रयम्।
ह्रस्वं दीर्घं प्लुतं चैव रसभावविभावकम्॥
— *नाट्यशास्त्रम्* १६. ११०. ११६

35 छन्दोहीनो न शब्दोऽस्ति न च्छन्दः शब्दवर्जितम्।
तस्मात्तूभयसंयोग नाट्यस्योद्योतकः स्मृतः॥ – XIV.47

36 वाचि यत्नस्तु कर्त्तव्यो नाट्यस्येयं तनुः स्मृता।
अङ्गनेपथ्यसत्त्वानि वाक्यार्थं व्यञ्जयन्ति हि ॥२॥
वाङ्मयानीह शास्त्राणि वाङ्निष्ठानि तथैव च।
तस्माद्वाचः परं नास्ति वाग् हि सर्वस्य कारणम्॥ – XIV.2.3

37 वृत्तैरेव तु विविधैर्नानाच्छन्दःसमुद्भवैः।
काव्यबन्धास्तु कर्तव्याः षट्त्रिंशल्लक्षणान्विताः॥ – *NŚ* XV.227

38 *Viṣṇudharmottara Purāṇa*, part III, 97.12. The seven Vedic metres are Gāyatrī, Uṣṇik, Anuṣṭup, Bṛhatī, Paṅkti, Triṣṭup, and Jagatī.

The later tradition understood *śilpa* as externalization of the inner substances, or making many forms out of one element.[39] Bharatamuni also says that *śilpa*s can be innumerable.[40] He makes a distinction between *śilpa* and *kalā* when he says that *nāṭya* combines all *śilpa*s and all *kalā*s.[41]

Nāṭya not only combines all *śilpa*s, as a Veda it also initiates *śilpa* of all types.[42] While the concept of *anukaraṇa* or *anukṛti* comes from the Brāhmaṇa texts, it has been defined in the context of *nāṭya* and has been supplemented with two other terms *anukīrtana* and *anudarśana*. *Anukīrtana, anukaraṇa,* and *anudarśana* – these three concepts have been envisaged *NŚ* to define the creative process of *nāṭya*.[43] The former is again redefined in the context of theatre as *bhāvānukīrtana*.[44]

*Chanda*s should have rhythmic patterns and the aesthetics of rhythm involves *varṇa*s (letters) in numerical combinations. Thus the rhythm of mathematical numbers therefore plays an important role in this aesthetics. Correspondences and interrelations are established through retaining the same numbers in diverse categories.

Śilpa inculcates *alaṁkāra* in a piece of art. *Alaṁkāra* is a dynamic aesthetic concept. *Alaṁkāra* as not only a vital concept in literary theory, but it is equally important in music and

---

39 एकस्यैव पदार्थस्य नानारूपप्रकल्पनम्।
वाङ्मनःकर्मभिर्यत् तच्छिल्पमित्यभिधीयते॥ – *BP* III.76.3-4

40 न शक्यमस्य नाट्यस्य गन्तुमन्तः कथञ्चन।
कस्माद् बहुत्वाज्ज्ञानानां शिल्पानामप्यनन्ततः॥ – *NŚ* VI.6

41 न तच्छ्रास्त्रं न तच्छिल्पं न सा विद्या न सा कला।
न स योगो न तत्कर्म यन्नाट्येऽस्मिन् यन्न दृश्यते ॥ ११६॥
(सर्वशास्त्राणि शिल्पानि कर्माणि विविधानि च।
अस्मिन्नाट्ये समेतानि तस्मादेतन्मया कृतम॥)

42 सर्वशास्त्रार्थसंपन्नं सर्वशिल्पप्रवर्तकम्। – I.95

43 भविष्यतश्च लोकस्य सर्वकर्मानुदर्शकम्। – *NŚ* I.14

44 त्रैलोक्यस्यास्य सर्वस्य नाट्यं भावानुकीर्तनम्। – *NŚ* I.107

dance. The combination of particular *svaras* (notes), which enhances *rakti* or *rāga* involving peculiar use of *varṇas*, is *alaṁkāra*.[45] Employment of *alaṁkāra* generates various layers in *svaras*.[46] *Alaṁkāra* is also employed in instrumental music, particularly in *avanaddha* type of instruments. There *alaṁkāra* leads to harmony amongst various instruments. Even *laya* that brings excellence in music becomes *alaṁkāra*.[47]

There is a search for unity of experience in all the divisions, which Bharatamuni has termed *rasa-vimarda* or *rasavyatikara*[48] and other *ācārya*s have defined as *sampalva;* and it encompasses various layers of time and space for the realization of *puruṣārtha*, eventually to achieve what the Upaniṣads termed

---

45 विशिष्टं वर्णसन्दर्भमलङ्कारं प्रचक्षते। – *स. र.* १. ६. ३
विशिष्टानां स्वराणां यः सन्दर्भो रभिवर्धनः।
वर्णाश्चित्रप्रयोगस्तमलङ्कारं प्रचक्षते ॥
— पण्डितमण्डली, भको. पृ. ३३

46 रचितास्ते त्वलङ्काराः सप्तस्वरमुखाक्षरैः।
एषु सर्वेषु रागेषु स्वराणां कारणं हि तत्।
अन्योन्यस्वरवर्णानां सान्तानां तु प्रयोगतः।
ये जायन्ते वर्णगुम्फास्तेऽलङ्काराः प्रकीर्तिताः ॥
— *सं. उप. सारो.* ३.११९-१२५

47 उत्कर्षहेतुरन्योन्याल्लयरूपा अलङ्क्रिया।
य आतोद्यान्तराणां हि परस्परसमन्वयः॥
तमलङ्कार इत्येवमूचे स भरतो यथा।
चित्रः समो विभभश्च चतुर्थश्छिन्न एव च॥
तदा चानुसृतो ज्ञेयोऽलङ्कारः प्रतिविद्युतः॥
दुर्गोऽवकीर्णोऽप्यर्धविकीर्णश्चापि तथा परः॥
परिक्षिप्त एकरूपस्तथैव नियमान्वितः॥
साचीकृतः समलेखश्चित्रलेखस्तथैव च।
सर्वसमवायकृतो दृढ इत्येकविंशतिः॥
— नान्यदेवः, *भको.*, पृ. ३४

48 न ह्येकरसजं काव्यं नैकभावैकवृत्तिकम्।
विमर्दे रागमायाति प्रयुभं हि प्रयत्नतः। – *NŚ* VII, after 119

as *bhūmā* (the infinity). A *nāṭaka* (play) therefore tends to become *mahārasa, mahābhoga udāttavacanānvitam, mahāpuruṣasañcāraṁ.*[49]

[49] महारसं महाभोगमुदात्तवचनान्वितम् ।
महापुरुषसञ्चारं साध्वाचारजनप्रियम ॥ – *NŚ* IXX.140

6

Narrating the Nation
Kālidāsa's Cultural Geography of India[1]

C. Rajendran

KĀLIDĀSA is one of the very few poets of ancient India who has given a panoramic picture of India through creative works like plays and poems. When we read his works like *Raghuvaṁśa* and *Meghasandeśa*, above everything else, they sometimes appear to be traveller's documents since they contain interesting descriptions of the various regions of the vast subcontinent. They show the poet's deep emotional involvement with the terrain and intimate connection with the geographical area which is now India. It should be pointed out that his descriptions are not abstract paintings of nature in general. They are region specific and full of accurate details. Kālidāsa is always more or less accurate about the geographical details of the region he describes; he invariably describes the rivers, mountains, forests, and other geographical features of places which he has to describe. Nor does he fail to mention the flora and fauna characteristic of the various regions. As a poet of five senses, he is also deeply immersed in the varied splendour of the regions portrayed in his poems. He portrays with great sensitiveness the changes brought forth by seasonal variations and he is conversant with the lifestyle of the people

---

[1] Paper presented at Leipzig University, Germany on 2 May 2013.

with such a vividness as if he has first-hand knowledge of the things he describes. It is precisely because of these features that a perusal of Kālidāsa's works generates a real-like experience in the reader which cannot be gained from any other source. Consequently, the geographical details portrayed by him become vivid experiences rather than dull second-hand enumerations with which one cannot relate in any manner. But above all this, Kālidāsa was subconsciously giving shape to his vision of a nation with which he could emotionally relate. This vision has several complex strands. Over and above, we do find glimpses of the idea of a nation of varied culture emerging from these details, however faint the contours and boundaries of it may be.

It can be argued that there is no evidence to prove the existence of the present-day India as a political entity at the time of Kālidāsa, who, by general consensus lived during the Gupta period. Even if it could be proven that he belonged to a different era, there is no evidence to suggest that he had the notion of a politically unified India with a centralized power structure. This should be clear from the fact that instead of writing about India as a whole, he was always writing about various regional kingdoms of the subcontinent. It is various regions like Suhma, Aṅga, Vaṅga, Kaliṅga, Pāṇḍya, Aparānta, Prāgjyotiṣa, Uttarakosala, Mithilā, Vidarbha, Avantī, Kerala, and Utkala which time and again appear in his works, and their clear-cut differences are well known to him. It is true that it will be difficult to read the notion of modern India in the writings of the poet of a very distant era when the political set-up was based on different considerations altogether. Despite all this it is the essence of real India, and its distinct culture which we find infused in the works of the poet. There seems to be a unity above all diversity in Kālidāsa's works as epitomized by the symbols like myths, festivities, pilgrim centres, places of worship, sacred spaces, and lifestyle in general. It is largely the writings of Vālmīki, Vyāsa, and Kālidāsa which created the image of India in the psyche of generations, an ideal, which was ultimately consummated with establishment of India as a political entity.

The notion of India in Kālidāsa's writings has definitely a political strand, which is epitomized in his concept of *cakravartin* (the emperor and overlord of all kings) which notion figures in most of his works, especially in *Abhijñānaśākuntalam* and *Raghuvaṁśa*. *Abhijñānaśākuntalam* has a deeper political significance in that it celebrates the birth of Bharata to whose name Bhāratavarṣa owes its origin. It is significant that the sages of the hermitage of Kaṇva offer blessings to King Duṣyanta, who is a royal sage (*rājarṣi*), that his progeny will be a *cakravartin*. The motif recurs on several occasions in the play and is reinforced when Duṣyanta recognizes the characteristic signs indicating an emperor in his son. However, it is *Raghuvaṁśa* which can be rightly considered as the work having a broad Indian canvas. Even if Kālidāsa celebrates the glory of the rulers of the Uttarakosala region through this epic, the terrain gets enlarged when the ideal of *cakravartin* is realized through conquest as in the case of Raghu.

In his conquest of the quarters (*digvijaya*) done as a part of his *viśvajit* sacrifice, Raghu marches forward to different directions thus turning the epic into an exploration of India. Region after region is portrayed with most vividness. Of course, it is from the point of view of the conqueror that the whole description is visualized. First he reaches the eastern region of Suhmas marked by the great ocean dark due to the forests of palm trees. Then he reaches the Vaṅga country erecting pillars of victory in between the patches of land lying in between the streams of Gaṅgā. Raghu then crosses the Kalama River with a bridge made by the row of elephants and conquers the Mahendra mountain to reach the Kaliṅga region. After the fierce battle, his victorious army drank the liquor made of coconut trees in bowls made of the betal leaves. Kālidāsa then describes how Raghu proceeds through the seashore abounding in areca-nut trees to the south, the region traversed by Sage Agastya in the past. The prowess of even the Sun becomes weak in the south, but not that of Raghu which could not be tolerated by the Pāṇḍyas. They present him with the best of the pearls collected from the confluence of the river Tāmraparṇī and the ocean as if they were their accumulated fame. Here his army enjoys the waters of river Kāverī imparting the smell of the rut of elephants, thereby making the river the object of jealousy to ocean, her husband. Then they reach the Malaya mountain with valleys having profuse pepper groves (*marica*) and frequented by green pigeons. There, the dust of the cardamon (*elā*) raised by the hoofs of the horses of the marching army trampling them is raised to the temples of the marching elephants full of rut having a similar fragrance. The sandal trees of the region had deep grooves on them due to the habitual coiling of snakes and hence the chains of elephants did not slip down from them.

Moving further, the army reaches Malaya and Dardura mountains covered with sandal trees, looking like the breasts of the region. Continuing the erotic imagery, Kālidāsa refers to the Mt. Sahya itself which looks like the hip of the region and the ocean her garment far removed, to be enjoyed by the marching army. Alluding to the myth of the creation of the west coast (Aparānta) as reclaimed by Paraśurāma, Kālidāsa describes the army in the vicinity of the mountain as resembling the western sea though far removed by the latter in the past. The women of Kerala abandon their ornaments in fear and the dust raised by the marching army settle on their curls of hair in the place of fragrant powder. The pollen grain of the *ketaka* flowers, raised by the breeze of the river Muralā becomes the pigment of perfume for the armour of the soldiers. The murmur of the black palm trees tossed by the wind was subdued by the tingling sound of the decked horses on march. Kālidāsa points out that if, in the past, the ocean had gifted land to Paraśurāma when he requested, it now gave tributes to him through the kings of the western region. A verse here refers to the black bees falling on the cheeks of elephants fragrant with rut from the date palms (*kharjūrī*),[2] but the presence of the palm on west coast is problematic and also, Aruṇagirinātha has not commented on it. Kālidāsa further winds up the conquest of the west coast with the statement that Raghu regarded the Trikūṭa mountain, identified with the hills near Junnār,[3] itself as the victory pillar which was marked with the incisions of his intoxicated elephants.

An interesting feature of Raghu's march is that after subduing the south, he goes abroad, first to the Persian region by land. He describes the women of the region as Yavanīs, probably suggesting that they are outside the purview of India. He also refers to the wine intoxicated faces of the women and the bearded faces of the men of the place. The soldiers remove their fatigue by drinking wine on the skin of the antelopes spread in the vineyards. After subduing them, Raghu marches ahead to the northern region. The river Vaṅkṣu, which is a better reading than Sindhu[4] and which is identified with river Oxus is mentioned along with the profuse *kumkuma* trees on its banks, the pollen of the flowers of which are tossed away by the horses from their shoulders, after they overcome their fatigue with exercises on the river bank. Bhagwat Saran Upadhyaya identifies the region as the doab formed by modern Wakshab and Akshab noted for its saffron flowers.[5] When the Hūṇas of the region are subdued by Raghu, the cheeks of

---

[2] Kālidāsa, *Raghuvaṁśa* IV.57.

[3] See *India in Kalidasa*, p. 12.

[4] Ibid., p. 57.

[5] Ibid., p. 18.

their wives become reddened with constant weeping. Kālidāsa mentions the rulers of the Kāmboja country, located in the Ghalcha-speaking country to the north-east of Kashmir[6] as bending their heads to Raghu like *aṅkolā* trees which, when elephants are tied to them, bend themselves.

After subduing the kings of the north-west, Raghu ascends the Himalaya to conquer the regions around it. He is engaged in fierce battle with the foresters there. The hoofs of the horses raise dust of minerals as if increasing the number of peaks. But the lions in the caves just stay unperturbed as they feel equal to the marching army. The breezes, with a whispering sound on the birch leaves, containing particles of water from Gaṅgā relieved him. The soldiers rested on the rocks fragrant with the contact of the navel of the musk deer, under the shades of *nameru* trees. The luminous plants get reflected in the chains around the neck of elephants tied to *sarala* (*Pinus deodara*) trees thus becoming the lamps without oil at night. The elephants left their marks on *devadāru* (*Cedrus libani*) trees caused by the friction of their ropes thereby giving the hunters an idea. Raghu then crosses the river Lauhitya to reach Prāgjyotiṣa wherein the king readily paid homage in the form of elephants. The king of Kāmarūpa worships the shade of the feet of Raghu.

If this account of the Himalayas is from the conquering army's perspective, Kālidāsa has compensated it with a magnificent description of the mountain in *Kumārasambhava*.[7] This is a classic example of the fusion of geography and mythology and relevant to Kālidāsa's vision of India itself. Kālidāsa here brings forth the extraordinary features – mythological and material – of the Himalaya which

6 *India in Kalidasa*, p. 61.

7 See also, C. Rajendran, 2009, "The Snow Did not Destroy His Glory", *Kālidāsa's Perceptions on Himalaya* Pandanus, Prague: Charles University, pp. 55-63.

make it different from just any other mountain. It is interesting to note that while the properties of the Himalaya emerging from this description are physical, the description in the sixth canto focuses on his human form. The very first verse of the first canto describes Himalaya as the lord of mountains stretching as the measuring rod of earth in the north with two tips sinking into the eastern and western seas. To highlight the splendour of the Himalaya, Kālidāsa refers to a mythical story of Mother Earth assuming the shape of a cow who condensed in her body all her essence, to escape from the clutches of Vena, who almost drained her of all her prosperity. At that time, Pṛthu, the son of Vena intervened and holding her back allowed all the beings of the universe to get whatever they wanted in the form of milk from her udder. The mountains assigned Mt. Mahāmeru the task of milking the earth and made the Himalaya a calf to facilitate milking. It was in this manner that the mountain obtained all the splendours constituting the essence of the prosperity of earth, including brilliant gems and precious herbs.[8] Kālidāsa refers to the wealth of ores in the peaks of the Himalayas, which provide water nymphs with materials for their make-up and which colour the tips of the clouds around, generating the notion of an untimely sunset. He further refers to the origin of the title of the "King of the Mountains" involving the entitlement to enjoy the fruits of sacrifice given to Himalaya by Lord Brahmā. This was in recognition of the Himalaya being the source of accessories used in sacrifices and his capacity to support the earth.

To the imagination of Kālidāsa, the height of the Himalaya makes interesting things happen. The Sun, who is circling

---

[8] Cf. *gaurbhūmiracalā sarve kartāro 'tra payāṁsi ca* ।
auṣadhyaúcaiva bhāsvanti ratnāni vividhāni ca ।
vatsaśca himavānāsīddogddha merurmahāgiriḥ ।
– quoted by Mallinātha on I.2

underneath the mountain, has to use his upward rays to make the lotus buds left behind by the seven sages blossom. The divine *siddhas* station themselves at the foot of the mountain when they want to escape the vigour of the sunlight so that the clouds on the middle slopes shade them; however, when they are harassed by the sudden rain, they have to resort to the sunny peaks. Not so agile do the horse-faced damsels (*aśvamukhī*) inhabit the mountains, who, even when the paths with petrified snow trouble their toes and heels, cannot give up their slow gait, burdened as they are by their heavy hips and breasts. In the case of the hunters, it is the water oozing from the glaciers which creates problem by washing away the bloodspots of the lions which have killed the elephants. They, however, detect the path of the lions with the help of the pearls taken by them from the forehead of the elephants and which then dropped out of their claws. The hunters enjoy the wind which is the vehicle of the water particles of the river coming from river Bhāgīrathī when afflicted by the fatigue caused by their pursuit of deers, with the peacock plumes which decorate their crest being tossed by it. Himalaya's caves are also mentioned on several occasions. The caves give refuge even to owls, as in the case of darkness which seeks protection from the sun. The clouds act as curtains there for the Kimpuruṣa women who become shamefaced when their lovers suddenly disrobe them.

No less interesting is the world of trees, plants and herbs in the Himalaya which have some unique features. Kālidāsa refers to *deodār* or *devadāru* which is perpetually tossed by the wind from Bhāgīrathī. The place selected by Śiva to undertake penance is characterized by *devadāru* trees being tossed by the water flow of Gaṅgā[9] and Śiva actually sits under a *devadāru* tree.[10] Another tree is birch (*bhūrja*), seen aplenty in the

[9] *Kumārasambhava* I.54.

[10] Ibid., IV.44.

Himalaya region, the barks of which are used by *vidyādhara* damsels to write their love letters using the red mineral dye and consequently which look red like the spots on the elephants indicating their age. It is an attested fact that birch bark, along with palm leaf was extensively used in ancient India for writing purposes. Kālidāsa refers to *sarala* trees which emit fragrance from the juice oozing from them when elephants rub their trunks against their branches to ease their itch. In *Meghasandeśa* it is described that the branches of *sarala* trees rub each other and produce forest fire.[11] The mountain is also full of bamboos which have holes on their stems and when the air coming from the caves fills the stems blowing through the holes, they produce musical notes. Kālidāsa fancies that the great mountain wants to accompany the *kinnaras*, the celestial singers who start singing.[12] In *Meghasandeśa,* the *yakṣa* exhorts the cloud to sound like a drum to the ongoing musical concert when the *kinnara* women sing the victory of the three cities by Śiva to the accompaniment of the sweet music coming from the bamboo holes filled by wind.[13] Luminous herbs are another striking feature of Himalaya. They light up the interiors of the caves and serve as oilless lamps during the amorous sports of forest dwellers and their consorts.

Coming to the fauna, the animals mentioned include lions, deer, elephants, peacocks and yaks (*camari*), and *śarabhas*, the fabulous eight-footed animals. The perpetually mobile yaks toss their white tails shining like moonlight. They thus toss chowries in the form of their white hair, and make the appellation of the "king among mountains" appropriate for the Himalaya by providing the royal sign. Kālidāsa mentions the plateau of Himalaya which is fragrant with the smell of

---

11 *Meghasandeśa* I.53.

12 *Kumārasambhava* I.8.

13 *Meghasandeśa* I.58.

the musk deer that Śiva undertakes his penance.[14] An animal with which Kālidāsa has little sympathy is the wretched *śarabha* which we are told will just jump at the cloud with futile fury and obstruct his path just to hurt itself. The *yakṣa* tells the cloud in no uncertain terms to shatter their herd with thunderous rain, for who indeed do not become butts of ridicule when engaged in futile activities.[15]

Kālidāsa mentions two mythical cities in the Himalaya, viz. Oṣadhiprastha and Alakā, but it is certain that the latter is the archetypal model for the former. Both of them, however, are more of dream cities which are inhabited by celestial beings like *yakṣa*s, *kinnara*s, and *vidyādhara*s, and unearthly phenomena like the wish-yielding tree. Alakā, the pinnacle of glory in *Meghasandeśa*, can be easily recognized by the cloud on the upper slope of Himalaya, on Mt. Kailāsa, as if seated on her lover's lap with Gaṅgā, appearing like her garment falling down. The city is endowed with many-storeyed mansions. Oṣadhiprastha looks as if it is Alakā transplanted or heaven itself overflowing. Encircled by Gaṅgā, and with ramparts made of precious gems, and luminous plants lighting up ramparts, it is beautiful even in defence.

Among the peaks of Himalaya mentioned by Kālidāsa, Kailāsa, described in *Meghasandeśa*, doubtlessly occupies the pride of place. The snow clad and hence transparent peak is aptly described here as the very mirror of goddesses. The peak, white as moon lotuses is imagined as the accumulation of the roaring laughter of Śiva. The fragrant peak Gandhamādana is described as the park of the City of Oṣadhiprastha.

Many of these regions reappear later in *Raghuvaṁśa* when Sunandā, the companion, describes various kings assembled

---

[14] *Kumārasambhava* I.54.

[15] *Meghasandeśa* I.56.

to court princess Indumatī. Here Sunandā mentions kings hailing from various parts of India like Magadha, Aṅga, Avantī, Anūpa, Śūrasena, Kaliṅga, Vidarbha, Nāgapura, and finally Uttarakosala, the place of Aja. Of special interest is Avantī, the place wherein Ujjayinī, the fond city of the poet is located. As in *Meghasandeśa*, where Ujjayinī is described at great length, here also Kālidāsa mentions the Mahākāla Temple and the gardens of the city and the beautiful garden shaken by the breeze from river Śiprā. He refers to the Anūpa kingdom wherein flows Revā, encircling the city of Māhiṣmatī, a river described in *Meghasandeśa*, as falling down scattered in the stony valley of Vindhya. The place is also connected with the story of Kārtavīrya. When Suṣeṇa of Śūrasena kingdom is described, river Yamunā is mentioned as joining Gaṅgā in Mathurā with all the Kṛṣṇa legends like the taming of Kālīya and also the splendour of Vṛndāvana, as well as the splendid caves of Govardhana wherein peacocks dance. In Kaliṅga, Indumatī is invited to stroll on the beaches of the sea which are accompanied by the murmur of palm forests and the breeze fragrant with clove flowers (*lavaṅga*) brought from other islands. In the kingdom of Pāṇḍyas, Indumatī can revel in the vales of Malaya mountain covered with *tamāla* trees and full of areca-nut trees intertwined with betal leaves and sandal trees encircled by cardamom creepers. Thus this description of Sunandā becomes an invitation to various regions of India replete with natural splendour and mythological allusions.

Yet another vision of India, this time an aerial one, is presented by Kālidāsa when he describes a victorious Rāma coming back to Ayodhyā with Sītā in the Puṣpaka aerial car. Here the journey is actually a visit to the sites of memories of Rāma and the mood is that of nostalgia and pain alike. The description, even though steeped in mythology sometimes becomes a realistic picture of India as gleaned from the sky. Rāma refers to the ocean divided by the bridge built by him up to the Malaya mountain and all its mythological association, the huge water creatures, waves and conch shells. The coastal lines with *tamāla* and *tālī* trees manifest gradually, and the breeze with the pollen of *ketaka* flowers come to decorate Sītā. Then the car flies over the Janasthāna region where Sītā was abducted. The Mt. Mālyavan with its *kadamaba* trees and *kandalī*s and peacocks, the Pampā River, river Godāvarī, Pañcavaṭī, the pleasure lake called Pañcāpsara, Citrakūṭa mountain, the glorious confluence of Gaṅgā and Yamunā, and the river Sarayū all add to this aerial vision. The confluence of Gaṅgā and Yamunā is the location of the city of Pratiṣṭhāna, which is viewed from the heavens by Urvaśī and Citralekhā in *Vikramorvaśīya*.

If this vision is more or less centred on the southern parts of India, Kālidāsa seems to compensate this with another aerial view of the vast northern Indian subcontinent in *Meghasandeśa*. Here the poet has immortalized the region between Vindhya mountain and the mythical Alakā of the north through his poetic descriptions from the point of view of the yearning *yakṣa* against the backdrop of the onset of rain. One feature of this description is the personification of rivers as beautiful ladies, who enjoy the amorous companionship of the cloud. Even mountains appear as living beings with a personality of their own. Nevertheless, the vision of India is firmly rooted in geographical facts, and we are feasted with the romantic details of each region steeped in mythology and folklore. Kālidāsa refers to various regions like the Daśārṇa with Vidiśā as its capital, Avantī with its capital Ujjayinī, Daśapura, Brahmāvarta, the confluence of Gaṅgā and Yamunā, and the Himalaya region. He refers to the impending departure of the royal geese from both the Vindhya region and the Daśārṇa region at the onset of monsoon. Vidiśā, the capital city of Daśārṇa is alluded to. It is the capital city of Agnimitra also, who is the hero of *Malavikagnimitra*.[16] Ujjayinī is selected for special treatment and her mansions having damsels of haunting glances are mentioned. So are the river Śiprā and the temple of Mahākāla. In Avantī, aged people are familiar with the story of Udayana. The famous temple of Skanda at Devagiri is also referred to. The next region is Daśapura. Brahmāvarta comes next, which became historic as the site wherein Arjuna vanquished his enemies with the shower of arrows in the great Mahābhārata war. Then the cloud reaches the Himalaya region after crossing the river Gaṅgā. The other rivers mentioned include Revā, Vetravatī, Nirvindhyā, Sindhu, Śiprā, Gambhirā, Carmaṇvatī, and Sarasvatī. The mountains in the path include Vindhya, Āmrakūṭa, Nichais, and Devagiri.

To conclude, it can be seen that through his plays and poems, Kālidāsa was giving shape to his unique vision of India with all her mythological associations, cultural diversity, cities, villages, forests, pilgrim centres, mountains, rivers and ethnologically diverse populace viewed from an aesthetic angle. This vision continues to inspire the Indian psyche, however far we are from the poet and his times.

References

Chandra Rajan, 1997–2002, *The Complete Works of Kalidasa* (in two vols.), New Delhi: Sahitya Akademi.

Chaturvedi, Acharya Sitarama (ed.), 1980, *Kālidāsa Granthāvalī*, Varanasi.

Rajendran, C., 2009, "The Snow Did not Destroy His Glory", *Kalidasa's Perceptions on Himalaya* Pandanus, Prague: Charles University, pp. 55-63.

Unni, N.P. (ed.), 2009, *The Complete Works of Kalidasa* (2 vols.), Delhi.

Upadhyaya, B.S., 1968, *India in Kālidāsa*, Delhi.

---

[16] *Mālavikāgnimitra*, *The Complete Works of Kalidasa*, ed. N.P. Unni, p. 144.

7

History and Background of the Sanskrit Commentary-tradition

Uma C. Vaidya

Introduction

THE world-renowned literature in Sanskrit, which covers almost all branches of knowledge and which dates back to the times immemorial, is always assisted by the commentaries thereon. In ancient India, this commentary literature was developed to such an extent that a full-fledged science about commentary writing can be traced through the study. These commentaries enjoy the major share in fame and popularity that the Sanskrit literature has gained through the centuries. The Sanskrit literature sought a place on the universal map of scholarship on account of its own merits which are underlined by the wonderful commentaries.

The modern research methods are keen about the historical viewpoint towards the topic concerned. In this light if one tries to trace the origin of this commentary type of literature and to present the history of this literary form he comes to the conclusion that the deliberate and conscious efforts of commentary writing are comparatively late but the seeds of this type of compositions are as old as the Vedic texts themselves. In ancient India, the only method of imparting knowledge was the method of oral transmission and therefore this method of direct teaching was the first and foremost type of commentary which was solely oral and therefore audible. From this viewpoint, commentaries can be classified under various heads. Apart from these oral commentaries, there were pictorial commentaries too. It is found that sometimes pictures are drawn to explain the thoughts which are presented in verses or in particular paragraphs. Such pictorial commentaries form an important part of Illustrated Manuscripts. Even a dancer, choosing a particular theme from a text and giving stage performance also comments on the verse or passage through the medium of performing art. These two types of commentaries are visual. The third one is the most popular and that is writing of the commentary and this is a readable type. It is not that all these types were used for all the texts but these are the progressive steps on this long march of framing the science of commentaries.

The available historical records unanimously agree to the point that *R̥gveda* (in Sanskrit) is the first literary composition in the history of world literature and therefore it is not improper to trace the origin of this commentary type of literature in *R̥gveda,* at least somewhere in Vedic literature. It is observed that *pāṭhabheda*s (i.e. alternative readings) or the different *uccāraṇa-paddhati*s (methods of pronunciation) are the steps in the same direction. *Padapāṭha* (i.e. the word analysis) of the Vedic *mantra*s also can be treated as the early offshoot of the then blossoming commentary literature.

Before proceeding with some more details about the commentaries, the thorough knowledge about the word commentary is very necessary. The verb "to comment" or the Sanskrit root *vi* + *ā* + *khyā* suggests the meaning as "the extensive and authentic explanation of the basic text". Therefore, the word commentary is rendered in Sanskrit as *vyākhyā* or *vyākhyāna*. So also, the words like *vr̥tti, vārttika, bhāṣya, ṭīkā,* and *cūrṇi* are used as synonyms but these different words have different shades of meanings and the point will be explained in due course. There are some fundamental questions, answers to which will help to know the real nature of the commentary form. The questions are: What is a commentary? Why is a commentary? How is a commentary? When is a commentary? Where is commentary? and which are the commentaries? Authentic and definite answers to these questions are the very purport of this article. The available information will transform the hypothesis into a theory that through the study of ancient Indian commentary literature a full-fledged science of it can be safely composed. Any science has to explain the concerned matters with three fundamental points – definition, classification, and analysis. If one examines the collected information about the commentaries on these three criteria, the results are quite satisfactory.

As a matter of fact, commentary writing seems to be a global phenomenon. Commentaries are written in various languages like Hebrew, Latin, Sanskrit, and Pāli; but commentaries in Sanskrit are unique for its style, scope, varied field, and for its qualitative and quantitative supremacy. The term "commentary literature" is very extensive and encompasses large area of the ancient Indian literature. In India it was a long and continuous process of writing commentaries on the basic texts. An uninterrupted chain of commentaries was formed irrespective of religion, language, matter, and manner of the text and thus one finds commentaries not only on Vedic texts but also on the Buddhist texts; not only written in Sanskrit but written in Pāli too. It is also found that commentaries are written not only on the basic texts but on the commentaries too. The commentaries on scientific or *dārśanika* texts are more in number than the commentaries on the literary or ornamental compositions. However, this article is confined to the basic information about Sanskrit commentaries and that the period taken care of is till the eighteenth century CE. It is proposed to take review of the commentary literature as a whole but special reference is made to Sāyaṇa, Śaṅkara, and Patañjali. These three commentators were great scholars. Their scholarship was not restricted to their own field of specialization but had studied almost all branches of Sanskrit studies and apart from the great commentaries that they have written; the composition of some basic texts is also to their credit. Patañjali, the Vyākaraṇācārya and the founder of the *yoga* system had flourished in the second century BCE. His *Vyākaraṇa-Mahābhāṣya* is the oldest, simplest, and finest specimen of commentary literature. Then flourished Śaṅkara, in the eighth century CE, the renowned scholar of Advaita Vedānta, the staunch follower of Vedic religion and a versatile genius who has written commentaries on *Prasthānatrayī,* i.e. *Brahmasūtras* of Bādarāyaṇa–Vyāsa, the ten principal Upaniṣads, and *Bhagavad-Gītā.* Then the famous and authentic commentator of Vedic texts followed in fourteenth century CE, whose name was Sāyaṇa. He commented especially on the Saṁhitās, Brāhmaṇas, Āraṇyakas, and Upaniṣads. Sāyaṇa's view and principle of commentary were a point of high debate for Western scholars.

Nature of a Commentary

A commentary is a particular method of the treatment to the original work. If the original work is a scientific or *dārśanika* text then the treatment to it will be fixed and if it is a literary composition, some different method will be adopted for the commentary. When this idea was deep-rooted in the mind of scholars, deliberate attempts were made to frame the norms of a commentary and to prepare the guidelines for the same and therefore three classes of commentaries are clearly marked as Vedic, philosophical or *dārśanika*, and literary commentaries. These three classes have their different norms and aims too but in general a commentary is expected to be a faithful representation of the natural and straightforward meaning of the original, apart from the inherent philosophical value of the doctrine propounded by the commentator. It is found that if the arrangement of the original work is rather astray or remote for the meaning to be conveyed, it is expected from the commentator to join the parts together with his commentary as to show the original work as a homogeneous product.

The commentaries are many a time referred to as interpretations. There are two methods of interpretations: one is critical and the other is traditional.[1] The second method is applied by commentators like Sāyaṇa. This method takes the doctrine or principle for granted and proceeds from this assumption to find that the doctrine, the work under examination, for instance, *Bhagavad-Gītā* (hereafter referred to as *BG*). Every school of Vedānta tries to fetch its own doctrine from the verses of *BG*, many a time shutting its eyes to all contradictory passages or more often trying to interpret them in a far-fetched manner, so as to confirm their own doctrine. In this class of commentaries the interpreter has a certain tradition coming down from of yore and he moves always in the groove where he has once placed himself.

On the other hand, the critical method presupposes an attitude of absolute impartiality considering the work by itself, without a leaning to any one particular doctrine and therefore there are many chances to commit a mistake in applying this method and very ridiculous conclusions may be arrived at. The reasons for such conclusions are sometimes due to the insurmountable prejudices due to birth, race, and other surroundings or owing to want of patience or lack of sufficient material to go upon. The example of *Gītā* verses will be explained soon. Of course, this critical method (as opposed to the purely traditional one) was not unknown to the old Sanskrit

---

1 V.S. Ghate, *The Vedanta*, Pune: BORI, 1926, p. 51.

writers especially in the domain of philosophy and the Mīmāṁsakas had laid down the canons of interpretation.

SYNONYMS FOR COMMENTARY

As stated earlier in ancient India commentary writing was a continuous process and therefore progressive steps on this march can easily be traced. At different stages, the commentaries were known by different technical terms. The most popular term in this connection is *bhāṣya*.

1. *Bhāṣya*

The commentaries written by Sāyaṇācārya, Śaṅkarācārya, and Patañjali are titled as *bhāṣya* and therefore the *Sāyaṇabhāṣya* in the field of Vedas, *Śāṅkarabhāṣya* in the Vedānta field, and *Pātañjala-Mahābhāṣya* in the field of Vyākaraṇa are the well-known treatises. *Bhāṣya* is a major part of commentary. It is even more than a commentary[2] because besides explaining the meaning of a *sūtra* and besides elaborating its implications through dialects, it admits a creative part, i.e. formulation of new like propositions with their own commentaries. The off-quoted definition of *bhāṣya* explains the word, as follows:[3]

> The knowers of *bhāṣya* know *bhāṣya* as a text where the meaning of *sūtra*s is explained with the words conformable to the *sūtra*s and where its own words are explained.

In other words *bhāṣya* explains the text and explains itself. The word is derived from the root √*bhas* (*vyaktayam vāci*) by Pāṇini 3.1.124 and used in the sense of *bhāva-karman* and *kāraṇa*. Therefore the words *yatra varṇyate* give the sense of locative and *yaiḥ varṇyate* give the sense of instrumental. There is a regular connection of the term *bhāṣya* with the *sūtra* and *bhāṣya*

---

[2] Filliozat, *An Introduction to the Commentaries on Patanjali's Mahabhashya*, Pune: BORI, 1991, Preface, pp. 5-6.

[3] Ibid.

therefore indicates the commentaries on *sūtras* only. The other definition of a *bhāṣya*[4] explains the word as follows:

> The work where the method of objection and refutation is adopted is called as *bhāṣya*.

In this form of a commentary, *bhāṣyakāra* is free to comment either positively or negatively on the topic concerned. The concept of *bhāṣyaṅgas* as seen through the definition was fully developed at the time of Kuṇḍin (5th Saṁvat, Vikrama Pūrva). *Baudhāyana Gṛhyasūtra* uses the word *vṛttikāra* for Kuṇḍin and it seems equivalent with the word *bhāṣyakāra*: (1) *vākyārthavamana*, (2) *sūtrānusarala śabdānvayaḥ*, (3) *śabdaspaṣṭakaraṇam*, and (4) *bhāṣyapadavarṇana* are the necessary components of a *bhāṣya*. In this type of commentary the commentator is free to support, or to criticize the original text but the writing must be evidenced by authentic statements.

2. *Vṛtti*

The traditional meaning of the term *vṛtti* is that work in which prominence is given to the meaning of the aphorism[5] and thus the other name for *vṛtti* is *sūtravṛtti*. Pāṇini has framed 3,999 rules of Sanskrit grammar and made a very brief science of grammar. This brevity creates ambiguity and it becomes very difficult to get exact meaning of the aphorism as desired by the grammarian and thus some explanation is required and that actually is titled as *vṛtti*. *Kāśikā* is the most important *sūtravṛtti* on Pāṇinian grammar and Pt. Narayana Mishra gives some information[6] about the *vṛtti*-type of commentary. The essence or purport of the grammatical theories, which are scattered in *vṛtti-granthas*, *bhāṣya-granthas* and in the works

---

4 S.N. Mishra, *Kāśikā* (part I), Varanasi: Chaukhamba Sanskrit Samsthana, 1996, p. 1 fn.

5 Ibid.

6 Ibid.

known as *Dhātuparāyaṇa* and *Nāmaparāyaṇa* is collected in this work, i.e. *Kāśikā*. It is found that *vṛttikāra* expresses tremendous faith in the author of the basic text and also exhibits his loyalty to the thoughts and opinions presented by the author. He very rarely expresses his likes or dislikes regarding these opinions but is very honest in explaining what the author has said. This particular tendency is highly criticized by the Western scholars and will be discussed soon. Another explanation of the term *vṛtti* in grammar is given as *śāstrapravṛttiḥ*,[7] i.e. "the reason for the very commencement of science", in this context, it is the science of grammar. Any science is built not only on the theories propounded, but by the explanation of those theories along with illustrations. Thus, the explanation or *vṛtti* is an important component of any science, especially of the grammatical science. Thus, by the word *śāstrapravṛttiḥ*, Patañjali probably means that explanation which gives rise to the science. *Nirukta* also comments in the same light when it says that *saṁśayavatyo hi vṛttayo bhavanti*. Kātyāyana also accepts the same meaning of the word *vṛtti* and explains the word *anuvṛtti* accordingly. It seems that the word *vṛtti* is equivalent to the word *vyākhyāna* because the characteristics of these two are the same. The thorough knowledge of any science cannot be acquired without a commentary on the rules. Thus, those works which explain the words separately (*padaccheda*), the cases (*vibhakti*s), the examples (*udāharaṇāni*), the counter-examples (*pratyudāharaṇāni*), etc. are also called *vṛtti*s or *vyākhyāna*s. Thus, as regards the *Pāṇinian Aṣṭādhyāyī* the aphorisms are to be called *sūtra*s and Pāṇini's oral explanation on them is a *vṛtti*. With this viewpoint the explanation of the term *vārttika* is as follows.

---

[7] Yudhisthira Mimamsaka, *Sanskṛtvyākaraṇaśāstra kā Itihāsa*, New Delhi: Bharatiya Prachyavidya Prakashana, 1950, p. 182.

3. Vārttika

This word is associated with the name of Kātyāyana and therefore the students of grammar take it for granted that the rules framed by Kātyāyana as the amendments to Pāṇinian rules are called *vārttika*s but the concept must be made clear. This word is explained variously. It is also referred to, as *vākya, vyākhyāna-sūtra, bhāṣya-sūtra, anutantra,* and *anusmṛti.*[8] Kaiyaṭa and Deva explain it as *vākya* and further state that the *sūtra*s do not use the verbs so they do not fulfil the criterion as *ekatin vākyam*, but *vārttika*s use the verb and therefore are called *vākya*s. Kaiyaṭa, in his *Pradīpa,* uses the word *vyākhyā-sūtra* in the sense of a particular type of commentary and Nāgeśa comments on the word as *vyākhyānasūtreṣviti vārttikeṣvityarthaḥ*. *Bhāṣya*s or *vyākhyāna*s were written on *vārttika*s and thus they are called *vyākhyāna-sūtras*. *Vārttika*s are also called *bhāṣyas-sūtra*s by Bhartṛhari in his *Mahābhāṣyadīpikā* and in his *Svopajña-ṭīkā* on *Vākyapadīya* (Brahma-Kāṇḍa). He has called them as *anutantra*. Sāyaṇa in his *Dhātuvṛtti* called this *vārttika*-type as *anusmṛti*. In short, Bhartṛhari, Kumārila, Jinendrabuddhi, Kṣīraswāmī, Helārāja, Hemacandra, Haradatta, Sāyaṇa, and Nāgeśa unanimously agree that *vārttikakāra* is *vākyakāra*. It is also pointed out that a *vyākhyāna* bears five distinguishing characteristics. All these on a small scale are called *vṛtti* and it is different from a *vārttika*. Yudhisthira Mimamsaka, in his *History of Sanskrit Vyākaraṇa-śāstra,* has clearly stated the difference between a *vṛtti* and a *vārttika* by making two different chapters on *vṛttikāra*s and *vārttikakāra*s[9] (i.e. chapter 14 and chapter 8, respectively). Kātyāyana, Bhāradvāja, Sunāga, Kroṣṭra, Vaḍava, Vyāghrabhūti, and Vaiyāghrapadya are recorded as *vārttikakāra*s and Pāṇini himself, Svobhūti, Vyāḍi, Kuni,

[8] Yudhisthira Mimamsaka, op. cit., p. 281.

[9] Ibid., chapters 8 and 14.

Māthura, Vararuci (other than the *vārttikakāra* Kātyāyana) Devanandī, Durvinīta, Cullibhaṭṭi, Nirlūra, Cūrṇi, and Jayāditya-Vāmana are recorded as *vṛttikāras*. If it is *vṛttervyākhyānam vārttikam*, then one has to note that *vārttikas* which are framed by Kātyāyana have got the base of *vṛttis* earlier framed by *vṛttikāras* on the Pāṇinian rules. Therefore, the graph of the evolution of this grammatical treatise will show that *sūtras*, *vṛttis*, *vārttikas*, and *vyākhyānas* (or *bhāṣyas*) was the order of the gradual development.

The famous definition of *vārttika* as *uktanukta-duruktanam* . . . is found in *Parāśara Upapurāṇa*. According to it, *vārttika* is that construction which thinks about what is said, what is not said, and what is said inadequately. But it seems that this definition is not for grammatical *vārttikas* framed by Kātyāyana but for those treatise which are written on *bhāṣyagranthas* such as *Ślokavārttika* by Kumārila on *Śābara-Bhāṣya*, *Tantra-Vārttika* by Kumārila on *Śābara-Bhāṣya*, and *Sureśvara-Vārttika* by Sureśvara on *Śaṅkara-Bṛhadāraṇyaka-Bhāṣya*. These are *vārttikas* in the true sense of the term.[10] But in the field of grammar, *vārttikas* are those explanations of Pāṇinian rules which help to understand the changes in the language.

4. *Vyākhyā, Vyākhyānam*

These two words are very popular to denote the sense of a commentary. In Sanskrit *vi + ā + khyā* means to explain fully so *vyākhyā* or *vyākhyāna* means "that which explains fully". Even *Mahābhāṣya* uses the word *vyākhyāna* and says *na kevalam carcāpadāni vyākhyānam*. Just splitting of words is not a *vyākhyāna*, but examples, counter examples, and filling the sentences by appropriate words constitute a *vyākhyāna*[11] on the work. In a commentary titled as *Bhāṣāvṛtti*, Sṛṣṭidharaswāmī

---

10 Yudhisthira Mimamsaka, op. cit., p. 281.

11 Ibid., p. 401.

has categorically marked five characteristics of *vyākhyāna* and they are: (i) splitting of *padas* (*padacchedaḥ*), (ii) the meaning of the words (*padārthoktiḥ*), (iii) the dissolving of the compounds (*vigrahaḥ*), (iv) the construe (*vākyayojana*), and (v) arguments and counter arguments (*pūrvapakṣasamādhāna*). In this type of a commentary, the commentator takes liberty to comment either positively or negatively on the basic text.

5. Pārāyaṇa

It is another form of commentary where additional information regarding the word formation (of both, the verbal forms and the nominal forms) is explained. When one goes through various types of literature on grammar he finds this type of composition in *prakriyā-granthas*. *Prakriya-granthas* have very important place in Pāṇinian grammar. It is very true that the aim of this type of treatise is not to comment upon Pāṇinian rules but to use them for practical purpose of word formation. Generally, the commentaries stress on the theoretical part of the text and any commentator hardly thinks of the application of those rules. However, *prakriyā-granthas* have the sole aim to simplify the process of word formation and thus they stress on the easy methods for students of this science. Though Pāṇini's numbering of *sūtras* was convenient for his infrastructure of *Aṣṭādhyāyī*, *sūtras* required for the word formation are scattered all over *Aṣṭādhyāyī* and students have to gather them from here and there. Consequently students lose their interest in grammatical studies. To avoid this problem, the old students, who were experts in the process of word formation, arranged the old material in proper order according to the requirements and finally this activity formed the base for the composition of *Siddhāntakaumudī* and *Prakriyākaumudī* the two were very popular in this field. The other two, process-oriented treatises were *Prakriyāratnam* and *Rūpamālā* but they are not available. The point therefore is, though the tradition does not count *prakriyā-granthas* as the commentaries, a student finding out the techniques of commentary can safely call them as applied commentaries, and these works prove to be more helpful for the students rather than theoretical explanations, arguments, and counter arguments on the topic.

6. *Ṭīkā and Ṭippaṇī*

Ṭippaṇī is generally used to indicate a brief comment on a particular word and it is hardly used in the sense of a whole treatise as a full-fledged commentary. On the contrary, the word *ṭīkā* is quite frequently used in this field. The commentaries written by Mallinātha on Sanskrit *mahākāvya*s are called *ṭīkā*s. These commentaries are of literary-type and not the philosophical ones. They are mainly on classical compositions and help to enhance the sentiment presented through the poems. These *ṭīkā*s are light in nature because the topic on which they comment itself is light. The commentator has a chance to display his appreciation of the event while commenting because it is not the establishment of any theory but just sharing of the experience which the poet has presented. He, then, explains the embellishments if any and teaches to appreciate the passage. But *ṭīkā*s are not always light in nature. The philosopher grammarian Bhartṛhari has written a commentary on his own text of *Vākyapadīya* which is called *Svopajña-ṭīkā* and nobody will dare to call it as a light commentary. In vernacular languages the word *ṭīkā* is used in the sense of criticizing with negative aspect but in Sanskrit root *ṭīk* means to comment in general, either positive or negative. Mallinātha has written a commentary on Nyāsa which itself is a commentary on *Kāśikā* (and *Kāśikā* is a commentary on Pāṇini) and Sāyaṇa quotes him. So it seems that Mallinātha flourished before Sāyaṇa and he had made *ṭīkā*-type of commentary very popular. [The word "Mallināthī" in Marathi became the symbol of a good comment.]

7. Cūrṇi

This word is not used as a general term for commentaries but it makes special reference to *Mahābhāṣya* of Patañjali. One explanation of the word is *carati iti cūrṇiḥ – grantha-viśeṣaḥ.*[12] It means that a special type of treatise which has open access in the field suggesting thereby varied coverage of the book. *Mahābhāṣya* of Patañjali is not only a commentary on Pāṇinian rules but it is a compendium of various philosophical principles and it is an *ākaragrantha* for various branches of knowledge. Bhartṛhari has referred this fact in his *Vākyapadīya.* Another explanation of this word is *cūrṇayati khaṇḍayati aśeṣapaṇḍitānām tarkam iti;*[13] that which smashes the argumentation of all scholars is called *cūrṇi.* All the special features of *Mahābhāṣya* are the features of a *cūrṇi.* It is all that the teacher of teachers may say about a topic. From this kind of ancient *bhāṣya*s one can imagine what was a lecture or debate of scholars at that time. Sometimes the *bhāṣya* seems to be a report by a person who was present at the seminar and who witnessed the discussion. The massive introduction of debates in *bhāṣya* had led to a designation of *Mahābhāṣya,* viz. *cūrṇi.* It displays all applications of intelligence to the concerned subject.

8. Saṁgraha

This is also a technical form of literature which seems like the commentaries but does not fit in the criteria of a commentary. *Saṁgraha* is an abridged edition of *Sūtrabhāṣya.*[14] This is how it is defined in Bharata's *Nāṭyaśāstra. Mahābhāṣya, Pradīpa, Udyota* and *Vākyapadīyaṭīkā* of Puṇyarāja mention the *saṁgraha* by Vyāḍi and say that a *saṁgraha* is also an important part of the science concerned. Thus, *Paribhāṣāsaṁgraha* and *Tarkasaṁgraha* are the

---

[12] Yudhisthira Mimamsaka, op. cit., p. 313.

[13] Ref. 2, p. 2.

[14] Ref. 7, p. 263.

important compositions of Vyākaraṇa and Nyāya-Vaiśeṣikas, respectively.

9. Niryukti, Vivṛtti, and Vivaraṇa

The two more words used in the sense of a commentary are *niryukti* and *vivṛtti*, derived from the roots *nir* + *yuj* and *vi* + *vṛ*, respectively. The noun *vivaraṇa* is derived from *vi* + *vṛ* which means to open, to disclose, to reveal, to explain, to expound. Thus, *vivaraṇa* is that type of commentary which unlocks the words from its aphoristic terseness, which reveals the principles hidden, which expounds the theories, in short, it explains every point which is necessary to understand the text. The root *vṛ* along with its preposition *vi* means to surround or to encompass. So *vivṛtti* is that explanation which encompasses the text from all sides. *Nirukta-laghu-vivṛtti* is the text of this type. Root *yuj* always carries two opposite meanings, i.e. to connect and to cut or to disconnect as per reference. In connection with the commentaries it means dissolving of the compounds in a sentence or to analyse the words into *prakṛti* and *pratyayas*, and again to arrange them in a particular order to suit the meaning; thus *yukti* or *niryukti* is that arrangement of words which will enable one to get the whole reference and meaning of the text and it is a special feature of a commentary and thus *niryukti*, *vivṛtti*, and *vivaraṇa* are all the technical names for a commentary. In some sciences *vārttika*, type of literature is called *niryukti* and according to them the *cūrṇis* are *vyākhyāgranthas*.[15]

Names of the Commentaries

Apart from the technical words used for a commentary, almost all commentaries have their own names and thus the technical name stands for its clan and genre, the name of the author or

---

15 K.V. Abhyankar, *Vyākaraṇa Mahābhāṣya* (Prastāvanā Khaṇḍa) (part VII), Bhūmikā, p. 2.

of the text on which it is written stands in the place of father's name and name of the commentary given by the commentator stands as its own name. For example, in the name *Vedārthaprakāśa-ṛgbhāṣya*, the word *Vedārthaprakāśa* is the name of the commentary, *Ṛg* is the name of the book and *Bhāṣya* is the type of the commentary. It is not that all the names include all these points but each contains either of them. These names also indicate the aim of commentary writing and they are very apt as far as their meaning is concerned (*anvarthaka*). In short, the titles, even being very brief and ornamental, throw light on the name of the text (the original one), the commentator's name, name of the commentary itself, purpose of the commentary, and suggest its supremacy or usefulness in understanding the texts. [Thus, the name of the commentary is "a history in capsule".] The point can be explained with a few illustrations.

The popular way to call a commentary is with the name of the author as *Brahmasūtra-Śāṅkarabhāṣya*. As a matter of fact, Śaṅkara's commentary works are famous as *Śāṅkarabhāṣya* but he has many commentaries to his credit. Thus they are specified by the name of the text. His other *bhāṣya*s are titled as *Śāṅkara-Gītābhāṣya* and *Śāṅkara-Upaniṣadbhāṣya*. It is called *Lekhakānusārī-bhāṣyam*. *Sāyaṇācārya-bhāṣya* on Vedic Saṁhitās have a common name though he has written commentaries on different texts and it is called as *Vedārthaprakāśabhāṣya*. The commentary throws light on the meaning of the Vedas and thus the title is very apt (*anvarthaka*). It is very interesting to go through the list of commentaries given at the end of the project. There is a commentary titled as *Locana* on the text of *Sāhitya-Darpaṇa*. Without *Locana* it is very difficult to see the reflections in the mirror (in the form of literature). This metaphorical name not only pleases the mind but also expresses the importance and propriety of the said commentary. Bhaṭṭojī Dīkṣita's *Siddhāntakaumudī* is traditionally considered as an original work and not as a commentary but many characteristics of a commentary are seen in it. It is called as *Kaumudī*, cool and pleasing as the stars. The Pāṇinian *sūtras* are terse and always cause fatigue to the reader. They are very difficult to understand and thus Bhaṭṭojī has extracted important theories which are easy to understand and the student therefore feels as if he is under the stars and not under the hot sun. Moreover, there are again two commentaries on this text which are named as *Bāla-manoramā* and *Prauḍha-manoramā* suggesting thereby their utility for a certain group of readers as the primary and higher secondary students of the school. Curiously enough Paṇḍitarāja Jagannātha has written a commentary for ruling out the theories in *Prauḍha-manoramā* and in consistency with his nature, the scholar has given the name as *Manoramākucamardinī* to his text. The *Prauḍha-manoramā* of Bhaṭṭojī stands as a beautiful lady to the eyes of the *prauḍhas* (the grown-ups), her breast is pressed, i.e. taken to task by Jagannātha.

The personal rivalry between the scholars on the point of supremacy is reflected in the names of the works they have written. Many commentaries show the relation of a lamp and light in the names. Kaiyaṭa's famous commentary on *Mahābhāṣya* is titled as *Pradīpa* (naturally) throwing light on the text and Nāgeśa's commentary on the same is called *Udyota*, the light itself. The ancient scholar, Gārgya Gopāla Yajva by name, has written a commentary titled as *Jñānadīpa* on *Vṛttaratnākara*. Bhartṛhari has written a commentary on *Mahābhāṣya* which is called *Bhāṣyadīpikā*. There are other interesting names such as *Bhāmatī*, *Citprabha*, *Tattvaviśāradī*, *Nyāsa*, *Padamañjarī*, *Tattvādarśa*, *Śāstrārthakalā*, *Advaitamṛtavarṣiṇī*, *Nyāyanirṇayabhūṣaṇasāra*, and *Vaiyākaraṇadūṣaṇa*. Apart from these names, there are some titles which indicate the type of a commentary with some technical word like *Mīmāṁsāvṛtti* by Bhartṛhari, *Mahābhāṣya* by Patañjali, *Nyāyavārttikatātparyaṭīkā*, *Nīlakaṇṭhavyākhyā*,

Bṛhadvivaraṇa, etc. These are *vṛttis*, *vyākhyās*, *vivaraṇas*, *ṭīkās*, *bhāṣyas*, i.e. various types of commentary literature and in these names the very faith of Indian mind is reflected, ***te jasvināvadhitamastu.***

The Purpose of the Commentaries

Let us know about the aims and objectives of commentary literature. The main reason for the rise of this type of literature is the aphoristic style of the philosophical and scientific literature in Sanskrit. Most of the ancient Indian Sanskrit works are written in *sūtra*-style and therefore are brief in words though pregnant with meaning. This brevity in writing is consistent with method of oral transmission for imparting the knowledge. The work should be comprehensive and be easy to be memorized. These two requirements had given rise to this *sūtra*-style or the *śloka*-style of Sanskrit literature. [In modern terms it is the codification of a particular subject.] If such a codified knowledge remains in the custody of author, it may become redundant for others as it is inexpressive and intangible. Therefore, some explanation of these codified theories which is given either by the author or by his direct disciple or some scholar of the same school is very necessary. [This explanation is a "commentary" which can be explained as "decoding system" in modern language.] The suitable nature of Sanskrit language has also facilitated the *sūtra*-style. Along with the easy access to memory, lack of (or scarcity of) writing material and that of methods (as Max Müllar puts it) were also the reasons for giving rise to this style. Moreover, there is socio-historical reason behind this oral transmission and aphoristic nature of the treatise. There was a long chain of foreign invaders in ancient Indian history and they were very cruel to destroy the treasures of knowledge along with the treasures of wealth. Consequently, almost all Sanskrit original texts were written in the *sūtra*-style and we have *Pātañjala Yogasūtra*, *Gautama Nyāyasūtra*, *Jaiminīya*

Pūrvamīmāṁsā-sūtra, Pāṇini-sūtra (i.e. *Aṣṭādhyāyī*), etc. Sometimes the whole treatise was composed in the verse style and we also have *kārikā* style presented through *Gauḍapādakārikā* or *Sāṁkhyakārikā*, etc. Each *kārikā* can be called "a tablet" or "a capsule" studded with a theory of that particular branch of study. [This type of intentional codification naturally required a decoding system and that was the commentary.]

The other purpose of commentary is supported by the universal experience. When the literary work enters into antiquity it becomes more difficult to understand. As far as the new generation is concerned, references to the time and situation get lost, the composition loses its charm and for the modern reader it becomes insignificant. The gap between the reader and the author widens, and consequently the text becomes outdated. In such conditions, to bridge this gap, the reader requires some expert scholar who himself has understood the text properly and who also possesses the skills to explain it to him. The commentator therefore is to be well versed in different branches of knowledge and is also expected to be an expert in imparting the thought and poetic joy to his readers. He has to be aware of the customs, traditions and situations of those times when that particular piece of literature is composed. The literature being the mirror of the society, the commentator must be a keen observer of the social events and changes. He has to take the note of social reforms, at the same time, he has to take care of the interest of the readers, that too without causing any injustice to the poet himself. It is not easy to be a good commentator and thus it must be admitted that Patañjali, Śaṅkara, and Sāyaṇa had done a great job in this field. It is interesting to note that in India, in such a demanding situation the commentary literature branched out and gave shelter to its readers under the big umbrella of its leaves and colourful blossoms. The terse texts were simplified because of the commentaries and thus more and more readers took interest in reading even the "high-tech" books in ancient India. The commentary on the text had then become the symbol of status and number of commentaries on a text became the scale to measure the importance of the text. It is also found that some texts received so much importance not on their original strength but because they are commented by some eminent commentator. Sometimes even the insignificant purport if supported and strengthened by a strong and reputed commentator receives the status of a Śāstra or a Darśana. On the contrary it also happens that the commentary becomes more terse and tough than the basic text. The reader finds it easy to read the original text rather than to read it with the commentary. It is also observed that if a commentator is the direct disciple of the teacher who has authored the book or if he is a commentator, immediately following the author chronologically, then his sincerity in the studies, his faith in his teacher, his loyalty to the principles he is taught, and his love for the subject is reflected in his commentaries. In such conditions, the commentaries serve another purpose and, that is, the propagation of the views adopted by the commentator's school and thereby to establish the religious or academic supremacy. Here, the commentator deduces the principles from the basic texts but when there is a big time passage between the author of the text and the commentator and then the latter induces or imposes his own thoughts on the original text. Thus, the laps of time is one of the important reasons why the commentaries go astray from the text. Another important point, that to be marked in this context, is the superiority of the commentator to the author of the basic text. It is also noted that sometimes the commentator is so strong and dominating that he thrusts his own ideas upon the text and induces his theories thereon. It has happened with Śaṅkarācārya himself. All the modern scholars unanimously opine that the theory of illusion (i.e. Māyāvāda) is nowhere suggested in the Upaniṣads but Śaṅkara extracts it from them and supports it logically. [Like a dictator he takes the decision and like a democrat he makes the readers to agree with it.] Sometimes the commentaries are engaged in hairsplitting due to which the main point becomes subordinate and the commentator tries to exhibit his own skills in reasoning, grammar, and expressions. This desire of exhibiting own skills in this field also is one of the reasons why many commentaries are written on the same topic. These were mainly the academic reasons for commentary writing but there is one more psychological reason too. Along with the appreciation of any thought, theory, scene or sentiment, there arises a feeling to share the experience with somebody and to enjoy it more. Sometimes without sharing the experience also it gives rise to the individual interpretation of that particular scene or theory. When such a phenomenon takes place in the field of literature and when these appreciations are transformed into verbal cognates, it becomes a commentary. When the commentaries are written on the commentaries, it is found that the commentators are faithful followers of the cult and of the philosophy which is depicted in that particular text. The commentators were very sincere and loyal to their teachers, except in a few cases they had never shown any kind of disagreement or difference of opinion with their *guru*'s. In fact, they kept on defending them and, therefore, a long chain of scholars propagating certain doctrines originated as we see it in the case of Gauḍapāda, Govindayati and Śaṅkarācārya. This consequently gave the sectarian colouring to the commentaries and therefore not less than five systems of monism came into existence from the same Upaniṣadic texts. One more purpose served by the commentaries is to clarify the debatable point and doubts and this view is presented by Nāgeśa in the very first *paribhāṣā* of *Paribhāṣenduśekhara*: *vyākhyānato viśeṣapratipattiḥ*.

General Observations

The following observations can be put forth and the further studies will verify them:

1. The commentator explains each and every word of the line and the grammatical, etymological or metaphorical explanation of the word is sought and if there is no special comment on the word at least a synonym is given for the word.
2. The parallel instances from other compositions either by the same author or by different poets are invariably quoted and thus commentaries become the compendium of thoughts related to that particular topic.
3. The purpose of the commentary work is declared in its *maṅgalācaraṇa* verse and most of the commentaries declare it as *balanam sukhabodhāya*. It is also marked that most of the commentary works begin with a *maṅgalācaraṇa* of their own as if some new treatise is being written and then they comment on the first verse of the original text.
4. The commentators are so confident about their expositions that they declare: "not even a single syllable is without the proof and not even a single syllable is redundant".[16] This is the guiding norm for all the commentators and they were unbinding themselves with them. They neither added anything of their own to the original text nor did they omit anything from the text.
5. The commentary literature has a special feature of quotations relevant to the main text, from different

[16] Mallinātha on *Raghuvaṁśam* Sañjīvanī Ṭīkā, stanza 8, Poona: Chitrashala Press, p. 3.

branches of knowledge. Śaṅkarācārya, the famous Advaita philosopher, quotes *Kāmasūtra* of Vātsyāyana and Mallinātha commenting on *śṛṅgāra*-sentiment quotes of Śaṅkarācārya. It shows that the commentators have open access to all the fields at all the times and ancient Indian Sanskrit commentators, being experts in various branches of knowledge, travelled through different regions of literature. The oft-quoted adjective, i.e. *śrutismṛtipurāṇokta,* is applicable to the commentaries in the real sense of the term.

6. In some cases, it is seen that the commentator supersedes the poet or the author of the basic text. The composition of a literary work by the poet is a spontaneous overflow of feelings and it is an expression of his poetic genius. But for a commentator, a commentary is a thoughtful and deliberate composition. The poet has the topic of his choice, while the commentator has the limits of the original text.

In modern times, the eminent critics are requested to comment on a particular text (either positively or negatively) so that the work either gains popularity and the box office thereby or loses on both the fronts. In such a situation the merits or demerits of the work do not count but what counts is the advertising skills of the agency. It seems that such agencies did not exist in ancient times and thus commentaries were written after fifty to hundred years after the text. In many cases, the works are commented after the death of the poet and thus it was to become a posthumous commentary.

Statistically it is proved that in most of the cases the commentary is a requirement (necessity) and in other cases it is a luxury. For the philosophical texts on *ṣaḍ-darśanas* or grammar or the science of etymology, it is very difficult to understand the text without a commentary but some commentaries like that of Mallinātha not only initiate the reader in that subject but they teach the reader, how to relish and enjoy the text with the enhancement of *rasa* (i.e. sentiment). The commentaries being so useful, not only the intangible texts, but in modern times, even sports like cricket and hockey are also being commented. The new style of comparing the programme is also a type of commentary though the traditional image of a commentary is being changed.

As stated earlier, commentary writing is, no doubt, a global phenomenon but the progress and development of this literature in India are far superior in its qualitative and quantitative measures. In the traditional commentary literature in India it is found that in the field of Vedānta and grammar, many commentaries were written on the commentaries. There are various reasons for this phenomenon. (1) The basic texts on which a commentary is written are so terse that even with one commentary they are difficult to understand and thus another attempt is made to simplify the text. (2) The text being very terse it is also likely that *bhāṣya* on it is also terse and to understand this *bhāṣya* another commentary on it is required. (3) In some cases, the view presented by the first commentator (as the interpretation of the text) is not accepted by another scholar and he wants to interpret the basic text in some other way. Thus, to point out his dissatisfaction and to note his own views, he writes either a different commentary on the basic text or he writes a commentary on the first commentary. But in the case of commentaries on *Brahmasūtra-Śāṅkarabhāṣya*, it is found that the three main commentaries on it, i.e. *Bhāṣyaratnaprabhā* by Śrī Rāmānanda Yati, *Bhāmatī* by Vācaspatimiśra, and *Nyāyanirṇayavyākhyā* by Śrī Ānandajñāna follow the same path paved by Śrī Śaṅkara. These three commentators follow him, they adore him, and they regard Śaṅkara as Paramaśiva. But on the same text of *Brahmasūtras*, Rāmānuja and Madhva have also written the commentaries which interpret *Brahmasūtras* in exactly the opposite direction.

Śaṅkarācārya explains them with Advaita view while Madhva interprets them with Dvaita. These two find Śaṅkara far-fetching and imposing his own views on *Brahmasūtras*, but Śaṅkara's unparalleled genius and logical arguments have set aside all the objections on his commentary and all the views other than Advaita-Vedānta are refuted in the assembly of scholars. Due to these important reasons, the number of commentaries is increased. There are two broad levels on which a commentary functions. One is called external level and another is internal level. In Sanskrit, these levels can be called as "Tantra" and "Mantra", respectively. In other words these are the ways to learn a particular text. They are not altogether different but mutually helping each other though the method of functioning differs. The modern scholars, who often speak the language of textual criticism when they assess the works of their older generation, concentrate on the external form of the text. They try to find out many things about the text as they are trained in the Western style of studies. According to Aklujkar[17] the word commentary stands for the commentaries themselves but for him a commentary functions to find out the original manuscripts of the text (at least the oldest possible transcript), to establish the genealogies of the manuscripts, to ascertain the number of versions of recessions of the text and even the number of *kārikā*s, stanzas or prose passages. The internal level includes splitting of *pada*s, decision about the true meaning of a word in consistency with the reference, finding out inherent meaning if any, metaphorical explanations if any, and establishing the theories suggested through the text. Sometimes it is found that the commentators

---

17 Saroja Bhate and John Bronkhorst, *Bhartrhari: Philosopher and Grammarian*, New Delhi: Motilal Banarsidass, 1993, p. 13.

not only deduce the theories from the texts but they induce their own theories on the text. Principles of methodology do not clash anywhere though they may clash in individual instances of practice.

The three top commentators are taken care of do represent three main branches of oriental studies. Their commentaries have become the landmarks in the studies not only in their own branch but in the study of Sanskrit literature in general. Vedic commentaries represented by Sāyaṇa, *Prasthānatrayī*-commentaries headed by Śaṅkara, and the greatest commentary to the credit of Patañjali in the field of grammar are the topics of discussion. All these commentaries show that each field of study has its own method of commentary. The canons and guiding principles for each field are ascertained by the scholars in those fields and the commentators through the ages have followed them scrupulously. The Vedas being the first literature, commentaries on Vedas are also first in the chronological order. The number of commentaries exceeds in these three fields only.

"Nirukta" The First Commentary

Traditionally *Nirukta* is considered as the first commentary. It can be technically designated as a commentary. The Vedic *mantras* were seen by the sages in the times immemorial and the rigorous studies about them have not yet succeeded in fixing the dates unanimously. But fortunately the case with *Nirukta* and its commentators differs. Yāska is dated back to seventh century BCE and there are no counter arguments for this date. In one of his lectures M.G. Dhadaphale[18] starts with *Nirukta*, the commentary on *Nighaṇṭu* and in the course of his lecture he comments on the Pāli-commentaries. The gist of it

[18] M.G. Dhadaphale, Presidential speech on *Veda and Avesta*, Brihanmaharashtra Marathi Prachya Vidya Parishad Sangamner, November 1999 .

is as follows: *Nirukta* is the oldest traditionally recorded commentary on the collection of words in the Vedas, i.e. the *Nighaṇṭu*. This *Nirukta* is also commented by eminent scholars like Durgā, Skanda, and Maheśvara. Durgā, at some place says that this collection of words is just the sample of how the words are to be commented. Another commentator named as Devarājayajvan says that Yāska has discussed only 350 words out of 1765. Thus, *Nirukta* is a guide, explaining the words, *Ṛk*s employing these words and giving thereby lessons about how to comment on a Vedic passage. The methodology of research and the result of research are two different things. *Nirukta* is a guide for the methodology of Vedic interpretation. The contribution of Yāska to the Sanskrit field in general and to the Vedic field in particular is that Yāska has not only produced a commentary on Vedas but has produced the commentators like Sāyaṇa and Bhaṭṭabhāskara.

Etymological explanation of the Vedic words is no doubt an important part of *Nirukta* but it is the limited only one part of the whole treatise. One may call it as the visible part but consistency in Vedic *mantra*s (and the refutation of the objections, raised by Kautsa), the discussion about the deities, the different schools in mythology (i.e. Naidāna, Nairukta or Aitihāsika) are the different important points of the science of commentary. Dhadaphale also informs that even in the Pāli literature we find that kind of commentaries which have *Nirukta* as their model. Such commentaries on the expositions of Buddha are called *arthakathās*, i.e. *vyākhyā-ṭīkā* and there is a special literary form developed which is called *Netti* (i.e. the Guide, Sanskrit version *Nettrī*) and *Peṭakopadeśa* (Piṭaka instructions) which lay down the guiding principle, fix the criteria and the methods of commentary theoretically. He refers to Bhikkhu Jñānamauli and says that these works are not important for the specific building that they have constructed but are useful for creating the base (i.e. foundation) for different buildings (dealing more with scaffolding rather than with architecture.). Similar is the nature of *Nirukta*. In fact, it is better to say that Yāska has given etiologies (*hetuvacanas*) rather than etymologies. In the Brāhmaṇa passages various reasons are given for the use of a particular word which are called *śabdapravṛttinimittas* by Patañjali and the explanation by Yāska is also called "etios" (*prayojana-hetu*) and thus he begins with the word *kasmāt*? As V.K. Rajavade counts and informs that Yāska has used the word for forty-two times and Durgā presupposes the word even if Yāska does not use it. The Pāli commentators also explain the word *nirvacana* in the same manner as *nibbacanam ti sahetukam vacanam*. In the explanations of *Nirukta* the "usage" (i.e. the reference to the context) is important and does not expect the stereotyped meaning of that particular word. Wittgenstein – the modern thinker says "ask not for meaning, ask for usage". The first dictionary of words in Greek is *Onamastica* (probably fourth century BCE). At least thousand years earlier we have *Nighaṇṭus*. These *Nighaṇṭus* not only enlist the original words but they also count the metaphorical terms (*alaṁkārika padas*) (*megha = parvata, camas* for *pṛthvī* or *elā*). The Pāli *Nighaṇṭus* also use such metaphorical words and they are scientifically called as *adhivacanas* in Pāli. Regarding the order of words used in *Nighaṇṭus* it is said that the alphabetical order was not under consideration. Raugeht also has to face this problem for his thesaurus. Durgā, the commentator of *Nirukta* and Śākapuṇi, one of the predecessors of Yāska, has presented different logical thoughts behind the order of words as presented in *Nighaṇṭus*.

Prātiśākhyas are a type of commentaries though its field of application is very narrow. But these *prātiśākhyas* had certainly provided the guidelines for commentaries. These are the treatises which explain a particular branch of knowledge, i.e. the Veda, from grammatical point of view. They mainly explain the *sandhis* in the *padapāṭha*, the accents and the pronunciation, etc. The number of *prātiśākhyas* available today is only five (*Ṛk* and *Taittirīya* by Śaunaka, *Vājasaneyī* by Kātyāyana, and also *Atharva* and *Ṛk-tantra prātiśākhya* by Śākaṭāyana) and all of them are commented. The Brāhmaṇas are the earliest expositions of the meaning of *mantras*[19] but they do not explain Vedic text word by word. The aim of the Brāhmaṇas is to point out the link between a *mantra* and its application to a ritual and not to paraphrase and explain every word of every hymn. The Brāhmaṇas enlighten us with the course of ritualistic activities and they do not advocate any bias against knowledge. To the contrary they often declare that the knowledge of the purpose of sacrifice is as much effective as its performance.

Ancient Commentaries and Modern Research Methodology

It can be deduced from what D.K. Santa has said in the introduction of his book[20] that the original Sanskrit texts are the collection of theories arrived at by the scholars of different branches of knowledge. These are the conclusions of their research through the years, but one does not know how these scholars arrived at these conclusions. That is to say, the reader does not know the research methodology used by these authors of the texts. One does not know how they have collected the data and how they have classified it? Because they themselves have not written anything about it. In those times, the conclusions were important than the method they have adopted to arrive at. But the later *paṇḍitas* thought about the research methods also and made a science of research methodology which then was called a commentary. Therefore,

---

19 Sudhakar Malaviya, *Aitareya Brāhmaṇa*, vol. II, Varanasi: Tara Printing, 1983, Intro., p. 9.

20 D.K. Santa, *Shodhavijnanakosh*, Pune: Pune Vidyarthi Griha Prakashan, 1985, Intro., p. 12.

it is a commentary that analyses the final conclusions, it separates the components, it explains the function of each component, and tries to understand the whole process of thought that has taken place in the mind of the author. A grammarian also starts with the finished forms and by the process of word formation he takes the reader to the components of the verbs and nouns as *prakṛti* and *pratyayas*, and supports his analysis by the rules which are the outcome of his studies. The commentators also follow the same method as they begin with the theories and reach up to the data. Therefore, the commentaries are the best examples of what is called research methodology in modern times. In a way a commentator and a grammarian, both of them start from the finished products and by their own research method they reach to the root cause of the text and of the word, respectively. There is one more point on which a commentary and grammar can be compared. The functions in commentaries for example the *padapāṭha* are mainly based on the grammatical principle of stem and suffix relation, and one agrees to the point that the principle *vākyatajani nāmāni*[21] is at its base. Just as there are sets of rules for acquisition of the vocal composition of the Veda, there is an established tradition for their interpretation too. This tradition is not an outcome of simple blind faith but the ancient sages have laid down different rules on scientific lines for the interpretation of Vedic texts and they have developed sound and steady fortifications in the form of six Vedāṅgas.

Demerits of Commentaries

It must be noted at this juncture that all the Western and Eastern, ancient and modern scholars have unanimously agreed to the point that the study of any ancient Indian

---

21 S.D. Laddu, *Evolution of the Sanskrit Language from Pāṇini to Patañjali*, Pune: CASS, 1974, pp. 16-18.

Sanskrit text is incomplete without the study of its commentary. Therefore, the scholars were very critical about their matter and manner. They were free and frank to note their own observations about the merits and demerits of commentary, and commentary literature in general. In this connection Swami Chidbhavananda says:

> The function of a commentary is to expand, explain, expound and extol the contents of a great book. It is but natural that numerous commentaries crop up round divinely inspired books. Several are the commentaries on Scriptural Trinity. If a person desires to extol or establish a particular creed or a school of thought it becomes his first and foremost duty to derive authority and sanction for it from this Scriptural Trinity. But it is observed that commentaries often suffer from a serious disadvantage. Consciously or unconsciously the authors have read the meaning of their own creeds and cults in these three sacred books.[22]

The point is seriously thought over by J. Bronkhorst[23] in connection with *Mahābhāṣya.* He is very critical in his thought and attacks on the sectarian views represented by the commentators as the pleaders of the author of the original text. He says:

> The commentators have a tendency to become the guardians of their tradition. The traditional tendency in our discipline has the unfortunate consequence that these initial theories have in many cases come to be looked upon as facts which one is not allowed to challenge unless one has very strong evidence. The formulation of other theories which are equally plausible, yet equally uncertain is often looked upon

---

22 Swami Chidbhavananda, *The Bhagavadgītā*, Tiruchirapalli, Madras: Tapovan Publishing House, 1967, p. 42.

23 J. Bronkhorst, *Three Problems Pertaining to the Mahābhāṣya*, Pune: BORI, 1987.

> as reproachable speculation. This is regrettable for it may and indeed does lead to situations in which one scholar blames another for being speculative, while at the same time accepting without questions, theories propounded in earlier centuries.

Another fault (demerit) regarding the commentary writing is seen in the tendency of hair splitting. The commentators who were experts in reasoning and in verbal plays often argue the point by hair-splitting method and show off their erudition rather than proving the point. Then, the commentary goes astray and the main point becomes subordinate. Bhaṭṭojī's *Śabdakaustubha* is cited as the example of this type. In an editorial a stanza is found on the name of Bhojarāja[24] which explains the demerits of the commentary. The commentaries sometimes do not explain the important points which are really difficult by saying that "the meaning is very clear". Sometimes they unnecessarily give extensive explanations of the points which are very clear and the explanations about the compounds, etc. are really unnecessary. Many times the commentaries create confusion by the undue and useless comments. In this way, the commentators create confusing state for the facts in the minds of the readers. The poet says that all the commentators are of the same type. Apart from the exaggeration, the point is that the commentator has to be aware of the flaws which may occur in his commentary. The stanza gives warning in a way to all those who want to explain the text. On this background the words of Mallinātha are very important and throw light on his attitude towards the commentaries.

At the beginning of his every commentary Mallinātha expresses his vow – *namūlam likhyate kiñcit nānāpek ṣitamucyate*[25]

---

24 Vedavrata, *Vyākaraṇa Mahābhāṣya* (1st edn.), Rohatak: Harayana Sahitya Samsthan, 1962, Editorial, p. 1.

25 See fn. 16.

(whatever that is written will be supported by the proof and that will be told which is not expected). The great commentators always keep themselves on the track, by fixing eye on their final aim in view. Generally, the commentators are found very true and loyal to their text but sometimes they go a step ahead and without crossing the thought, presented in the text, they include and insert their own theories cleverly.

These three great personalities represent three important branches of ancient Indian studies. Sāyaṇa, a comparatively modern commentator, stands for various branches of Vedic studies. He has not only commented on Vedic Saṁhitās but has also commented upon Brāhmaṇas and Upaniṣads. He was not only the oriental scholar but he was a minister to the great kings like Harihara and Bukkā. His scholastic expositions are inspired by the political intensions of religious propaganda. Therefore, survival and propagation of ritualistic tradition, (which has come down to him) was one of his aims of commentary writing.

As regards Śaṅkara's commentaries, everybody knows that his efforts were against the attack by Buddhist religion and his sole aim was to protect the Vedic preaching. It was not only against the Buddhist revolt but against all the branches of knowledge which consider the "activity" and "knowledge of activity" as the supreme goal, i.e. Mīmāṁsā, Nyāya, etc. and those which were coming in his way on his long march of philosophical expositions, were cut off by the sharp blazing sword of reasoning. Śaṅkara's commentaries are really the milestones in this field. Patañjali, amongst these three, is chronologically earlier and the great work he has done in the form of *Mahābhāṣya* is an ideal for all the later commentators, to whichever branch they may belong to.

References

Abhyankar, K.V., *Vyākaraṇa Mahābhāṣya* (Prastāvanā Khaṇḍa) (part VII).

Bhate, Saroja, and John Bronkhorst, *Bhartrhari: Philosopher and Grammarian*, New Delhi: Motilal Banarsidass, 1993.

Bronkhorst, J., *Three Problems Pertaining to the Mahābhāṣya*, Pune: Bhandarkar Oriental Research Institute, 1987.

Chidbhavananda, Swami, *The Bhagavadgītā*, Tiruchirapalli, Madras: Tapovan Publishing House, 1967.

Dhadaphale, M.G., Presidential speech on *Veda and Avesta*, Brihanmaharashtra Marathi Prachya Vidya Parishad Sangamner, November 1999.

Filliozat, Pierre, *An Introduction to the Commentaries on Patanjali's Mahabhashya* (Prof. K.V. Abhyankar Memorial Lectures), Pune: Bhandarkar Oriental Research Institute, 1991.

Ghate, V.S., *The Vedanta*, Pune: Bhandarkar Oriental Research Institute, 1926.

Laddu, S.D., *Evolution of the Sanskrit Language from Pāṇini to Patañjali*, Pune: Centre for Advanced Study in Sanskrit, 1974.

Malaviya, Sudhakar, *Aitareya Brāhmaṇa*, vol. II, Varanasi: Tara Printing, 1983.

Mallinātha, *Raghuvaṁśam*, Sañjīvanī Ṭīkā, Poona: Chitrashala Press.

Mimamsaka, Yudhisthira, *Sanskṛtavyākaraṇaśāstra kā Itihāsa*, New Delhi: Bharatiya Prachyavidya Prakashan, 1950.

Mishra, S.N., *Kāśikā* (part I), Varanasi: Chaukhamba Sanskrit Samsthana, 1996.

Santa, D.K., *Shodhavijnanakosh*, Pune: Pune Vidyarthi Griha Prakashan, 1985.

Vedavrata, *Vyākaraṇa Mahābhāṣya* (1st edn.), Rohatak: Harayana Sahitya Samsthan, 1962.

8

Archaeoastronomy in India

Subhash Kak

Abstract

OUR understanding of archaeoastronomical sites in India is based not only on a rich archaeological record and texts that go back thousands of years, but also on a living tradition that is connected to the past. Conversely, India has much cultural diversity and a tangled history of interactions with neighbouring regions that make the story complex. The texts reveal to us the cosmological ideas that lay behind astronomical sites in the historical period and it is generally accepted that the same idea also apply to the Haṛappan era of the third millennium BCE (Kenoyer 1998: 52-53).

In the historical period, astronomical observatories were part of temple complexes where the king was consecrated. Such consecration served to confirm the king as foremost devotee of the chosen deity, who was taken to be the embodiment of time and the universe (Kak 2002a: 58). For example, Udayagiri is an astronomical site connected with the classical age of the Gupta dynasty (CE 320–500), which is located a few kilometers from Vidiśā in central India (Willis 2001; Dass and Willis 2002). The imperial Guptas enlarged the site, an ancient hilly observatory going back at least to the second century BCE at which observations were facilitated by the geographical features of the hill, into a sacred landscape to draw royal authority.

Indian astronomy is characterized by the concept of ages of successive larger durations, which is an example of the pervasive idea of recursion, or repetition of patterns across space, scale and time. An example of this is the division of the ecliptic into twenty-seven star segments (*nakṣatra*s), with which the moon is conjoined in its monthly circuit, each of which is further sub-divided into twenty-seven sub-segments (*upa-nakṣatra*s), and the successive divisions of the day into smaller measures of thirty units. The idea of recursion underlies the concept of the sacred landscape and it is embodied in Indian art, providing an archaeoastronomical window on sacred and monumental architecture. It appears that this was an old idea because intricate spiral patterns, indicating recursion, are also found in the paintings of the Mesolithic period. Tyagi (1992) has claimed that they are unique to Indian rock art.

According to Vāstu Śāstra, the structure of the building mirrors the emergence of cosmic order out of primordial chaos through the act of measurement. The universe is symbolically mapped into a square that emphasizes the four cardinal directions. It is represented by the square *vāstu-maṇḍala*, which in its various forms is the basic plan for the house and the city. There exist further elaborations of this plan, some of which are rectangular.

It is significant that yantric buildings in the form of *maṇḍala*s have been discovered in North Afghanistan that belong to a period that corresponds to the late stage of the Haṛappan tradition (Kak 2000a; 2005b) providing architectural evidence in support of the idea of recursion at this time. Although these building are a part of the Bactria-Margiana Archaeological Complex (BMAC), their affinity with ideas that are also present in the Haṛappan system shows that these ideas were widely spread.

Chronology and Overview

India's archaeological record in the north-west has an unbroken continuity going back to about 7500 BCE at Mehrgaṛh (Kenoyer 1998; Lal 2002), and it has a rock art tradition, next only to that of Australia and Africa in abundance, that is much older (Pandey 1993; Bednarik 2000). Some rock art has been assigned to the Upper Palaeolithic period. There is surprising uniformity, both in style and content, in the rock art paintings of the Mesolithic period (10000–2500 BCE) (Tyagi 1992; Wakankar 1992).

The archaeological phases of the Indus (or Sindhu–Sarasvatī) tradition have been divided into four eras: early food-producing era (*c.* 6500–5000 BCE), regionalization era (5000–2600 BCE), integration era (2600–1900 BCE), and localization era (1900–1300 BCE) (Shaffer 1992). The early food-producing era lacked elaborate ceramic technology. The regionalization era was characterized by styles in ceramics, lapidary arts, glazed faience and seal making that varied across regions. In the integration era, there is significant homogeneity in material culture over a large geographical area and the use of the so-called Indus script, which is not yet deciphered. In the localization era, patterns of the integration era are blended with regional ceramic styles, indicating decentralization and restructuring of the interaction networks. The localization era of the Sindhu–Sarasvatī tradition is the regionalization era of the Gaṅgā–Yamunā tradition which transforms into the integration era of the Magadha and the Mauryan dynasties. There is also continuity in the system of weights and lengths between the Haṛappan period and the later historic period (Mainkar 1984).

The cultural mosaic in the third millennium BCE is characterized by the integration phase of the Haṛappan civilization of north-west India, copper and copper/bronze age cultures or central and north India, and Neolithic cultures of south and east India (Lal 1997). Five large cities of the integration phase are Mohenjo-Daṛo, Haṛappā, Ganwerīwālā,

Rākhīgaṛhī, and Dholāvīrā. Other important sites of this period are Kālībaṅgan, Rehman Ḍherī, Nausharo, Koṭ Dījī, and Lothal.

A majority of the towns and settlements of the Haṛappan period were in the Sarasvatī Valley region. Hydrological changes, extended period of drought, and the drying up of the Sarasvatī River due to its major tributaries being captured by the Sindh and Gaṅgā rivers after an earthquake in 1900 BCE led to the abandonment of large areas of the Sarasvatī Valley (Kak 1992). The Haṛappan phase went through various stages of decline during the second millennium BCE. A second urbanization began in the Gaṅgā and Yamunā valleys around 900 BCE. The earliest surviving records of this culture are in Brāhmī script. This second urbanization is generally seen at the end of the Painted Gray Ware (PGW) phase (1200–800 BCE) and with the use of the Northern Black Polished Ware (NBPW) pottery. Late Haṛappan was partially contemporary with the PGW phase. In other words, a continuous series of cultural developments link the two early urbanizations of India.

The setting for the hymns of *Ṛgveda*, which is India's most ancient literary text, is the area of Sapta Saindhava, the region of north India bounded by the Sindh and the Gaṅgā rivers although regions around this heartland are also mentioned. *Ṛgveda* describes the Sarasvatī River to be the greatest of the rivers and going from the mountains to the sea. The archaeological record, suggesting that this river had turned dry by 1900 BCE, indicates that *Ṛgveda* is prior to this epoch. *Ṛgveda* and other early Vedic literature have astronomical references related to the shifting astronomical frame that indicate epochs of the fourth and third millennium BCE which is consistent with the hydrological evidence. The *nakṣatra* lists are found in the Vedas, either directly or listed under their presiding deities, and one may conclude that their names have not changed. Vedic astronomy used a luni-solar year in which an intercalary month was employed as adjustment with solar year.

The shifting of seasons through the year and the shifting of the northern axis allow us to date several statements in the Vedic books (Sastry 1985). Thus *Śatapatha Brāhmaṇa* (2.1.2.3) has a statement that points to an earlier epoch where it is stated that the Kṛttikā (Pleiades) never swerve from the east. This corresponds to 2950 BCE. *Maitrāyaṇīya Brāhmaṇa Upaniṣad* (6.14) refers to the winter solstice being at the mid-point of the Śraviṣṭhā segment and the summer solstice at the beginning of Maghā. This indicates 1660 BCE. *Vedāṅga Jyotiṣa* mentions that winter solstice was at the beginning of Śraviṣṭhā and the summer solstice at the mid-point of Āśleṣā. This corresponds to about 1300 BCE.

*Nakṣatra*s in *Vedāṅga Jyotiṣa* are defined to be twenty-seven equal parts of the ecliptic. The *nakṣatra* list of the late Vedic period begin with Kṛttikā whereas that of the astronomy texts after CE 200 begin with Aśvinī (α and β Arietis), indicating a transition through two *nakṣatras*, or a time span of about 2,000 years.

The foundation of Vedic cosmology is the notions of *bandhu* (homologies or binding between the outer and the inner). In Āyurveda, the medical system associated with the Vedas, the 360 days of the year were taken to be mapped to the 360 bones of the developing foetus, which later fuse into the 206 bones of the person. It was estimated correctly that the sun and the moon were approximately 108 times their respective diameters from the earth (perhaps from the discovery that the angular size of a pole removed 108 times its height is the same as that of the sun and the moon), and this number was used in sacred architecture. The distance to the *sanctum sanctorum* of the temple from the gate and the perimeter of the temple were taken to be 54 and 180 units, which are one-half each of 108 and 360 (Kak 2005a). Homologies at many levels are at the basis of the idea of *recursion*, or repetition in scale and time. The astronomical basis of the Vedic ritual was the reconciliation of the lunar and solar years (Kak 2000a; 2000b).

Texts of the Vedic and succeeding periods provide us crucial understanding of the astronomy and the archaeoastronomy of the historical period throughout India. The medieval period was characterized by pilgrimage centres that created sacred space mirroring conceptions of the cosmos. Sacred temple architecture served religious and political ends.

The instruments that were used in Indian astronomy include the water clock (*ghaṭī yantra)*, gnomon (*śaṅku*), cross-staff (*yaṣṭi yantra*), armillary sphere (*gola-yantra*), board for sun's altitude (*phalaka yantra*), sundial (*kapāla yantra*), and astrolabe (Gangooly 1880). In early eighteenth century, Mahārāja Sawāī Jai Singh II of Jaipur (r. 1699–1743) built five masonry observatories called Jantar Mantar in Delhi, Jaipur, Ujjain, Mathurā, and Varanasi. The Jantar Mantar consists of the *rāma yantra* (a cylindrical structure with an open top and a pillar in its centre to measure the altitude of the sun), the *rāśivalaya yantra* (a group of twelve instruments to determine celestial latitude and longitude), the *jaya prakaśa* (a concave hemisphere), the *laghu samrāṭ yantra* (small sundial), the *samrāṭ yantra* (a huge equinoctial dial), the *cakra yantra* (upright metal circles to find the right ascension and declination of a planet), the *digāṁśa yantra* (a pillar surrounded by two circular walls), the *kapāla yantra* (two sunken hemispheres to determine the position of the sun relative to the planets and the zodiac), the *ṣaṣṭāṁśa yantra* (to display a pinhole image of the sun over a sixty-degree meridian scale), and the *nāḍīvalaya yantra* (a cylindrical dial).

Pre-Historical and Haṛappan Period

The city of Moheṅjo-Daṛo (2500 BCE), like most other Haṛappan cities (with the exception of Dholāvīrā as far as we know at this time), was divided into two parts: the acropolis and the lower city. The Mohenjo-Daṛo acropolis, a cultural and administrative centre, had as its foundation a 12 m high platform of 400 x 200 m. The lower city had streets oriented according to the cardinal directions and provided with a network of covered drains. Its houses had bathrooms. The city's wells were so well constructed with tapering bricks that they have not collapsed in 5,000 years. The Great Bath (12 x 7 m) was built using finely fitted bricks laid on with gypsum plaster and made watertight with bitumen. A high corbelled outlet allowed it to be emptied easily. Massive walls protected the city against flood water.

The absence of monumental buildings such as palaces and temples makes the Haṛappan city strikingly different from its counterparts of Mesopotamia and Egypt, suggesting that the polity of the Haṛappan state was de-centralized and based on a balance between the political, the mercantile, and the religious elites. The presence of civic amenities such as wells and drains attests to considerable social equality. The power of the mercantile guilds is clear in the standardization of weights of carefully cut and polished chart cubes that form a combined binary and decimal system.

Mohenjo-Daṛo and other sites show slight divergence of 1° to 2° clockwise of the axes from the cardinal directions (Wanzke 1984). It is thought that this might have been due to the orientation of Aldebaran (Rohiṇī in Sanskrit) and the Pleiades (Kṛttikā in Sanskrit) that rose in the east during 3000 to 2000 BCE at the spring equinox; the word *rohiṇī* literally means rising. Furthermore, the slight difference in the orientations amongst the buildings in Mohenjo-Daṛo indicates different construction periods using the same traditional sighting points that had shifted in this interval (Kenoyer 1998).

Moheṅjo-Daṛo's astronomy used both the motions of the moon and the sun (Maula 1984). This is attested by the use of great calendar stones, in the shape of ring, which served to mark the beginning and end of the solar year.

DHOLĀVĪRĀ

Dholāvīrā is located on an island just north of the large island of Kutch in Gujarat. Its strategic importance lay in its control of shipping between Gujarat and the delta of the Sindhu and Sarasvatī rivers.

The layout of Dholāvīrā is unique in that it comprises of three "towns", which is in accord with Vedic ideas (Bisht 1997; 1999a; 1999b). The feature of recursion in the three towns, or repeating ratios at different scales, is significant (*fig.* 8.1). Specifically, the design is characterized by the nesting proportion of 9:4 across the lower and the middle towns and the castle. The proportions of 5/4, 7/6, and 5/4 for the lower town, the middle town, and the castle may reflect the measures related to the royal city, the commander's quarter, and the king's quarter, respectively, which was also true of Classical India (Bhat 1995).

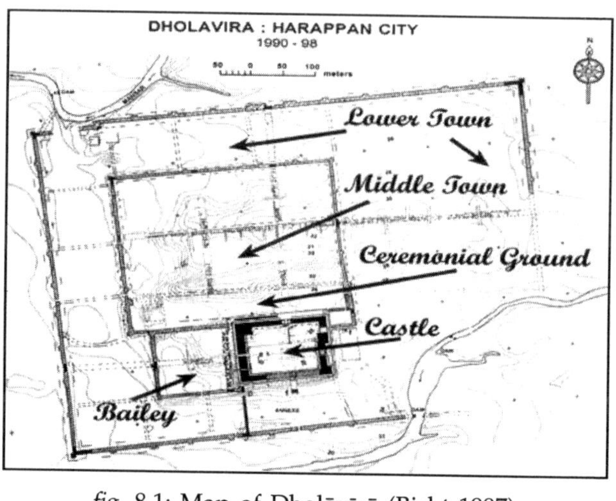

fig. 8.1: Map of Dholāvīrā (Bisht 1997)

A Dholāvīrā length, D, has been determined by finding the largest measure which leads to integer dimensions for the various parts of the city. This measure turns out to be the same as the *Arthaśāstra* (300 BCE) measure of *dhanuṣ* (bow) that equals 108 *aṅgulas* (fingers). This scale is confirmed by a terracotta scale from Kālībaṅgan and the ivory scale found in Lothal. The Kālībaṅgan scale (Joshi 2007; Balasubramaniam and Joshi 2008) corresponds to units of 17.5 cm, which is substantially the same as the Lothal scale and the small discrepancy may be a consequence of shrinkage upon firing.

The analysis of the unit of length at Dholāvīrā is in accord with the unit from the historical period (Danino 2005; 2008). The unit that best fits the Dholāvīrā dimensions is 190.4 cm, which when divided by 108 gives the Dholāvīrā *aṅgula* of 1.763 cm. The subunit of *aṅgula* is confirmed when one considers that the bricks in Haṛappā follow ratios of 1:2:4 with the dominating size being 7 x 14 x 28 cm (Kenoyer 1998). These dimensions can be elegantly expressed as 4 x 8 x 16 *aṅgulas*, with the unit of *aṅgula* taken as 1.763 cm. It is significant that the ivory scale at Lothal has twenty-seven graduations in 46 mm, or each graduation is 1.76 mm.

With the new Dholāvīrā unit of D, the dimensions of Moheṅjo-Daṛo's acropolis turn out to be 210 x 105 D; Kālībaṅgan's acropolis turn out to be 126 x 63 D. The dimensions of the lower town of Dholāvīrā are 405 x 324 D; the width of the middle town is 180 D; and the inner dimensions of the castle are 60 x 48 D. The sum of the width and length of the lower town comes to 729 which is astronomically significant since it is 27 x 27, and the width 324 equals the nakṣatra year 27 x 12.

Continuity has been found between the grid and modular measures in the town planning of Haṛappā and historical India, including that of Kathmandu Valley (Pant and Funo 2005). The measure of 19.2 m is the unit in quarter-blocks of

Kathmandu; this is nearly the same as the unit characteristic of the dimensions of Dholāvīrā. It shows that the traditional architects and town planners have continued the use of the same units over this long time span.

REHMAN ḌHERĪ

A third-millennium seal from Rehman Ḍherī, showing a pair of scorpions on one side and two antelopes on the other, that suggests knowledge of Vedic themes (*fig.* 8.2). It has been suggested that this seal represents the opposition of the Orion (Mṛgaśiras, or antelope head) and the Scorpio (Rohiṇī of the southern hemisphere which is fourteen *nakṣatra*s from the Rohiṇī of the northern hemisphere) *nakṣatra*s. The arrow near the head of one of the antelopes could represent the decapitation of Orion. It is generally accepted that the myth of Prajāpati being killed by Rudra represents the shifting of the beginning of the year away from Orion and it places the astronomical event in the fourth millennium BCE (Kak 2000a).

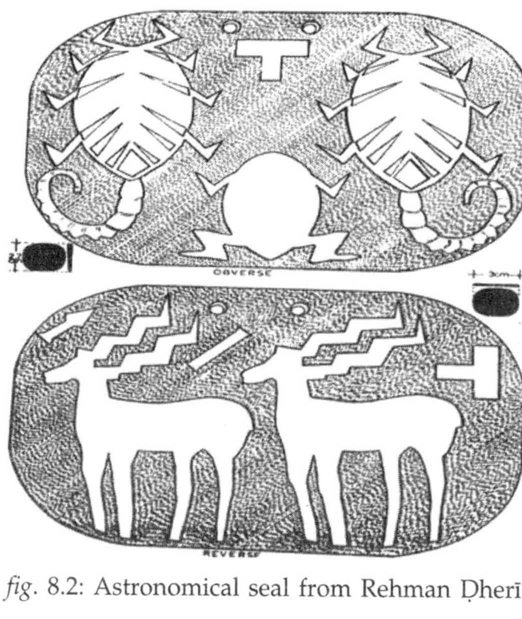

fig. 8.2: Astronomical seal from Rehman Ḍherī

Neolithic and Megalithic Sites

Interesting sites of archaeoastronomical interest include the Neolithic site of Burzahom from Kashmir in north India, and megalithic sites from Brahmagiri and Hanamsāgar from Karnataka in south India.

BURZAHOM, KASHMIR

This Neolithic site is located about 10 km north-east of Srinagar in the Kashmir Valley on a terrace of Late Pleistocene-Holocene deposits. Dated to around 3000–1500 BCE, its deep pit dwellings are associated with ground stone axes, bone tools, and gray burnished pottery. A stone slab of 48 x 27 cm, obtained from a phase dated to 2125 BCE shows two bright objects in the sky with a hunting scene in the foreground (*fig.* 8.3). These have been assumed to be a depiction of a double star system (Kameswara Rao 2005).

BRAHMAGIRI, KARNATAKA

The megalithic stone circles of Brahmagiri in the Chitradurga district of Karnataka in south India, which have been dated to 900 BCE, show astronomical orientations (*fig.* 8.4). This site is close to Siddapur where two minor Aśokan rock edicts were found in 1891. Kameswara Rao (1993) has argued that site

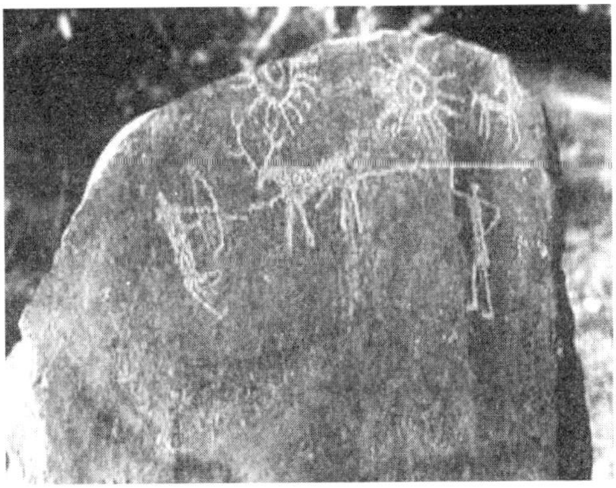

fig. 8.3: Burzahom sky scene

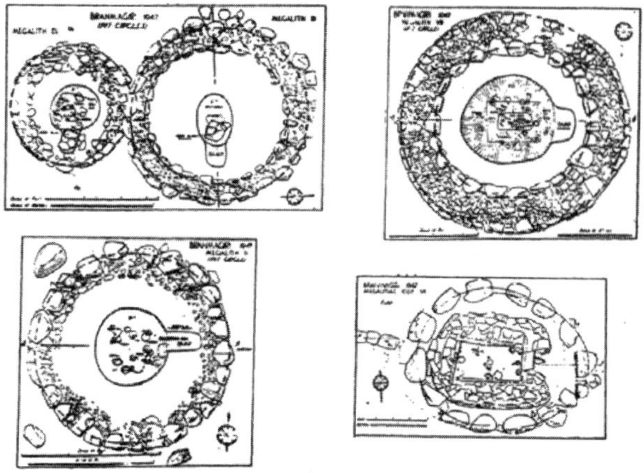

fig. 8.4: Megalithic stone circles of Brahmagiri

lines from the centre of a circle to an outer tangent of another circle point to the directions of the sunrise and full moon rise at the time of the solar and lunar solstices and equinox.

HANAMSĀGAR, KARNATAKA

Hanamsāgar is a megalithic site with stone alignments pointing to cardinal directions (*fig.* 8.5). It is located on a flat area between hills about 6 km north of the Kṛṣṇā River at latitude 16° 19' 18" and longitude 76° 27' 10". The stones, which are smooth granite, are arranged in a square of side that is about 600 m with fifty rows and fifty columns (for a total of 2,500 stones), with a separation between stones of about 12 m. The stones are between 1 to 2.5 m in height with a maximum diameter of 2 to 3 m. The lines are oriented in cardinal directions. There is a squarish central structure known as *cakrī kaṭṭi*.

It has been argued that the directions of summer and winter solstice can be fixed in relation to the outer and the inner squares. Kameswara Rao (2005) suggests that it could have been used for several other kinds of astronomical observations such as use of shadows to tell the time of the day, the prediction of months, seasons and passage of the year.

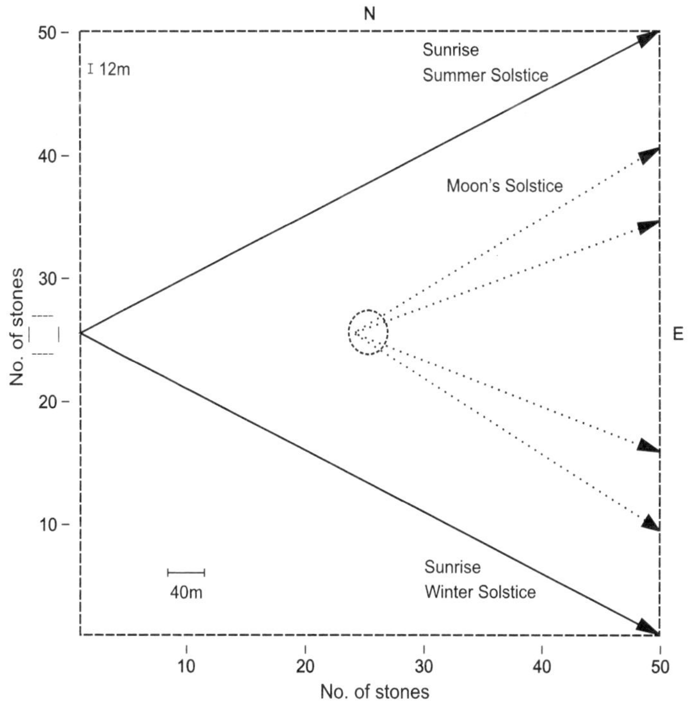

fig. 8.5. Alignments at Hanamsāgar

The Plan of the Temple

The sacred ground for Vedic ritual is the precursor to the temple. The Vedic observances were connected with the circuits of the sun and the moon (Kak 1993; 1995; 1996). The altar ritual was associated with the east–west axis and we can trace its origins to priests who maintained different day counts with respect to the solstices and the equinoxes. Specific days were marked with ritual observances that were done at different times of the day.

In the ritual at home, the householder employed three altars that are circular (earth), half-moon (atmosphere), and square (sky), which are like the head, the heart, and the body of the Cosmic Man (*Puruṣa*) (*fig*. 8.6). In the Agnicayana, the great

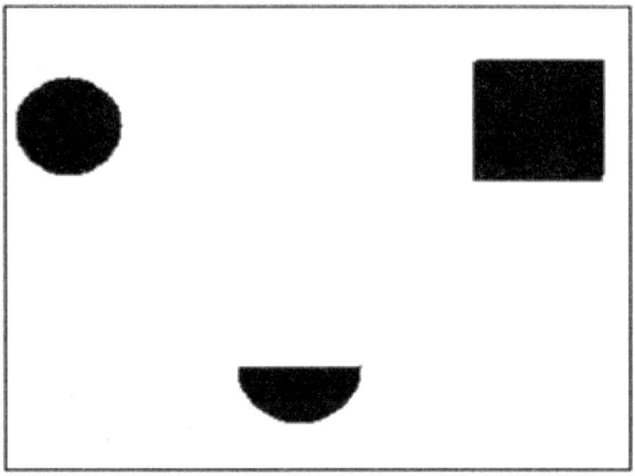

fig. 8.6: The three altars of the Vedic house: circular (earth, body), half-moon (atmosphere, *prāṇa*), square (sky, consciousness)

ritual of the Vedic times that forms a major portion of the narrative of *Yajurveda*, the atmosphere and the sky altars are built afresh in a great ceremony to the east. This ritual is based upon the Vedic division of the universe into three parts of earth, atmosphere, and sky that are assigned numbers 21, 78, and 261, respectively. The numerical mapping is maintained by placement of twenty-one pebbles around the earth altar, sets of thirteen pebbles around each of six intermediate (13 x 6 = 78) altars, and 261 pebbles around the great new sky altar called the *uttara-vedī*, which is built in the shape of a falcon (*fig*. 8.7); these numbers add up to 360, which is symbolic representation of the year. The proportions related to these three numbers, and others related to the motions of the planets, and angles related to the sightings of specific stars are reflected in the plans of the temples of the historical period (Kak 2002b; 2006a; 2009; Kaulācāra 1966).

The Agnicayana altar is the prototype of the temple and of the tradition of architecture (*vāstu*). The altar is first built of 1,000 bricks in five layers (that symbolically represent the

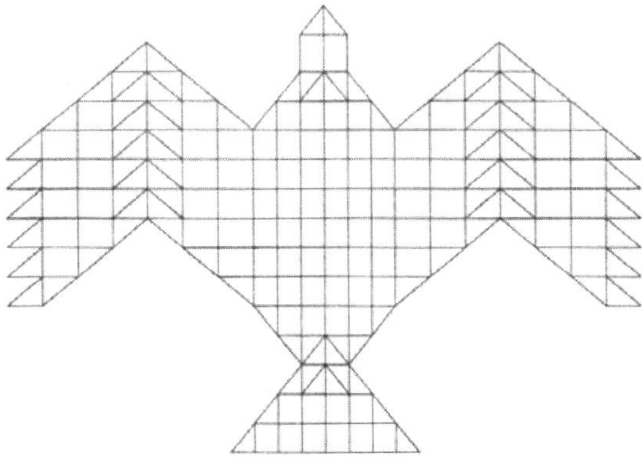

fig. 8.7: The falcon altar of the Agnicayana

five divisions of the year, the five physical elements, as well as five senses) to specific designs. The altar is constructed in a sequence of ninety-five years, whose details are matched to the reconciliation of the lunar and solar years by means of intercalary months.

In the ritual ground related to the Agnicayana ceremony, the *uttara-vedī* is fifty-four units from the entrance in the west and the perimeter of the ritual ground is 180 units (Kak 2005a). These proportions characterize many later temples. The connection of the *nakṣatra*s to the solar months is provided in *fig*. 8.8 for which we have textual evidence in the *Ṛgveda*.

THE TEMPLE COMPLEX AT KHAJURĀHO

The town of Khajurāho extends between 79° 54' 30" to 79° 56' 30" East and 24° 50' 20" to 24° 51' 40" North, in Chhatarpur district, in Madhya Pradesh (*fig*. 8.9). The temples of Khajurāho were built during ninth-twelfth centuries CE by the Candela kings. Originally there were eighty-four temples, of which twenty-three have survived. Of the surviving temples, six are associated with Śiva, eight with Viṣṇu, and five with the goddess (Singh 2009b).

At the eastern edge of the temple complex are the Dantla

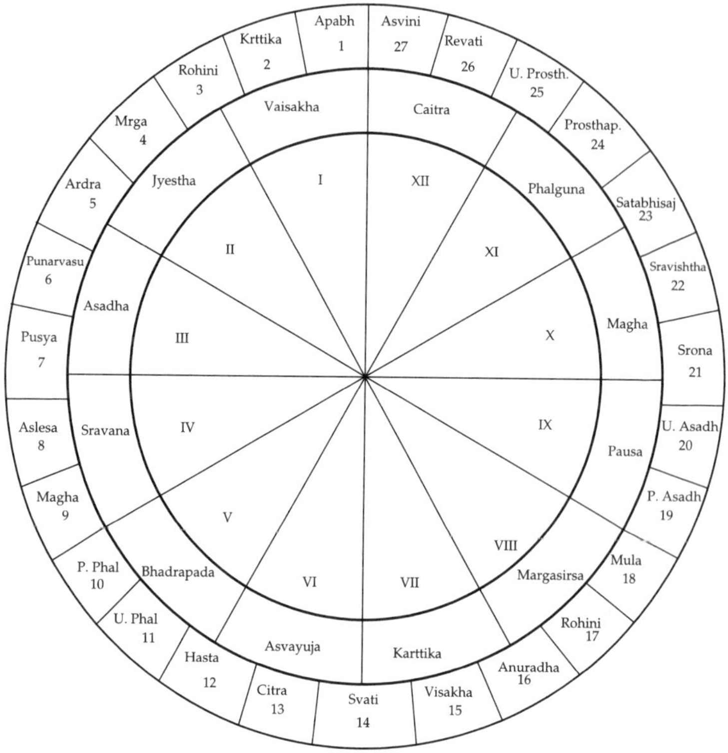

fig. 8.8: Mapping of the *nakṣatra*s to the solar months

hills, with a peak of 390 m at which is located a shrine to Śiva, which is a reference point for the temple entrances. All the temples excepting the Caturbhuja face the east. The south-eastern edge has the Lāvaṇya hill that is separated from the Dantla hills by the eastward flowing river Khudar. At the foothills of the Lāvaṇya hill at a height of 244 m is the shrine of Goddess Durgā as Mahiṣāsurmardinī.

The shrines to Śiva and Durgā on the Dantla and Lāvaṇya hills span the polarities of spirit (*Puruṣa*) and matter (*Prakṛti*), which are bridged by the river between the hills. The temples of Khajurāho are popular pilgrimage centres during two spring festivals: Śivarātri that falls on the new moon of Phālguna

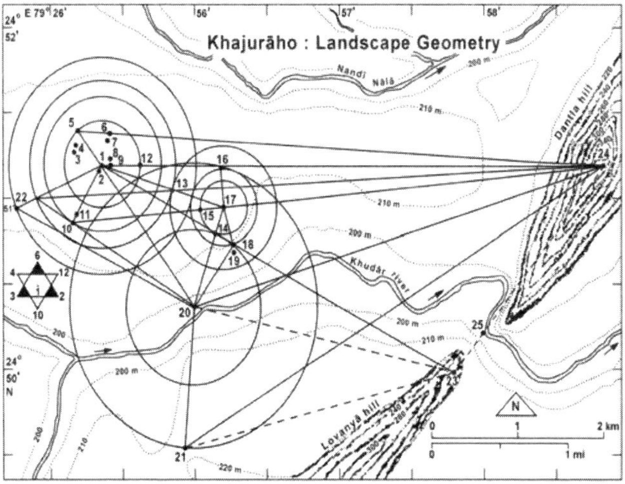

fig. 8.9: Khajurāho landscape geometry and topography (Singh 2009b)

(February/March), and Holī, which falls on the full moon of Caitra (March/April).

The Lakṣmaṇa Temple, one of the oldest of the complex, is considered the *axis mundi* of the site. It was built by the King Yaśovarman (925-50) as symbol of the Candela victory over the Pratihāras and a record of supremacy of their power. This temple is oriented to the sunrise on Holī.

The groups of temples form three overlapping *maṇḍala*s, with centres at the Lakṣmaṇa (Viṣṇu), the Javeri (Śiva), and the Duladeva (Śiva) temples. Their deviation from true cardinality is believed to be due to the direction of sunrise on the day of consecration (Singh 2009).

The temple, as a representation of the cosmos and its order, balances the *asura*s (demons) and the *deva*s (gods), as well as inheres in itself other polarities of existence. In the Lakṣmaṇa Temple, Viṣṇu is depicted in a composite form with the usual calm face bracketed by the faces of lion and boar. The conception of the sanctum is as a *maṇḍala* (Desai 2004).

The planetary deities (*grahas*) encircle the temple in the following arrangement:

	Sūrya (Sun)	
Soma (Moon)		*Maṅgala* (Mars)
Bṛhaspati (Jupiter)		*Budha* (Mercury)
Śani (Saturn)		*Śukra* (Venus)
Gaṇeśa		*Durgā*

Gaṇeśa and Durgā are the deities of the ascending and the descending nodes of the moon, respectively. The temple is envisioned like Mt. Meru, the axis of the universe, and the planets move around it.

The Udayagiri Observatory

Udayagiri (hill of [sun]-rise] is one of the principal ancient astronomical observatories of India. It is located at 23°31' N latitude on the Tropic of Cancer in Madhya Pradesh, about 50 km from Bhopal, near Vidiśā, Besnagar and Sāñcī. An ancient site that goes back to at least the second century BCE, it was substantially enlarged during the reign of the Gupta emperor Candragupta II Vikramāditya (r. 375–414). This site is associated with twenty cave temples that have been cut into rock; nineteen of these temples are from the period of Candragupta's reign (Dass and Willis 2002).

It appears that the ancient name of Udayagiri was Viṣṇupadagiri, or the "hill of the footprint of Viṣṇu", and the name Udayagiri is after the Paramāra ruler Udayāditya (*c.* 1070-93). The hill is shaped like a foot (*fig.* 8.10). A saddle connects the northern and southern hills, and a passageway is located at the place where the northern hill meets the saddle. The Gupta period additions and embellishments at Udayagiri were concentrated around this passage. Most of the cave temples are located around the passageway.

On the summer solstice day, there was an alignment of the sun's movement with the passageway. The day mentioned

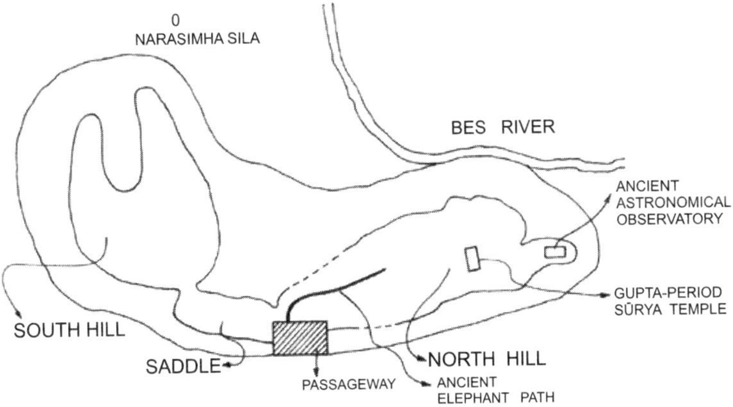

fig. 8.10: Udayagiri layout (Balasubramaniam 2008)

in the dated Candragupta II Vikramāditya period inscription in Cave 6 has been calculated to be very close to the summer solstice of the year CE 402. On this day, the shadow of the Iron Pillar of Delhi, which was originally located at the entrance of the passageway, fell in the direction of the reclining Viṣṇu panel (Balasubramaniam 2008).

On the northern hilltop, there exists a flat platform commanding a majestic view of the sky. Several astronomical marks have been identified at this platform, indicating that this was the site of the ancient astronomical observatory.

Medieval Pilgrimage Complexes

Medieval pilgrimage centres fulfilled many functions including that of trade and business. They were important to the *jyotiṣī* (astrologer) who would make and read the pilgrims' horoscope. The better astrologers were also interested in astronomy and this knowledge was essential for the alignment of temples and palaces.

Every region of India has important pilgrimage centres, some of which are regional and others pan-Indic. The most famous of the pan-Indic centres are associated with Śiva

(Varanasi), Kṛṣṇa (Mathurā, Dwārkā), Rāma (Ayodhyā), Viṣṇu (Tirupati), and the twelve-yearly rotation of the Kumbha Melā at Prayāg, Haridwar, Ujjain, and Nashik. For pilgrimage centres such as Citrakūṭ, Gayā, Madurai, Varanasi, Vindhyācal, and Khajurāho, the question of alignments of temples to cardinal directions or to direction of the sun on major festivals has been studied by scholars (Singh 2009b). Here we will consider the sun temples of Varanasi (Malville 1985; Singh 2009a; 2009b).

THE SUN TEMPLES OF VARANASI

Varanasi is an ancient city dating from the beginning of the first millennium BCE, whose Vedic name is Kāśī (Sanskrit for "radiance"), a name that continues to be used together with Banaras. Of its many temples, the most important is Kāśī Viśvanātha Temple, or "Golden Temple", dedicated to Lord Śiva, the presiding deity of the city. Because of repeated destruction by the sultans and later by Aurangzeb, the current Viśvanātha is a relatively modern building. It was built in 1777 by Mahārānī Ahilyābāī of Indore, and its *śikhara* (spire) and ceilings were plated with gold in 1839, which was a gift from Mahārājā Ranjit Singh (Singh 2009a; 2009b).

Śiva represents both the axes of the universe as well as that of one's inner being. One of the great festivals celebrated in Varanasi is Śivarātri which is celebrated on the 13th day of the dark fortnight of the Phālguna month (February–March). On that day you can see the sun rise in the east with the new moon just above it, which is represented iconographically by Śiva (as the sun) wearing the moon on his head.

There are several pilgrimage circuits in Varanasi for circumambulating the city. The Pañcakrośī circuit has 108 shrines on it, and the four inner circuits have a total of 324 shrines. It is also known for the circuit of the Āditya shrines. The Ādityas are the seven or eight celestial gods, although their number is counted to twelve in later books. In Purāṇic India, they were taken to be the deities of the twelve solar months. The Āditya temples (*fig.* 8.11) were also razed during the centuries of Muslim rule, but have been re-established at the same sites and are now part of the active ritualscapes (Singh 2009a).

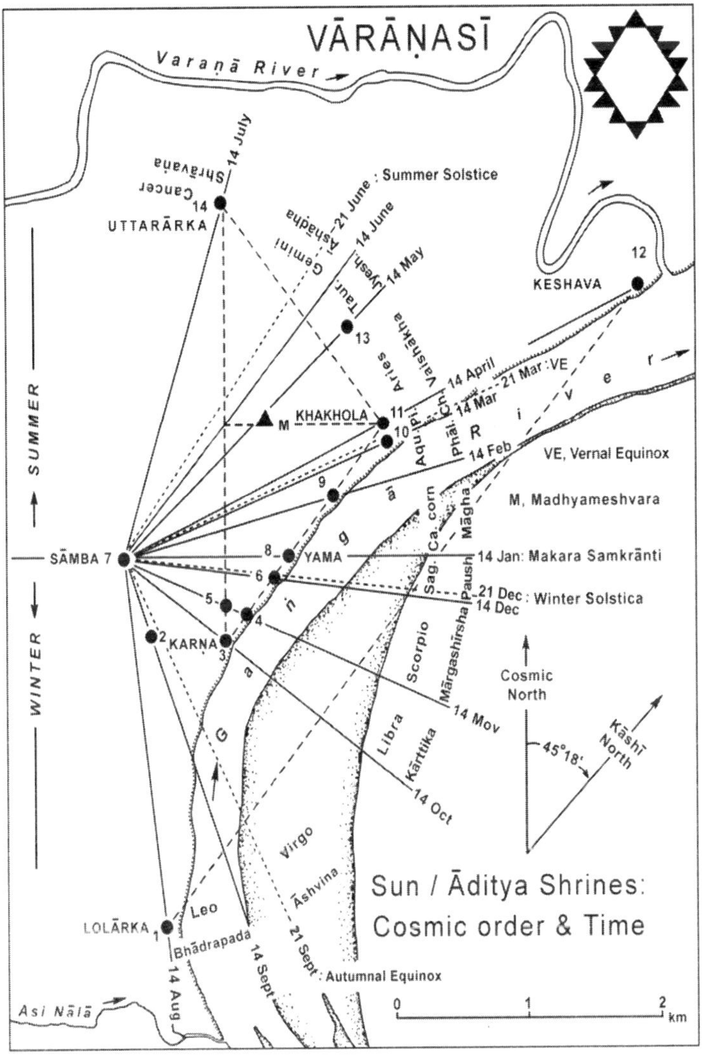

fig. 8.11: Sun shrines, cosmic order and cyclic orientation of time (Singh 2009a)

Several Āditya shrines have been located with the aid of descriptions in the Kāśī Khaṇḍa and pilgrimage guides (Singh and Malville 1995; Singh 2009a; 2009b). Six of these lie along one side of an isosceles triangle with a base of 2.5 km. The triangle surrounds the former temple of Madhyameśvara, which was the original centre of Kāśī. Pilgrims walking along the triangle are symbolically circumambulating the cosmos.

Sacred Cities

There are numerous sacred cities in the Indian subcontinent that were either built to an archetypal master plan or grew organically by virtue of being connected to a specific celestial deity. Some of the important sacred cities are: 1. Varanasi, 2. Vijayanagara, 3. Ayodhyā, 4. Mathurā, 5. Bhaktapur, 6. Tirupati, 7. Kañcīpuram, 8. Dwārkā, and 9. Ujjain.

Robert Levy viewed the Indian sacred city as a structured "mesocosm", situated between the microcosm of the individual and the macrocosm of the culturally conceived larger universe (Levy 1991). Such a city is constructed of spatial connected *maṇḍala*s, each of which is sustained by its own culture and performance. The movements of the festival year and rites of passage constitute a "civic dance", which defines the experience of its citizens.

The life cycle passages and festivals dedicated to the gods affirm the householders' moral compass, identities and relationships. But there also exist other deities, represented generally by goddesses, who point to the forces of nature outside of moral order. These are brought into the larger order through tāntric invocations and amoral propitiatory offerings. Performances invoking the goddess are the responsibility of the king and the merchants.

SACRALITY AND ROYAL POWER AT VIJAYANAGARA

The city of Vijayanagara (also known as Hampī) was founded

in the fourteenth century and sacked in 1565 (*fig.* 8.12). The best known kings associated with Vijayanagara are Harihara I and II and Bukkā Rāya I (*c.* 1336–1404), and Kṛṣṇadevarāya and his half-brother Acyutadevarāya (1509-42). From the mid-fourteenth century to 1565, the city was the capital of the Vijayanagara Empire. According to the Persian ambassador Abdur Razaaq (CE 1442):

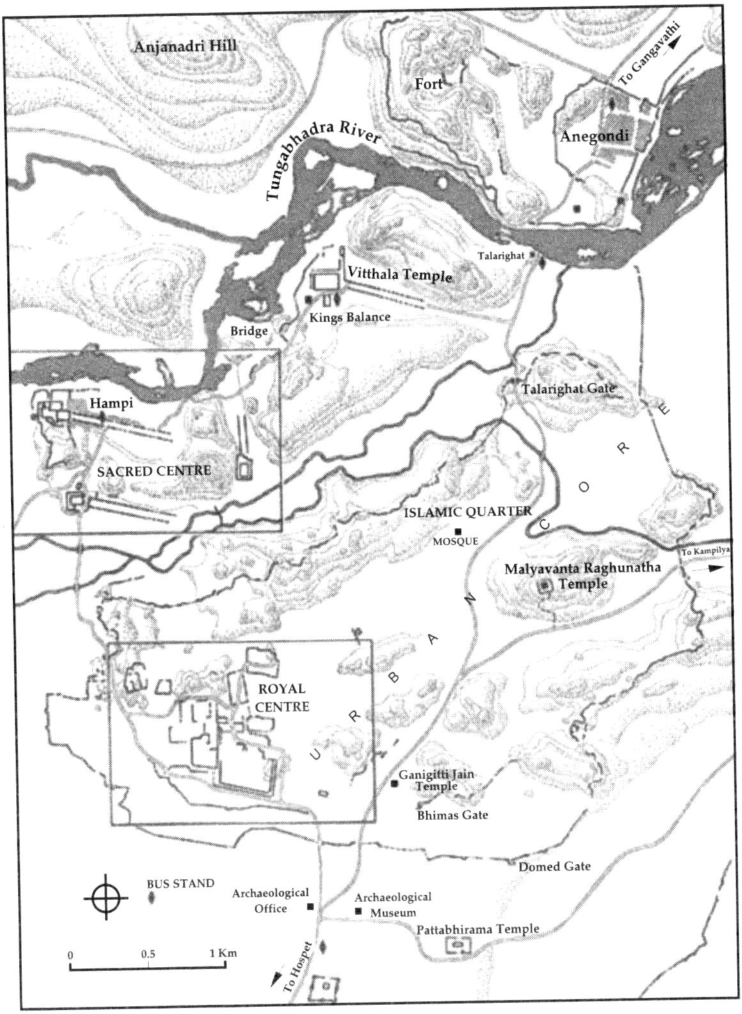

fig. 8.12: Vijayanagara city

> The city of Vijayanagara is such that the pupil of the eye has never seen such a place like it, and the ear of intelligence has never been informed that there existed anything to equal it in the world.

Hampī had for centuries been an important pilgrimage city due to its mythic association with river Goddess Pampā and her consort Virūpākṣa, or Pampāpati. An inscription dated CE 1163 records a *mahādāna*, a religious offering in the presence of Lord Virūpākṣa of Hampī by the Kaḷacuri king Bijjala. The region was part of the kingdom of Kampiladeva until 1326 when the armies of Mohammed Bin Tughlaq defeated the king and imprisoned the two sons of Saṅgama, Hukkā and Bukkā. Some years later the sultan sent the two as governors of the province. In 1336 they broke free from Tughlaq allegiance and established the Saṅgam dynasty with its capital at Vijayanagara.

The destruction of Vijayanagara in 1565 was captured vividly in the account of Robert Sewell (1900):

> They slaughtered the people without mercy; broke down the temples and palaces; and wreaked such savage vengeance on the abode of the kings that, with the exception of a few great stone-built temples and walls, nothing now remains but a heap of ruins to mark the spot where once the stately buildings stood. . . . They lit huge fires in the magnificently decorated buildings forming the temple of Viṭṭhalaswāmi near the river, and smashed its exquisite stone sculptures. With fire and sword, crowbars and axes they carried on day after day their work of destruction. Never perhaps in the history of the world has such havoc been wrought so suddenly on so splendid a city; teeming with a wealthy and industrious population in the full plenitude of prosperity one day and on the next seized, pillaged and reduced to ruins amid scenes of savage massacre and horrors beggaring description.

Hampī has a strong association with *Rāmāyaṇa* and the names of many sites in the area bear names mentioned in the epic. These include Ṛṣimūka, Mālyavanta and Mataṅga hills along with a cave where Sugrīva is said to have kept the jewels of Sītā. The site of Anegundi is associated with the kingdom of Aṅgad, son of Vāli. The Āñjaneya Parvata, a hill to the west of Anegundi, is the fabled birthplace of Hanumān.

Hampī is also linked with the river goddess Pampā and the legend of her marriage to Lord Virūpākṣa or Śiva. Each year, in the month of Caitra (March–April), this marriage is re-enacted, with the priests of Virūpākṣa Temple devoutly performing every ritual from Phalapūjā (betrothal) to Kalyāṇotsava (marriage) in the temple.

The Sacred Centre of the city lies south of the Tuṅgabhadrā River, and it is dominated by four large complexes of the Virūpākṣa, Kṛṣṇa, Tiruveṅgalanātha (Acyutarāya) and Viṭṭhala temples. The major temples are either close to cardinality, departing by an average of 10', or are oriented to major features of the sacred landscape.

Further south of the Sacred Centre is the Royal Centre, which is divided into the public and private realms. The division is achieved by a north–south axis, which passes almost precisely between the king's 100-column audience hall in the east and the queen's large palace in the west. The Rāmacandra Temple pierces the axis by connecting the private and the public domains. In the homology of the king and the deity, the king is able to inhere in him the royalty and divinity of Rāma.

The Vīrabhadra Temple is on the summit of Mataṅga hill, which is the centre of the *vastu-maṇḍala* and the symbolic source of protection that extended outward from it along radial lines. As viewed from a point midway between the audience hall and the queen's palace, the *śikhara* of the Vīrabhadra lies only 4 minutes of arc (4') from true north. The ceremonial gateway in the corridor west of Rāmacandra Temple joined with the summit of Mataṅga hill departs from true north by 0.6 minutes of arc (0.6') (Malville 2000).

The orientations of the major axes of the small temples, shrines, and palaces of the urban core are in marked contrast to those. The smaller structures are rotated away from cardinality for the four directions by 17°, suggesting that they were influenced by the position of the rising sun in the morning when it crosses the zenith.

The bazaar streets of the Virūpākṣa, Viṭṭhala and Kr̥ṣṇa temples are set between 13° and 15° south of east. Malville speculates that there may be some link between these orientations and the rising point of the star Sirius.

Conclusion

Interest in archaeoastronomy and art, as connected to temples and ancient monuments, has increased in India as the country's prosperity has increased. This increase is also owing to the major archaeological discoveries that have been made in the past few decades and the importance of temple tourism.

The principal authority over significant sites is the Indian Archaeological Survey of India (ASI) and its sister institutions that function at the state level as Departments of Archaeology and Museums. In 1976, the Indian government initiated projects to excavate three great medieval cities: Fatehpur Sikri in Uttar Pradesh, Champaner in Gujarat, and Vijayanagara in Karnataka, which are Unesco World Heritage sites. The wealth of discoveries made in these cities is strengthening the movement to expose and preserve other sites in the country. The efforts at excavation, conservation, and research can only be expected to increase. In particular, greater attention will be given to the archaeoastronomical aspects of the monuments.

Acknowledgement

I am thankful to R. Balasubramaniam, Michel Danino, McKim Malville, and Rana P.B. Singh for their advice. The essay is dedicated to the memory of R. Balasubramaniam who passed away in December 2009.

This article is the unabridged version of an essay written for the International Council on Monuments and Sites (ICOMOS). An abridged version appeared as a chapter titled "India" on pp. 101-10 in the book *Heritage Sites of Astronomy and Archaeoastronomy in the Context of the Unesco World Heritage Convention: A Thematic Study*, ed. Clive Ruggles and Michel Cotte that was published jointly by ICOMOS and the International Astronomical Union (IAU), Paris, in 2010.

References

Balasubramaniam, R., 2008, "On the Mathematical Significance of the Dimensions of the Delhi Iron Pillar", *Current Science*, **95:** 766-70.

Balasubramaniam, R. and J.P. Joshi, 2008, "Analysis of Terracotta Scale of Harappan Civilization from Kalibangan", *Current Science*, **95:** 588-89.

Bednarik, R.G., 2000, "Early Indian Petroglyphs and Their Global Context", *Purakala*, **11:** 37-47.

Bhat, M.R., 1995, *Varahamihira's Brihat Samhita*, Delhi: Motilal Banarsidass.

Bisht, R.S., 1997, "Dholavira Excavations: 1990-94", in *Facets of Indian Civilization: Essays in Honour of Prof. B.B. Lal*, ed. J.P. Joshi, New Delhi: Aryan Books International, vol. I, pp. 107-20.

———, 1999a, "Urban Planning at Dholavira, a Harappan City", in John McKim Malville and Lalit M. Gujral (eds.) *Ancient Cities, Sacred Skies: Cosmic Geometries and City Planning in Ancient India*, New Delhi: Aryan Books International for Indira Gandhi National Centre for the Arts, pp. 11-23.

———, 1999b, "Harappans and the Ṛgveda: Points of Convergence", in *The Dawn of Indian Civilization*, ed. G.C. Pande, Delhi: Centre for Studies in Civilizations, pp. 393-442.

Danino, M., 2005, "Dholavira's Geometry: A Preliminary Study", *Puratattva*, **35:** 76-84.

———, 2008, New Insights into Harappan Town-planning, Proportions and Units, with Special Reference to Dholavira", *Man and Environment*, **33:** 66-79.

Dass, M.I. and M. Willis, 2002, The Lion Capital from Udayagiri and the Antiquity of Sun Worship in Central India", *South Asian Studies*, **18:** 25-45.

Desai, D., 2004, "Manifestation of Order in Art: The Iconic Scheme at Khajuraho", in *Ṛta: The Cosmic Order*, ed. Madhu Khanna, New Delhi: D.K. Printworld.

Gangooly, P. (ed.), 1880, *Surya Siddhanta, Translated with Notes and Appendix by Rev. Ebenezer Burgess*, New Delhi: Motilal Banarsidass, 1960.

Joshi, J.P., 2007, *Excavations at Kalibangan, The Harappans*, vol. II, part I, New Delhi: Archaeological Survey of India Report, 2007.

Kak, S., 1992, "The Indus Tradition and the Indo-Aryans", *Mankind Quarterly*, **32:** 195-213.

———, 1993, "Astronomy of the Vedic Altars", *Vistas in Astronomy*, **36:** 117-40.

———, 1995, "The Astronomy of the Age of Geometric Altars", *Quarterly Journal of the Royal Astronomical Society*, **36:** 385-96.

———, 1996, "Knowledge of Planets in the Third Millennium BC", *Quarterly Journal of the Royal Astronomical Society*, **37:** 709-15.

———, 2000a, *The Astronomical Code of the Ṛgveda*, New Delhi: Munshiram Manoharlal.

———, 2000b, "Birth and Early Development of Indian Astronomy", in *Astronomy Across Cultures: The History of Non-Western Astronomy*, ed. Helaine Selin, Kluwer, pp. 303-40.

———, 2002a, "*The Aśvamedha: The Rite and Its Logic*, Delhi: Motilal Banarsidass.

———, 2002b, "Space and Cosmology in the Hindu Temple", Presented at Vaastu Kaushal: International Symposium on Science and Technology in Ancient Indian Monuments, New Delhi, 16-17 November.

———, 2005a, "The Axis and the Perimeter of the Temple", presented at the Kannada Vrinda Seminar, *Sangama 2005*, held at Loyola Marymount University, Los Angeles.

———, 2005b, "Early Indian Architecture and Art", *Migration and Diffusion: An International Journal*, **6:** 6-27.

———, 2006a, "Art and Cosmology in India", *Patanjali Lecture*, University of Massachusetts, Dartmouth, 5 May.

———, 2006b, "Cosmology and Sacred Architecture in India", in *Sangama: A Confluence of Art and Culture During the Vijayanagara Period*, ed. Nalini Rao, Delhi: Originals.

———, 2009, "Time, Space and Structure in Ancient India", presented at the Conference on *Sindhu–Sarasvati Civilization: A Reappraisal*, Loyola Marymount University, Los Angeles, 21-22 February 2009.

Kameswara Rao, N., 1993, "Astronomical Orientations of the Megalithic Stone Circles of Brahmagiri", *Bulletin, Astr. Soc. India*, **21:** 67-77.

———, 2005, "Aspects of Prehistoric Astronomy in India", *Bulletin, Astr. Soc. India*, **33:** 499-511.

Kaulacara, R., 1966, *Śilpa Prakāśa*, A. Boner and S. Rath Sarma (eds.), Leiden: E.J. Brill.

Kenoyer, J.M., 1998, *Ancient Cities of the Indus Valley Civilization*, Karachi: Oxford University Press.

Lal, B.B., 1997, *The Earliest Civilization of South Asia*, New Delhi: Aryan Books International.

———, 2002, *The Saraswati Flows on: The Continuity of Indian Culture*, New Delhi: Aryan Books International.

Levy, R., 1991, *Mesocosm: Hinduism and the Organization of a Traditional Newar City in Nepal*, Berkeley: University of California Press.

Mainkar, V.B., 1984, "Metrology in the Indus Civilization", in *Frontiers of the Indus Civilization*, ed. B.B. Lal and S.P. Gupta, New Delhi: Books and Books.

Malville, J.M., 1985, "Sun Worship in Contemporary India", *Man in India: A Quarterly Journal of Anthropology*, **65:** 207-33.

———, 2000, "The Cosmic Geometries of Vijayanagara", in *Ancient Cities, Sacred Skies: Cosmic Geometries and City Planning in Ancient India*, ed. J.M. Malville and L.M. Gujral, New Delhi: Indira Gandhi National Centre for the Arts and Aryan Books International, pp. 100-18.

Maula, E., 1984, "The Calendar Stones from Mohenjo-Daro", in *Interim Reports on Fieldwork Carried Out at Mohenjo-Daro 1982-83*, vol. 1, ed. M. Jansen and G. Urban, Aachen and Roma, pp. 159-70.

Pandey, S., 1993, *Indian Rock Art*, New Delhi: Aryan Books International.

Pant, M. and S. Funo, 2005, "The Grid and Modular Measures in the Town Planning of Mohenjodaro and Kathmandu Valley", *Journal of Asian Architecture and Building Engineering*, **4:** 51-59.

Sewell, Robert, 1900, *A Forgotten Empire: Vijayanagara*, Kessinger Publishing, 2004 (repr.).

Sastry, T.S. Kuppanna, 1985, *Vedanga Jyotisa of Lagadha*, New Delhi: Indian National Science Academy.

Shaffer, J.G., 1992, "The Indus Valley, Baluchistan, and Helmand Traditions: Neolithic Through Bronze Age", in R. Ehrlich (ed.), *Chronology in Old World Archaeology*, Chicago: The University of Chicago Press.

Singh, Rana P.B., 2009a, *Banaras, Making of India's Heritage City*, Planet Earth & Cultural Understanding Series, No. 3, Newcastle upon Tyne: Cambridge Scholars Publishing.

———, 2009b, *Cosmic Order and Cultural Astronomy: Sacred Cities of India*, Planet Earth & Cultural Understanding Series, No. 4, Newcastle upon Tyne: Cambridge Scholars Publishing.

Singh, Rana P.B. and J.M. Malville, 1995, "Cosmic Order and Cityscape of Varanasi (Kashi): Sun Images and Cultural Astronomy", *National Geographical Journal of India*, **41:** 69-88.

Tyagi, G.S., 1992, "Decorative Intricate Patterns in Indian Rock Art", in M. Lorblanchet (ed.), *Rock Art in the Old World*, New Delhi: Indira Gandhi National Centre for the Arts.

Wakankar, V.S., 1992, "Rock Painting in India", in M. Lorblanchet (ed.), *Rock Art in the Old World*, New Delhi: Indira Gandhi National Centre for the Arts.

Wanzke, H., 1984, "Axis Systems and Orientation at Mohenjo-Daro", in *Interim Reports on Fieldwork Carried Out at Mohenjo-Daro 1982-83*, vol. 2, ed. M. Jansen and G. Urban, Aachen and Roma, pp. 33-44.

Willis, M., 2001, "Inscriptions at Udayagiri: Locating Domains of Devotion, Patronage and Power in the Eleventh Century", *South Asian Studies*, **17:** 48.

9

Universal Premise in Early Nyāya

Kisor K. Chakrabarti

TRADITIONAL Indian logic is dominated by the study of an argument called *nyāya*. In a *nyāya*, the conclusion is typically of the form that something is qualified by something. The former is the subject (*pakṣa, dharmin*) and the latter is the probandum (*sādhya*). The conclusion is based on the premise that the subject is characterized by what is called the probans (*sādhana, hetu*) and the premise that the probans is pervaded (*vyāpta*) by the probandum. The last premise takes either of these forms: (a) whatever is characterized by the probans is characterized by the probandum or (b) whatever is characterized by lack of the probandum is characterized by lack of the probans. The former is called the statement of universal inclusion (*anvaya*) and the latter, that of universal exclusion (*vyatireka*). If the general notions of probans and the probandum are replaced by the variables *a* and *b*, respectively, the universal inclusion may be put as: all *a* is *b*, and the universal exclusion as: all non-*b* is non-*a*. Thus either "all *a* is *b*" or its contrapositive "all non-*b* is non-*a*" is a required premise in a *nyāya*. The following is a common example: whatever is originated is non-eternal, such as a pot, etc. (or whatever is eternal is non-originated, such as space, etc.). Sound is originated. Therefore, sound is non-eternal. This argument is often stated concisely as: sound is non-eternal because of being originated like a pot, etc. (and unlike space, etc.).

It may be gathered from the above that a universal statement of the form "all *a* is *b*" or of the form "all non-*b* is non-*a*" is a required premise (part, step: *avayava*) in a *nyāya*. However, many modern scholars have held that a universal premise was not used in a *nyāya* before the Buddhist logician Diññāga (fifth century CE) or that the evidence for such a premise before then is unclear.[1] We shall examine this claim with special reference to early Nyāya.

One reason for this claim is the use of examples in such an argument. An example (*dṛṣṭānta*) is a particular instance where the probans and the probandum are both present or both absent acceptable to both sides of the argument. (Since space is limited, we below consider only cases of presence of the probans and the probandum.) It is accepted by both parties that the probans and the probandum are both present together in the given instance; accordingly, it is argued that the probandum is present in the inferential subject where the probans is known to be present. Such an argument is analogical. The inferential subject is similar to the cited example in the respect that both possess the probans. Hence the inferential subject should also possess the probandum. (Cases of absence of the probandum

---

[1] ". . . this reasoning still was from particular to particular by analogy." – A.B. Keith, *Indian Logic and Atomism*, Oxford: Clarendon Press, 1921, p. 87; "Both the *Sūtra* and the *Bhāṣya* formulate inference as based on the likeness of the case . . . to example. . . . " – H.N. Randle, *Fragments from Diṅnāga*, p. 75; ". . . one giving an argument is conceived to be citing examples . . . to suggest the plausibility of his hypothesis." – K.H. Potter, in Chi's *Buddhist Formal Logic*, London: Royal Asiatic Society, 1969, pp. xliv-xlv; "It is the Buddhist logician Diṅnāga . . . who seems to have been the first to make this explicit . . ." – J. Ganeri, "Indian Logic" in *Handbook of the History of Logic* (*HHL*), vol. I, North Holland: Elsevier, 2004, p. 326.

and the probans and the consequent argument from dissimilarity may be worked out analogously.) Thus it is an analogical argument from particulars to particulars without any universal premise. This looks more convincing when we look at the abbreviated statement of another common specimen of such an argument: the hill is fiery because it is smoky like a kitchen hearth (and unlike a lake). The hill is a particular where fire is inferred from the similarity of the hill to the kitchen hearth in the respect that both are smoky.

But the mere fact that the universal premise is not explicitly stated in the abbreviated versions of the arguments is not sufficient to prove that the premise is not implied. In a case of inferring fire from smoke it is understood that smoke is caused by fire and thus that all smoky things are fiery. In a natural reading that such a universal premise is implied makes sense particularly when from the beginning Nyāya philosophers have supported causal connections and held it to be non-deviant (*avyabhicārin*).

It may also be noted that although short versions of arguments explicitly citing only examples without universal premises are found in many places, examples are often left out in short versions of arguments in Gotama's *Nyāyasūtra* (*NS*: sixth century BCE), the earliest available work of the Nyāya school.[2] Gotama wrote in aphorisms that are extremely condensed partly because keeping it very short helped

---

[2] Solid evidence for the dates of early philosophers like Gotama is hard to come by and the estimates made by different scholars vary widely. In this connection many scholars prefer to assign the most recent possible date. We find this unwarranted, for it could miss the target by a big margin. We think that we should assign neither the earliest possible date nor the latest possible date but the most likely date in the light of available evidence. However, the discussion of the evidence and different opinions for these dates will take a lot of space and must be skipped here.

memorization and handing it down orally in the ancient times; there is little doubt that because of the age-old and continuing oral tradition Gotama also expected the aphorisms to be expanded with examples and other implied material by teachers for the benefit of the students. Gotama many times supplied only the inferential subject, the probandum and the probans without stating explicitly either the universal premises or the supporting examples. (Sometimes he even supplied only the probans so that the subject and the probandum must be gathered from the context of preceding or succeeding aphorisms though examples in the form of counter-examples to refute (what are judged to be false) universal propositions are effectively used in some places.) Here is a specimen:

> Perception is inference because of being knowledge of [objects of which only] a part is given. – *NS* 2.1.30

Here "perception" is the subject, "being inference" is the probandum and "being knowledge of objects of which only a part is given" is the probans. The argument may be reformulated as:

> All knowledge of objects of which only a part is given is inference, e.g. knowledge of a building of which only the front is given, etc. Perception is knowledge of objects of which only a part is given. Therefore, perception is inference.

It is unnatural to read such an argument as merely from particular to particular by analogy. Though examples are implied, so is implied the general premise that examples seek to support. (More on the role of examples later.) "Perception" can be taken as a singular term; but on a natural reading it may be taken as a general term and the argument seeking to prove that all perceptions are cases of inference. (Gotama criticizes and rejects this view with powerful arguments that show a high level of development in epistemology.) Thus on a natural reading the argument proceeds from the general claim that knowledge of objects of which only a part is given is inference to the case in interest that perception being knowledge of objects of which only a part is given is inference. The underlying principle (not mentioned explicitly) is: what is true of a wider class is also true of a class included in (or of a member of) the wider class.

Here is another specimen of an argument in *Nyāyasūtra*:

> Hypothesization (*arthāpatti*) is not a source of knowledge because of being inconclusive. – 2.2.3

In this case "hypothesization" is the inferential subject, "not being a source of knowledge" is the probandum and "being inconclusive" is the probans. The argument may be reformulated as:

> Nothing inconclusive is a source of knowledge [in the strict sense], e.g. a state of doubt, etc. Hypothesization is inconclusive. Therefore, hypothesization is not a source of knowledge.

Once again, it would be quite unnatural to take this argument as merely from particular to particular by analogy. Though examples are implied, so is there the implicit general premise that nothing inconclusive is a source of knowledge [in the strict sense]. "Hypothesization" can be a singular term. But on a natural reading it can be a general term and the argument seeking to prove the general proposition that no case of hypothesization is a source of knowledge (a view that Gotama upon examination rejects).[3] Once again, the argument proceeds

[3] According to J. Ganeri, "the conclusion of the *Nyāyasūtra* demonstration is a singular proposition" (*HHL*, p. 327). While the conclusion can be a singular proposition, in some cases the conclusion can also be naturally interpreted as a universal proposition with the quantifier understood as it may be expected not only in an aphoristic work like *Nyāyasūtra* but also in a highly condensed commentary such as *Nyāyabhāṣya*. In yet other →

from the universal proposition that nothing inconclusive is a source of knowledge (that Gotama accepts) to the case at hand that hypothesization being inconclusive is not a source of knowledge (that Gotama rejects). Here also the underlying logical principle is: what holds of a general class holds also of a class included in (or of a member of) that general class.

Thus it is clear that the use of examples within an argument in many Sanskrit logical works does not by itself show that universal premises are not used in early Nyāya. In some specimens of Gotama's own arguments examples are left out though implied as are left out the universal premises that too are implied. Thus, in spite of being condensed, these arguments on a natural reading rest on universal premises, such as that knowledge of an object only a part of which is given is inferential, what is inconclusive is not a source of knowledge, and so on. Accordingly, an examination of the earliest available Nyāya arguments in *Nyāyasūtra,* far from lending support to the said interpretation of modern scholars, casts doubt upon it. It may be noted that the modern interpretation may be challenged from the evidence available in *Nyāyasūtra* itself. We shall find more such evidence from *Nyāyasūtra* itself later though as we proceed we take into account another old work as well.

→ cases the conclusion can be naturally interpreted as a particular proposition (again with the quantifier understood). (For example, *NS* 4.1.29 and 4.1.30.) Accordingly, we do not think that (although Gotama does not use universal or particular quantifiers explicitly) a substantial point of contrast between Gotama and Aristotle is that while for the former the conclusion is a singular proposition, for the latter the conclusion is a universal or a particular proposition (*HHL*, 327). Indeed, in spite of important differences, the deductive core of Gotama's *nyāya* has significant affinity with Aristotle's syllogism. For more discussion, see Kisor Chakrabarti, *Logic of Gotama* (*LG*), Honolulu: University of Hawaii Press, 1978, chaps. III and VII.

It goes without saying that one should not look only at short versions of arguments but also at longer versions. A more articulated version is found in Vātsyāyana's *Nyāyabhāṣya* (NB: second century BCE?, the earliest available commentary on the *Nyāyasūtra*) in the discussion of the pentapod (*pañcāvayava*) argument. We first quote the passage confining ourselves to the case of *sādharmya* (universal inclusion, more on this concept later):

> . . . the sentence "sound is non-eternal" is the Thesis (*pratijñā*). "Because of being originated" is the Reason (*hetu*).
>
> "What is originated is Non-eternal, such as a plate, etc." is the Exemplification (*udāharaṇa*). "Sound is so originated" is the Application (*upanaya*). "Therefore, because of being originated, sound is non-eternal" is the Outcome (*nigamana*).
>
> — *NB* 1.1.39[4]

We have earlier cited this argument briefly, viz. sound is non-eternal because being originated like a pot, etc. Immediately above we see how it has been presented in *NB* (in the universal inclusion mood) in five steps as recommended in *NS*.[5] We restate it as:

> Sound is non-eternal. Because of being originated. What is originated is non-eternal, like a plate, etc. Sound is so originated. Therefore, because of being originated, sound is non-eternal.

---

4 The word *hetu* stands for not only the inferential mark but also the second step of the pentapod argument that supplies the mark. We translate the former as "probans" and the latter as "reason". Similarly, the word *udāharaṇa* stands for an example but also for the third step of the pentapod that supplies universal premises with supportive examples. We translate the former as "example" and the latter as "exemplification".

5 More on the pentapod argument is given below. For a full discussion of the pentapod argument, see *LG*, chap. III.

It is clear that the third step includes not only an example but also a general proposition. "What is originated is non-eternal" lacks an explicit universal quantifier. But it naturally means "whatever is originated is non-eternal". When something non-existent comes into being it is said to be originated. Thus something originated is not eternal, for something eternal is never non-existent. Accordingly, the premise is not a particular proposition but a universal proposition. This shows that in a longer version such an argument in an early text contains a universal premise with a supporting example. *NB* says:

> . . . when the relation of the probans and the probandum is known decisively with the help of examples, the character . . . is offered as the probans and not by way of mere similarity or mere dissimilarity. – *NB* 1.1.39

This shows clearly what the role of an example is. It helps to show that two characters are related as the probans and the probandum. We shall see that the relation of the probans and the probandum holds according to *Nyāyasūtra* and *Nyāyabhāṣya* (and all logicians of the school) if and only if the former is non-deviant from the latter. Thus what an example helps to show is that the probans is non-deviant from or universally concomitant with the probandum. *Nyāyabhāṣya* adds explicitly that mere similarity or mere dissimilarity does not suffice for the relation of the probans and the probandum. Again, returning to the above specimen, on a natural reading "sound is non-eternal" means that all sounds are non-eternal. Thus the argument seeks to prove a universal conclusion with the help of a premise that includes a universal proposition. All this, the specific remarks on the role of examples and the explicit rejection of mere analogy in *Nyāyabhāṣya* in particular, casts very serious doubt on the claim that in the said early stages of the school arguments are merely analogical and from particular to particular.

For a closer look into the question of universal premises in early Indian logic we now look at the account of the pentapod argument given by Gotama in *NS*:

> The parts [of the pentapod argument] are the Thesis, the Reason, the Exemplification, the Application and the Outcome. – 1.1.32
>
> The Thesis is the statement of what is to be proved. – 1.1.33
>
> The Reason is [that from which we get] what proves the probandum by virtue of the universal inclusion (*sādharmya*) [stated] in the Exemplification. – 1.1.34
>
> So also by virtue of universal exclusion (*vaidharmya*). — 1.1.35
>
> The Exemplification is [that from which we get] an instance where that character (the probandum) is present in accordance with the universal inclusion [of the probans] with the probandum. – 1.1.36
>
> Or the opposite in the reverse case of that. – 1.1.37
>
> The Application is the characterization of the subject as so or not so depending on the Exemplification. – 1.1.38
>
> The Outcome is the restatement of the Thesis qualified by the probans. – 1.1.39

For our present purpose we shall confine ourselves to the Reason and the Exemplification. The Reason states the inferential mark or the probans (such as being originated in inferring non-eternality). In the traditional understanding that we follow in our account above and is shared by dozens of leading philosophers (including such illustrious names as Uddyotakara (sixth century CE), Jayanta Bhaṭṭa (ninth century CE), and Udayana (eleventh century CE, etc.), the probans proves the probandum (in part) by virtue of the universal inclusion (or universal exclusion) with the probandum. However, many modern scholars have interpreted and translated *sādharmya* and *vaidharmya* as similarity and dissimilarity, respectively.

This is one of the reasons why many in modern times interpret the *nyāya* demonstrations in early Indian logic as merely analogical arguments. Indeed, if these words are to be so interpreted, the arguments in early times are most likely analogical without universal premises.

Now it is true that the said two words can literally mean similarity and dissimilarity. But it should not be overlooked that these words are compounds and depending on the way the compounds are analysed still strictly following the rules of Sanskrit grammar these two words can also literally and explicitly mean universal inclusion and universal exclusion, respectively. Needless to say, if these concepts should be interpreted as universal inclusion and universal exclusion, Gotama has said in so many words in the account of the pentapod that a universal premise is required (along with examples). So the question is: when interpreting the aphorisms of Gotama on the pentapod argument, which of the two readings (the modern or the traditional) makes more sense?

To answer this question we first look at some observations on the probans and related topics found in *Nyāyasūtra*. Since the aphorisms are very cryptic, to throw more light it is useful to study not only what Gotama says on the probans but also on what is not a probans or is a pseudo-probans (*hetvābhāsa*). According to the aphorism *NS* 2.1.28: "[a certain inferential mark] is not a probans because of being contradicted (*vyāhata*)". (This is found in the discussion of the inner sense (*manas*) one function of which is to supervise (somewhat like the brain in modern terms) the five external sense-organs of sight, touch, etc.) It is implied that nothing contradicted can be a probans. (Gotama has also said in the context of discussing if authority is a source of knowing that something contradicted is not a source of knowing: *NS* 2.1.57.) One requirement of a probans then is that it should not be contradicted.[6] Another condition is that a probans should not contradict the conclusion (*NS* 2.2.6). Yet another condition is that a probans should not be as open to question as the probandum (*sādhyasama*) (*NS* 2.2.8). (It is implied that a probans should be better grounded and acceptable to both sides in the debate.) A further condition is that a probans should not be such that while it seeks to prove the presence of probandum in the inferential subject, the probans is counterbalanced by an equally matching rival inferential mark that seeks to prove absence of the probandum in the inferential subject (*prakaraṇasama*) (*NS* 2.2.7). A final condition is that a probans should not be deviant (*savyabhicāra*) (*NS* 2.2.5).[7]

For our purpose the last condition is critically important. *Nyāyasūtra* says explicitly that a deviant inferential mark is a pseudo-probans and is inconclusive (*anaikāntika*). As *Nyāyabhāṣya* explains a deviant mark is present not only where the probandum is present but also where the probandum is absent (*NB* 2.2.5). This is why it is not conclusive. Since it is present both where the probandum is present and where the latter is absent (even if such a mark is present in the inferential subject), we cannot conclude on this basis that the probandum is present for it may also be absent. Thus such a mark does not provide the logical guarantee for the conclusion that the probandum is present. For example, suppose it is argued that sound is eternal because it lacks touch (*NS* 2.2.22). Lacking touch is deviant; while some things lacking touch, such as space, are eternal, other things lacking touch, such as motion, are non-eternal (*NS* 2.2.23). So lacking touch is not a logically sufficient basis to conclude that something is eternal, for it

6 More on this is found in the discussion of the kind of pseudo-probans called *kālātīta*. See *LG*, chap. IV for an explanation of this kind of pseudo-probans.

7 These conditions and the concept of a pseudo-probans are explained in *LG*, chap. IV.

may also be non-eternal. Thus in spite of being cryptic *Nyāyasūtra* makes it clear that deviation cannot provide the proper inferential basis. This implies that to be a probans and conclusive a probans should be non-deviant (*avyabhicārin*). That is, the probans should be present only where the probandum is present and not where the latter is absent. Since *Nyāyasūtra* and *Nyāyabhāṣya* require that a probans should be non-deviant, it follows that the connection between the probans and the probandum is universal and not particular. The universal connection is either universal inclusion or universal exclusion as *Nyāyasūtra* says. The words *sādharmya* and *vaidharmya* are, as already said, ambiguous. These can literally mean similarity and dissimilarity, respectively, as also universal inclusion and universal exclusion, respectively. But when one adds the condition that a probans must not be deviant, to be consistent with that, these can only be construed as universal inclusion and universal exclusion. In other words, a deviant mark can fulfil the condition of similarity or dissimilarity. For example, in arguing for eternality from lacking touch, since some eternal things like space are eternal, one can argue consistently that since sound lacks touch it is eternal like space (that too lacks touch). Thus if mere analogy were the required inferential basis, a deviant mark cannot consistently be rejected as a pseudo-probans. This shows that a probans should not be related merely by way of similarity or dissimilarity but by way of universal inclusion or universal exclusion and, accordingly, a universal premise is required in *Nyāyasūtra* and *Nyāyabhāṣya*.

Gotama has thrown more light on the need for universal premises in the discussion of pseudo-rejoinders (*jāti*). He has listed twenty-four of them but we shall (to keep it short) look only at two of his aphorisms.[8] The aphorism *NS* 5.1.2 says:

[8] For more on pseudo-rejoinders see Kisor Chakrabarti, *Definition and Induction*, Honolulu: University of Hawaii Press, 1995, chap. VIII.

> In the case of drawing the conclusion based on universal inclusion (*sādharmya*) and universal exclusion (*vaidharmya*) counter arguments through that character and its absence are matching by similarity (*sādharmya-sama*) and matching by dissimilarity (*vaidharmya-sama*) [respectively].

The aphorism *NS* 5.1.3 says:

> That proof (i.e. *nyāya*) excels in the way does proving that something is a cow with the help of cow-ness.

Gotama here duly warns in his usual cryptic way that if an argument is based on mere similarity or mere dissimilarity without making use of universal connection, one could land in a logical stalemate: there could be equally matching counter arguments based on mere similarity or mere dissimilarity. But there is no stalemate and such counter arguments turn out to be pseudo-rejoinders if the argument is based on universal connection. As a specific case Gotama cites proving that something is a cow on the basis of cow-ness. In his view cow-ness is universal (*jāti*) and universals are objective common properties that generate sameness (*samāna-prasavātmikā jātiḥ*, *NS* 2.2.70). In other words, innumerable different cows are different from each other in some respects but are all still the same in the respect that they all possess cow-ness. This is true of other universals like substance-ness. There are an infinite number of substances and they differ from each other in many respects but they still are all identical in so far as each possesses substance-ness, i.e. each is a substance. Thus the connection between a universal and its instance admits of no exception: each cow has cow-ness and each thing with cow-ness is a cow. When one argues based on such universal connection, counter arguments based on mere similarity or mere dissimilarity are futile and are pseudo-rejoinders.

Nyāyabhāṣya throws more light (we confine ourselves only to matching with similarity due to limited space) with an example:

> Illustration: the soul has motion because of having a quale (*guṇa*) that is a causal condition of motion in a substance. A stone is a substance having a quale that is a causal condition of motion and also has motion. The soul is so and, therefore, has motion. If the conclusion is drawn thus, it may be counter matched on the basis of similarity itself. The soul is motionless, for a ubiquitous substance is motionless; *ākāśa* (the substratum of sound) is ubiquitous and motionless; the soul is so [i.e. ubiquitous] and, therefore, motionless. . . . Since there is no reason to make a difference [to the epistemic status of the two arguments], there is matching by similarity.
>
> — *NB* 5.1.2

In this illustration the conclusion that the soul has motion is drawn on the basis of its similarity with a stone (that has motion) in the respect that both have a quale that is a causal condition of motion in a substance. The conclusion is drawn on the basis of this similarity alone without using the universal premise that whatever has a quale that is a causal condition of motion has motion (a false universal proposition in Gotama's view). The matching counter argument shows that the soul is motionless because it is similar to the substratum of sound (that is motionless in Gotama's view) in the respect that both are ubiquitous. The counter argument too is drawn based on this similarity alone without the universal premise that whatever is ubiquitous is motionless (accepted by Gotama). Thus such arguments and counter arguments based on analogy alone without universal premises can lead to logical stalemate.

Nyāyabhāṣya also makes clear, following Gotama, how the stalemate is resolved:

> If the probandum is sought to be proven on the basis of mere similarity or mere dissimilarity, there could be lack of decisiveness (*avyavasthā*). But this is not rationally justifiable if there is a character [i.e. a probans] that can make a difference. On the basis of the common character of cows or

> the particular universal called cow-ness, it is proven that something is a cow . . . by way of excluding horses, etc. . . . and not on the basis of difference in qualia, etc. – *NB* 5.1.3

Nyāyabhāṣya says explicitly above that an analogical argument based on mere similarity or mere dissimilarity may not be decisive, for it can be equally matched by a counter analogical argument. But there is no lack of decisiveness if there is a character or a probans that can make a difference because of being universally concomitant with the probandum. Cow-ness is such a probans in proving that something is a cow, for the relation between cow-ness and being a cow admits of no exception. Other characters, such as being brown, lack universal connection, for just as a cow can be brown so also can be a horse. Of course, such other characters lacking universal connection may be used in a merely analogical argument but are not suitable for a *nyāya*.[9]

It is reasonable to conjecture that there was a pre-Gotama stage of development of Indian logic when analogical arguments based on similarity or dissimilarity without universal premises served as the norm for demonstration. *Nyāyasūtra* and *Nyāyabhāṣya* make a determined effort to raise it to a higher level by pointing out that such arguments may lead to logical stalemate and that the stalemate can be resolved by using universal premises. There is thus strong evidence that instead of the modern interpretation cited above it is the

---

[9] J. Ganeri has made the interesting suggestion that the Nyāya model may be an early attempt at "case-based reasoning" (*HHL* pp. 327-29). However, in the latter kind of reasoning one is not required to know the underlying general law. Since *Nyāyasūtra* and *Nyāyabhāṣya* require that the probans should be related to the probandum by way of universal inclusion or universal exclusion and should be non-deviant and further that mere similarity or mere dissimilarity without universal connection is inadequate for proof, we find this suggestion questionable.

traditional interpretation that is preferable if one carefully examines the account of the pentapod in *Nyāyasūtra* and *Nyāyabhāṣya* and related views on the pseudo-probans and pseudo-rejoinders.[10]

[10] Further evidence that *Nyāyasūtra* and *Nyāyabhāṣya* require the probans to be non-deviant from the probandum is found in the examination of inference as a source of knowledge, specially *Nyāyasūtra* and *Nyāyabhāṣya* 2.1.37 and 2.1.38. A fuller discussion would show that *Nyāyasūtra* and *Nyāyabhāṣya* made a great contribution to the development of logic, both deductive and inductive. It may be added that a careful study would also show that, in spite of extreme brevity, *Nyāyasūtra* and *Nyāyabhāṣya* have critically examined a number of central philosophical topics such as that the self is not the body, that the meaning of a word includes the universal, the particular and the form or the relationship, etc. in remarkable depth and rigour.

10

Gaṅgeśa on Showing Inference Failure

The Asādhakatā-Sādhakatva-Prakaraṇam from the Tattvacintāmaṇi

Stephen H. Phillips

atha asādhakatā-sādhakatva-prakaraṇam
Now on Showing Inference Failure[1]

Text (Tirupati 165; Calcutta 983)

atha hetv-ābhāsānām asādhakatvena sad-uttaratvam jāty-ādīnāṁ ca asādhakatā-sādhāraṇyena para-asādhakatā-sādhakatayā sva-vyāghātakatvād asad-uttaram।

Pūrvapakṣin: In so far as pseudo-provers (*hetv-ābhāsa*) show the ineffectiveness or failure (of an opponent's inference), to cite one would be a good response (in a debate). And (so-

---

[1] The Sanskrit text is taken from the Tirupati Vidyapeetha edition of the inference chapter, Anumāna-Khaṇḍa, of the *Tattvacintāmaṇi* by Gaṅgeśa, with the commentary of Rucidatta and sub-commentary by Dharmarājādhvarin, ed. N.S. Ramanuja Tatacharya, vol. 2, part 2, Sanskrit Vidyapeetha Series 33, Tirupati, 1999, pp. 165-90. Also consulted – but only very occasionally favoured as indicated – has been the Calcutta Asiatic Society edition: *Tattvacintāmaṇi* by Gaṅgeśa, Anumāna-Khaṇḍa, with the commentary of Mathurānātha, ed. Kamakhyanath Tarkavagish, Calcutta: Asiatic Society, 1884–1901, repr., 1991, part 1, pp. 983-96.

Much of the best work in epistemology and logic of the Navya- →

called) "futile rejoinders" (*jāti*) and the like (mentioned in *Nyāyasūtra* and elsewhere) would not be good responses. It is by nature self-contradictory to try to show another's inference to fail because of a characteristic shared with the other's inference which does not produce inferential knowledge.

Comments: According to Gaṅgeśa's *pūrvapakṣin* – most of whose points Gaṅgeśa does not answer in his short *siddhānta* section at the end – there is a common problem with "futile

---

→ Nyāya School remains inaccessible except to traditional Sanskrit-speaking scholars. N.S. Ramanuja Tatacharya, a scholar of great accomplishment, read with me the inference chapter of Gaṅgeśa's *Jewel* up to this section more than a decade ago, and although we did not have the opportunity to read this one together, his instruction has been crucial. A few years after our work, I made a partial translation of the entire inference chapter to compose a summary for Sibajiban Bhattacharyya who helped me iron out a few rough spots: "The Inference Chapter of Gangesa's *Tattvacintamani*", *Development of Nyaya Philosophy and Its Social Context*, ed. Sibajiban Bhattacharyya (New Delhi, 2004) in the *Project of History of Indian Science, Philosophy and Culture*, ed. D.P. Chattopadhyaya, vol. 3, part 3, pp. 424-47. The translation here, however, is based on a fresh reading, and mistakes belong only to me. I wish to thank the participants of the workshop sponsored by the Indian Council of Philosophical Research, "Rendering of the Categories of Classical Indian Thought in the English Language", New Delhi, December 2011, for helpful criticisms of some of my earlier works and for insights about translation in general, in particular P.K. Mukhopadhyay.

In the transliteration, compounds are indicated by hyphens, and *sandhi* is broken. Beyond indication of *sandhi* breaks, no effort has been made to improve the *sandhi* representation. The Tirupati edition is practically mirrored, and violations of *sandhi* are left as they appear (some serving in effect as commas). Some punctuation has been simplified, however, and there are no paragraph indentations or designations other than the big breaks for translation and comment. In this way, the Sanskrit text here is an edition slightly distinct from the Tirupati edition, reflecting my reading.

rejoinders" (*jāti*). It is that they purport to show that an original inference relies on properties or reasoning that would prove the opposite such that the original inference would be blocked except that the rejoinder relies on similar reasoning or properties and thus is self-defeating in context. For example, "Sound is non-eternal, *since* it is produced, like a pot", is a good inference for which a *jāti* could be constructed, "Sound is eternal, *since* it is immaterial, like ether (*ākāśa*)". If the second inference blocks the first, then so does the first block the second. In contrast, pointing out a pseudo-prover would seem itself to be a proof of something, at a minimum that an original inference is wrong.

Although Gaṅgeśa does not in any thoroughgoing fashion answer the opponent whose voice dominates this section, his own views are explored by questions and objections put to the *pūrvapakṣin* throughout. Apparently, one should be able to see by the end what the right positions are, although many are not put in Gaṅgeśa's own authoritative voice. That is to say, few are spelled out in the *siddhānta* section at the end although we are treated to a couple of definitive definitions of inference failure.

Throughout this translation, the words "know", "inferential knowledge", etc. are used where earlier Nyāya translators (myself included) of *jñāna*, *anumiti*, and company have used "cognition", "inferential conclusion", etc. Use of the former group is only usually and not invariably more appropriate since there are no false bits of knowledge as the word. "Knowledge" is used in English or at least in philosophical English: there are only bits of apparent knowledge, *pramā-ābhāsa*, or false cognitions, *mithyā-jñāna*, as the words are used in Sanskrit. Nevertheless, unchallenged, unjustified (i.e. unselfconsciously justified) cognition, *jñāna*, counts, if true, as knowledge, *pramā*, according to Nyāya and most of the other classical schools. Furthermore, in the context of "inference for others" or formal *nyāya*, as Nyāya philosophers say – which provides the setting for this section and most of the latter half of Gaṅgeśa's inference chapter – all claims may be taken as challenged, such that the goal is to have not just unreflective knowledge but certified, reflective knowledge, *nirṇaya*, which in the debate context consists of a winning proof. In other words, a good inference that produces in this context inferential knowledge must not only obey the rules of (a) pervasion (i.e. entailment, *vyāpti*), and (b) an existential requirement of the prover being a property of the inferential subject (*pakṣa-dharmatā*) but also (c) the prover must face no defeaters or counterinferences. For elaboration, see the opening of the on-line entry, "Epistemology in Classical Indian Philosophy", in the *Stanford Encyclopedia of Philosophy*,[2] as well as below in further comments.

Text (Tirupati 165; Calcutta 983)

atha viruddhatva-ādi-jñānād eva sva-anumiter iva para-anumiteḥ pratibandhe kim asādhakatā-anumānena । *yad vacasi vādy-ukta-dūṣaṇa-avagamaḥ sa nigṛhīta iti samaya-bandhena kathā-pravṛttau dūṣaṇa-mātram udbhāvyam anyathā artha-antaratvād iti cet na* । *dvayaṁ hy uddeśyaṁ para-anumiti-pratibandhaḥ sthāpanāyāḥ asādhakatā-sādhanatvaṁ ca* । *tatra ādyam dūṣaṇa-mātra-jñānād eva* । *dvitīyaṁ tu liṅgatva-jñāpanāt* । *pratibandhakatva-vad anena api rūpeṇa dūṣakatva-saṁbhava ity abhiprāyeṇa vā asādhakatā-sādhanam* ।

***Objection (to the pūrvapakṣin)*:** What is the use of *inference* to inference failure, if the opponent's inferential knowledge is prevented simply by knowledge of contradictoriness and the others (the other inferential flaws), as would be the case with

[2] Stephen Phillips, "Epistemology in Classical Indian Philosophy", *The Stanford Encyclopedia of Philosophy* (Spring 2011 Edition), ed. Edward N. Zalta. URL = <http://plato.stanford.edu/archives/spr2011/entries/epistemology-india/>.

one's own (putative) inferential knowledge (which would be blocked by one's own knowledge of contradictoriness, etc.)? What you say, namely, that there is comprehension of vitiation as voiced by one of the debaters would itself be blocked (on your view). Thus by the blocking on the occasion, i.e. when a debate has commenced, it is simply the vitiating itself that should be brought forth. Otherwise, there would be irrelevance.

Pūrvapakṣin: Wrong. For there is a pair (of results) to be spelled out: (a) blocking of (production of) inferential knowledge for the other person, and (b) showing the failure (or ineffectiveness) of what the opponent would establish. Of the two, the former results from knowledge of vitiation alone. But the latter results from an inferential sign being made known. Like blocking, in this manner, too, vitiation is possible – or this is the gist that there can be a showing of inference failure.

Comments: There is a big difference between (a) a mere blocker of inference, such as awareness of a counter-example, and (b) a debater's being able both to block an opponent's inference by pointing out a fallacy and to state why the blocker does this job.

Text (Tirupati 166; Calcutta 984)

nanv evaṁ pañca-avayava-prayoga-apekṣā syāt anyathā nyūnatā-āpattir iti cet na । *dūṣaṇasya asādhakatā-vyāpyatvam aṅgīkṛtya kathā iti pakṣa-dharmatāyā eva udbhāvyatvāt* । *anyathā adhikatā-āpatteḥ* ।

Objection: In that case, it would all depend on employment of the five members (of the formal syllogism, an "inference for others", *para-artha-anumāna*, also called a *nyāya*). Otherwise, the difficulty would be (the fallacy called) "leaving something out" (*nyūnatā*).

Pūrvapakṣin: Wrong. Debate proceeds on the presupposition that vitiation is pervaded by inference failure (i.e. that vitiation entails such failure). Just the prover's being a property of the inferential subject should be brought forth. Otherwise, the difficulty would be (the fallacy called) extraneous addition (*adhikatā*, "putting something in").

Comments: Debate proceeds by formal presentations of inferences and attempts to block inferences on the part of each side. Beyond the logic of inference and the "pseudo-provers", there are presentational requirements that have been discussed by Gaṅgeśa earlier in addressing the "members" of a formal "inference for others", *para-artha-anumāna*, also called a *nyāya*. To call these "presentational" is not quite right since they are in Gaṅgeśa's view practically grammatical requirements in arousing the right expectations (*ākāṅkṣā*) in the hearer so that she or he can draw for themselves the desired conclusion and have inferential knowledge.

1. The inferential subject has the probandum (i.e. this will be proved: S*a*)
2. Since it has the prover (H*a*)
3. As shown in the example (illustrating the rule or pervasion: (x)(Hx → Sx))
4. With the subject as having the prover falling under the rule (H*a* → S*a*)
5. Therefore, the subject has the probandum (S*a* but also now proved).

Text (Tirupati 167; Calcutta 984)

nanv evaṁ kṛtakatvena anityatva-anumāne[3] *vyāptir na abhidheyā ubhaya-siddhatvād iti cet na* । *kathāyāṁ samaya-viṣayatayā dūṣaṇe tv asādhakatā-vyāpty-upasthiter āvaśyakatvāt anyathā kathakatva-virodhāt* ।

Objection: In that case, the pervasion would not have to be spelled out in the case of the inference to impermanence from being a product, since that would be accepted by both parties.

[3] The Calcutta edition adds *'pi*.

Purvapakṣin: Wrong. In debate, vitiating occurs, rather, according to the topic of the occasion. Setting in mind the pervasion involved in (showing) inference failure is required. Otherwise, what it is to be a debater would be controverted.

Comments: Buddhists and Naiyāyikas agree, for example, that if something is produced it is impermanent. The agreement does not rule out mentioning the pervasion if the topic demands.

Text (Tirupati 168; Calcutta 985)

nanv evaṁ kr̥takatvena-anumāne tad-vyāptim anaṅgīkr̥tya api kathā-sambhavāt yas tu kathā-ārambhe bādhakasya asādhakatva-vyāptiṁ na aṅgīkaroti taṁ prati tad-dūṣaṇatvaṁ prasādya pañca-avayava-prayogaḥ kartavya eva । *yat tu dūṣaṇe pakṣa-dharmatā-mātram udbhāvyaṁ tatra yatra vādinos tathā samayaḥ anyatra tu pañca-avayava-prayoga eva iti* । *tan na* । *kathā-saṁpradāya-virodhāt* ।

Objection: In the case of the inference from being a product (to impermanence), debate is possible for someone who does not accept that pervasion at all; indeed, debate is possible for someone who thus at the very beginning of the debate (on this or any topic) does not accept that there is a pervasion (an entailment) between blocking and inference failure. Against such a person, one making clear a vitiation would indeed have to employ the five members (of the formal syllogism, a *nyāya*). In contrast, merely bringing forth in vitiation the inferential subject's possessing the prover property may be an occasion like what you imagine for the two debaters. However, on other occasions there should indeed be employment of the five members (of a *nyāya*).

Pūrvapakṣin: Wrong. For it controverts our inherited positions about debate.

Comments: Rucidatta glosses *saṁpradaya-virodha*, "opposition to inherited positions", as the fallacy *apasiddhānta*, "incoherence" (with what is already known and certified).

The *pūrvapakṣin* at this point may be supposed to be a Naiyāyika who has inherited a tradition of rules of debate from *Nyāyasūtra* on. (Later, he seems to be a Prābhākara Mīmāṁsaka.) Roughly, 25 per cent of the *sūtras* of *Nyāyasūtra,* a comparatively enormous amount of text is devoted to debate and its tools.

Text (Tirupati 169; Calcutta 986)

atha asādhakatvaṁ na pakṣe sādhya-pratyaya-ajanakatvam । tena api tattvena ajñāna-daśāyāṁ pakṣe sādhya-bhrama-jananāt kadācid ajanakatvaṁ sad-hetāv api । nanv etat-kāle sādhya-viśiṣṭa-pakṣa-jñāna-ajanakatvaṁ tat । na hi dūṣaṇatva-jñāna-daśāyāṁ pakṣe bhrama-rūpā apy anumitiḥ sādhya-viśiṣṭa-pakṣa-jñānaṁ ca hetutvena jñāna-daśāyāṁ prasiddham iti cet na । sad-dhetāv asat-pratipakṣatā-daśāyām api pūrva-kāle sādhya-viśiṣṭa-pakṣa-jñāna-ajankatvam asti ity asādhakatā-prasaṅgāt ।

***Objection*:** (Showing) inference failure (of a putative prover, i.e. a putative prover's failing to produce inferential knowledge) amounts to (showing) (D^1) non-generation of the notion of the probandum with respect to the inferential subject (as one of its properties).

***Pūrvapakṣin*:** Sometimes when there is no (inferential) knowledge there is no such generation because there is generation of erroneous cognition of a probandum with respect to an inferential subject. This would happen (sometimes) too with a genuine (a good) prover, even according to that principle (you propose concerning contradiction and other fallacies as securing knowledge failure without showing inference failure).

***Objection*:** At such a time it (a putative prover) does not generate knowledge of an inferential subject as qualified by a probandum. For it is not the case that, although taking the form of erroneous cognition with respect to the subject (some kind of), inferential knowledge occurs when there is knowledge of vitiation. Furthermore, knowledge of a subject as qualified by a probandum is well known as occurring when the knowledge has proceeded by way of a (genuine) prover.

***Pūrvapakṣin*:** Wrong. The difficulty would be that, even on an occasion of a false (i.e. an unwarranted) charge of a counterinference (a counterbalancing inference) against a prover that is good (or genuine), non-generation of knowledge of the inferential subject as qualified by the probandum would count, at the time before (the counterbalancing was exposed), as inference failure.

***Comments*:** Counterinference (*sat-pratipakṣa*) is defined (Tirupati, p. 84):

> (An inference blocked by counterinference) is to have an inferential mark whose result is contradicted by that which (i.e. a counterprover), having been brought to mind, has equal power ("force", *bala*, evidential power), capable, that is to say, of bringing to mind the contradictory to the probandum (*sādhya-virodhy-upasthāpana-samartha-samāna-bala-upasthityā pratiruddha-kārya-liṅgatvaṁ tattvam*).

So even if one's prover in another context, where it is not being challenged by a counterinference, does in fact produce inferential knowledge, in the context of debate, where the opponent presents counterevidence of the right form which one cannot show flawed, one does not have, or no longer has, inferential knowledge.

In other words, against an original inference:

$$Ha \text{ and } (x)(Hx \rightarrow Sx), \text{ therefore } Sa$$

there is the counterinference:

$$Ja \text{ and } (x)(Jx \rightarrow \sim Sx), \text{ therefore } \sim Sa$$

and thus inference failure even if the basic requirement of epistemic logic is met:

$$(K)(^{Sp}Ha) \rightarrow (K)Sa.$$

(If a person comes to know that H-as-qualified-by-being-pervaded-by-S qualifies *a*, then that person comes to know that S*a*.) For the counterinference raises suspicion that one may have somewhere gone wrong.

In the current passage, the *pūrvapakṣin* does not have the right understanding of the epistemic significance of counterinference – in fact, he says practically the opposite of the right view – but he is on the right philosophic track, it seems, to worry about the impact of pseudo-fallacies, in particular, pseudo-counterinference.

Text (Tirupati 170; Calcutta 987)

atha pakṣe sādhya-bhrama-janakatvaṁ tat । bādha-viruddhayor api tattva-ajñāna-daśāyāṁ bhrama-janakatvād iti cet na । sad-dhetau sat-pratipakṣe 'sādhāraṇe ca tattvena jñāna-daśāyāṁ sādhya-bhrama-janakatvāt ajñāne sādhya-bhrama-ajanakatvāt । na api vyāpti-pakṣa-dharmatā-antara-rāhityam । sat-pratipakṣa-asādhāraṇa-sad-dhetur abhāvāt daśā-viśeṣe tasya doṣatvāt sādhya-aprasiddhau prakṛta-sādhya-vyāpty-aprasiddheś ca । na apy anaikāntika-ādy-anyatamatvam । yat-kiṁcid-anaikāntikatvasya ativyāpteḥ । prakṛta-sādhya-anaikānti-katvasya aprasiddhatvena kevala-anvayi-sādhane 'prasiddheḥ । aṁśataḥ siddha-sādhanāt sādhya-aviśeṣāc ca ।

Objection: That (showing inference failure) amounts to (D^2) (showing) generation of erroneous cognition of a probandum with respect to an inferential subject. (The fallacies of) the defeated (*bādha*) and the contradictory (*viruddha*) also generate error when there is no knowledge of the truth.

Pūrvapakṣin: No. For by your account (*tattvena*) error about the probandum would be generated in the case of a genuine (true) prover both when a (putative) counterinference was proffered and when (the fallacy) the unexampled was to occur (i.e. when the probandum seemed unexampled elsewhere, although in both cases there is in fact no error but only a challenge). Error about the probandum would not be generated if there were no knowledge (of it, i.e. if the probandum were not in general familiar).

Nor is (D[3]) correct: (Showing) a lack of either pervasion or the prover's being a property of the inferential subject. Since a genuine (true) prover would be absent in cases of counterinference and the unexampled (i.e. the probandum being unexampled elsewhere), it (the definition, D[3]) would be flawed with respect to some occasions (of putative inference). Also, if a probandum were not familiar, it would not be known whether there was a pervasion with (i.e. entailing) the probandum in question.

Nor is (D[4]) correct: (Showing) one or another of (the pseudo-provers listed as) the indecisive and the rest. This would cover too much in including whatever kind of indecisiveness. (For example) in so far as it were not well known whether indecisiveness held for a probandum in question, it (showing inference failure) would not be well known in the case of a proof of the "positive-only" variety. Furthermore, there could be no particular probandum because in part there would be (an attempt at) proof of something already established (and in part not).

Comments: The challenge is to come up with a definition that includes defeating by way of citing any of the fallacies, the pseudo-provers, *hetvābhāsa*, discussed by Gaṅgeśa in the immediately preceding section of his *Jewel*. In particular, the definitions here fall short of including cases of counterinference and the unexampled as well all the varieties of the "indecisive" which Gaṅgeśa takes to include the varieties of what he more commonly calls "deviation", *vyabhicara*. Counterinference involves showing neither a lack of pervasion nor a lack of the inferential subject's having the prover property. Because there would be insufficient evidence, the unexampled, similarly, is a fallacy even when there is a pervasion and the inferential subject does possess the probandum property. Also, there is a peculiar kind of indecisiveness, it is implied here, involving whether the opponent is familiar with the probandum. To fail the familiarity requirement is also something else, an additional test, other than the two better known and recognized requirements of pervasion and the prover's being a property of the subject. But several important proofs, and disproofs, hinge on it, for example, proving to the Buddhist that there is a self, i.e. proving it to someone who is not familiar with the concept, which, Gaṅgeśa says is an attempt that fails for this reason. (Thus on this score he goes against his "teacher" Udayana, as I try to explain in comments on that bit of the *Jewel* at the end of the section on "negative-only" inference where Gaṅgeśa takes up a traditional Nyāya proof of self, making this point.[4])

Text (Tirupati 173; Calcutta 987)

yat tu etat-kālīna-etat-pakṣīyatva-avacchinna-pratiyogika-etat-sādhya-pramā-karaṇatva-abhāvaḥ[5] *tat-tat-kāla-tat-tat-pakṣa-viṣaya-sādhyatva-abhimata-nityatva-ādi-pramā-janakatva-abhāvo vā asādhakatvam* । *na ca pratiyogy-aprasiddhiḥ* । *etat-kālīna-etat-pakṣīyatva-tat-tat-kāla-tat-tat-pakṣa-viṣayatvayor vyadhikaraṇayor eva pratiyogitā-avacchedakatvād iti tan na* । *sad-dhetoḥ sat-pratipakṣatva-ajñāna-daśāyām api tādṛśa-pramāyām akaraṇa-abhāvena asādhakatā-āpatteḥ na api tṛtīya-liṅga-parāmarśasya pramātvaṁ tat viruddha-ādau parāmarśa-abhāvāt sad-dhetau sat-pratipakṣe 'sādhāraṇe ca tat-pramātvāc ca na api anumiti-hetu-bhūta-pratiyogi-jñāna-viṣayatvaṁ tat sad-hetāv api pratipakṣatva-jñānasya anumiti-pratibandhakatvāt*

Objection: (Showing) inference failure is (D[5]) (showing) an absence of instrumentality for knowledge about a precise probandum where the countercorrelate (absentee) is specified

[4] In *Logic and Belief in Indian Philosophy*, ed. Piotr Balcerowitcz, Delhi: Motilal Banarsidass, 2010, pp. 502-04.

[5] Reading *abhāva* instead of *bhāva* with the Calcutta edition, p. 987.

by the precise time and precise inferential subject, or it is (D[6]) (showing) an absence of production of knowledge about such (a topic) as eternality taken to be the probandum, knowledge whose (intentional) object (*viṣaya*) is this or that (precise) time and this or that (precise) inferential subject.

And it is not the case that the countercorrelate is not well known. The reason is that two things not sharing the same location or substratum constitute exclusively the countercorrelates, two (distinct, intentional) objects as fixed by (precisely) this time and this inferential subject or (precisely) that time and that subject.

Pūrvapakṣin: The view is wrong. The difficulty is that even were there a genuine (true) prover at a time when there was no knowledge of a (putative) counterinference (and thus genuine inferential knowledge) we could have a case of (showing) inference failure (by your definition) in so far as there was a lack of the instrumentation for such knowledge (as requires counterinference refutation to restore the original knowledge).

It is also true that this would not be the knowledge that is appropriate to the third "consideration" (*parāmarśa*) of the inferential mark (that results in inferential knowledge). There is no such consideration in the case of (pointing out the fallacies of) the contradictory and the rest. Furthermore, in the cases of counterinference and the unexampled as well as in the case of a genuine (true) prover, there is knowledge.

There is not here, moreover, the (intentional) object belonging to the knowledge of an absential countercorrelate that gives rise to inferential knowledge. With respect to a genuine (a true) prover, sometimes an error – a cognition such as (putative) deviation or (putative) counterinference – (albeit false) nevertheless blocks inferential knowledge.

Comments: Here *pūrvapakṣin* expresses views more in line with

Gaṅgeśa's own. The problem of underinclusion remains, and there is the additional one that according to D^5 or D^6 a situation where there was no attempt to show inference failure would count as such.

When I see that my glasses are not on the table, the absence has as its countercorrelate (or absentee) the glasses that are absent – they would be the "absential countercorrelate" (and the table, the absence's location or substratum). The absential countercorrelate of an absence, ~S*a* (an absence of S at a location, *a*), would be S. (Refinement of the notion of the absential countercorrelate through the use of specifiers need not concern us at the moment.) Sometimes, but not all the time, when an inference is blocked, one knows that ~S*a* (thus ~K(S*a*) ≢ ~S*a*).

Text (Tirupati 174; Calcutta 988)

atha anumiti-pratibandhaka-pramā-viṣayatvam asādhakatvam sad-dhetau vyabhicāra-ādi-bhramaḥ pratibandhakaḥ । anumiti-pratibandhakatvaṁ ca vyabhicāra-ādi-pramāyās tṛtīya-liṅga-parāmarśa-vighaṭana-dvārā tulya-balatayā viṣayatayā vā iti cet na । satpratipakṣayor viruddhayor vāstava-tulya-balatva-abhāvena tad-bhramasya pratibandhakatvāt । na ca tulya-balatayā jñāyamānena bodhita-sādhya-viparyayakatva-jñānaṁ pratibandhakam tac ca pramā eva iti vācyam । tulya-balatā-jñānam eva hi pratibandhakam na tu jñāyamānatva-jñānam gauravād asiddheś ca । na ca sat-pratipakṣe anyatara-aṅga-vaikalya-pramā eva pratibandhikā iti vācyam । anyataratvaṁ tad-atad-vṛtti । na ca tad-atad-vṛtti-sāmāna-adhikaraṇyena jñāyamānasya doṣatvam । dharma-mātrasya vyabhicāra-jñānād anumity-uccheda-āpatteḥ । anyatara-aṅga-vaikalya-jñāna-upajīvyasya tulya-balatva-jñānasya eva pratibandhakatvāc ca । anyathā vyāpyatva-asiddhi-antarbhāva-āpatteḥ ।

Objection: (Showing) inference failure is (D^7) (showing) a bit of knowledge having an (intentional) object that blocks inference. In the case of a genuine (true) prover, an error about deviation or the like is the blocker. Furthermore, blocking inferential knowledge can occur either (a) by means of destruction of the third "consideration" (*parāmarśa*) of the inferential sign (that would result in inferential knowledge) on the part of our having knowledge of the likes of deviation, or (b) through the (intentional) object having equal force (in the case of counterinference).

Pūrvapakṣin: No. In the case of two counterinferences that contradict one another, the blocker would be an error about there being in fact equal force (equal evidence), in that in reality (factwise) there would be no equal force (i.e. were we to know all the evidence, we would see the one inference to be correct and the other to be erroneous).

Objection: The blocker is the cognition that makes known the controversion of the probandum through there being cognized equal force (equal evidence with that supporting an original inference). And that cognition (the blocker) is just a bit of knowledge (not necessarily a bit of inferential knowledge).

Pūrvapakṣin: That should not be alleged. For it is only cognition of there being equal force (in the case of a counterinference) that is the blocker. It is not (second-level) *cognition* of there being cognized (equal force or evidence). That is a (theoretically) cumbersome position and is unproved.

Objection: It is just the bit of knowledge that there is deficiency with one or the other members (of a formal inference or *nyāya*) that does the blocking, in the case of counterinference.

Pūrvapakṣin: That, too, should not be said. Being one or the other (as you say) involves the occurrence of something as φ that is not φ. And there being an (epistemic) flaw (*doṣa*) is not a matter of something's being cognized as having the same location or substratum as something occurring as φ that is not φ. This has the untoward consequence of the implosion of inference (altogether whenever counterinference is alleged), since there could be (with any inference and putative counterinference) knowledge that one property (or the other) deviates (i.e. that the one or the other counterinference is wrong).

Furthermore, it would be precisely the knowledge that there is equal force (or evidence), which comes to life through the knowledge that there really is deficiency in one or another member (of an original inference), that would be the blocker (in such cases). Otherwise, we would face the unfortunate circumstance of these cases being included in (the fallacy of) failure to show pervadedness (of the prover by the probandum, which is rightfully classified as distinct from "counterinference" as a fallacy).

Comments: The reasoning here all seems both clear and cogent except, perhaps, the principled objection to the proposal of a disjunctive test for showing inference failure, to wit, *being one or the other* of the fallacies on the traditional list. The *pūrvapakṣin* reasons that *being the other* means "not being oneself", something φ thought to be not φ in the context of the disjunction. This would seem to disallow the disjunctive form as illogical. Probably a better response would be that the false disjuncts are otiose and the definition cumbersome (*gauvava*).

But the main problem with D^7 is, in brief, that cases of overriding success could not be identified according to its terms. In other ways, too, D^7 is vague.

Text (Tirupati 175; Calcutta 989)

atha anaikāntika-ādi-jñānasya tat-tad-anumiti-prati-bandhakatvam asādhakatvam । *tathā hi idam anaikāntika-ādi-jñānam etat-sādhyavattayā etat-puruṣasya etat-kālina-etat-pakṣaka-anumiti-pratibandhakam etad-anaikāntika-jñānatvāt etad-anya-taj-jñāna-vat iti cet na* । *etat-sādhyavattayā etat-pakṣakatva-anumiteḥ kadācil liṅga-bhramāt prasiddhāv api etat-kālina-etat-puruṣasya tādṛśa-anumity-aprasiddheḥ* ।

Objection: (Showing) inference failure is (D^8) (showing) a cognition of indecisiveness or the like as blocking this or that bit of (putative) inferential knowledge. For in this way such cognition of indecisiveness or the like would block inferential knowledge as temporally indexed (*etat-kālina*) and as having (precisely) this (or that) inferential subject that would belong to (precisely) this (or that) person, in so far as it would have (precisely) this (or that) probandum, *since* it would be cognition of indecisiveness or the like as applying to (precisely) that, *like* cognition of something that is other to (the truth of precisely) that.

Pūrvapakṣin: No. Even were there well known to occur from error about an inferential sign sometimes (a notion of) inferential knowledge as having (precisely) this (or that) subject in so far as it would have (precisely) this (or that) *probandum*, no such inferential knowledge would be well known that belonged to (precisely) this (or that) *person*.

Comments: Modally conceived, D^8 is flawed because it proposes the existence of something that is not known to occur, knowledge, namely, that is merely possible but not actual as belonging to some particular person. Nyāya countenances possible entities, but not any conceived in general without known instances.

Text (Tirupati 176; Calcutta 989)

na api samīcīna-sādhya-viśiṣṭa-pakṣa-pratyaya-ajanakatvam । *bādha-viruddha-asiddheṣu sādhya-anadhikaraṇe pakṣe satya-sādhya-pratīty-aprasiddheḥ*[6] *vahnimati bāṣpe dhūma-bhramāt vahny-anumite. satyatvāc ca* ।

(The pūrvapakṣin continues): Nor is (showing) inference failure (D^9) (showing) a lack of generation of a correct notion of an

[6] Reading *aprasiddheḥ* instead of *prasiddhe* with the Calcutta edition, p. 990.

inferential subject as qualified by a probandum. In the case of (the fallacies) the defeated (*bādha*), the contradictory, and the unestablished, (a) the inferential subject, which is not a location of the probandum, would not be well known through confidence that there was a true probandum, and (b) there can be inferential knowledge of fire – which would be true – from an error about smoke when there is mist on (i.e. rising from) something that is (indeed) fiery.

Comments: It is to be stressed that this is a *pūrvapakṣa* or stretch of text devoted to opponent positions not necessarily endorsed by Gaṅgeśa himself, who, in this instance, would *not* find the true belief resulting from mistaking mist for smoke to be veritable inferential *knowledge* (*anumiti*) albeit there really is fire where the mist is seen rising. A Mīmāṁsaka, especially of the Prābhākara camp, on the other hand, would, we may presume, see this as a case of knowledge, since error, on that view, is a matter of a failure to cognize (e.g. a failure to recognize the cognition of smoke as a memory when the visual presentation is of mist): all cognition is by nature veridical. The mist considered smoke is an error, an error founded in a failure to cognize the distinctness between a remembering of smoke and a perception of mist, but the inferential cognition of fire, I take it, is not an error on this view. Often Gaṅgeśa presents Prābhākara views in a *pūrvapakṣa*, and probably we should see the current *pūrvapakṣin* as a Prābhākara.

Text (Tirupati 177; Calcutta 990)

na ca anya eva vahnis tatra bhāsate māna-abhāvāt tad-vahneḥ pratyabhijñānāt eka-vyaktike tad-asaṁbhavāc ca | *na ca sā anumitir liṅga-viṣayatvena bhramaḥ anumitau liṅga-bhāne māna-abhāvāt* | *kiṁ ca bhāvo 'bhāvo vā ubhayam api prameyam iti satya-anumitau bhāvatva-abhāvatvavati prameyatva-jñāne ekatra tayor abhāvād asatya-anumitiḥ syāt na ca anyataratvaṁ liṅgam tad-vyāptim aviduṣo 'py anumiteḥ vyartha-viśeṣaṇatvāc ca*

(*The pūrvapakṣin continues*): And it is false that it is just another fire that is appearing in this case, because there is no argument (for that position) and because from recognition (i.e. later perceptual recognition) of the fire (that is appearing in the occurrent "inferential knowledge") that would be impossible with regard to that which has (as its object) a single individual.

It is also false that the inferential knowledge would be an error in so far as the inferential sign is (taken as) its (or as part of its) object (its intentional object, *viṣaya*). For there is no argument (to that effect) with respect to the appearance of an inferential sign in the case of a bit of inferential knowledge.

Moreover, we would have a false bit of inferential knowledge when there was really a true bit of inferential knowledge to the effect that whether a presence or an absence both (or either) would still be the object of knowledge, since the two (presence and absence of φ) do not occur with respect to one and same thing. And it is not the case that the inferential sign would be (taken to be) one or the other (the presence or the absence). For there can be inferential knowledge even on the part of someone who does not desire to know the pervasion (the entailment on which it relies), and such inferential knowledge would suffer from useless qualification.

***Comments*:** Here let me repeat that in my reading Gaṅgeśa does not himself endorse the view that there would be genuine inferential knowledge in a case of dust, or mist, misperceived and mischaracterized as smoke from whose perception nevertheless a subject believes (rightly) that there is fire on a mountain at a place where there is indeed fire although unconnected causally to the dust actually perceived.

But concerning the last point in the passage, Gaṅgeśa should be taken to agree. There can be, he has told us earlier (in the *pakṣatā* section, Tirupati, p. 338[7]) that a person can have inferential knowledge without a desire to know. This is a traditionally recognized requirement appearing in the *Nyāya-sūtra* commentaries on *sūtra* 1.1.5, the so-called "inference *sūtra*", but he rejects it on the basis of everyday inferences that we make just as a matter of course (inferring clouds automatically from the sound of thunder, for instance).

Text (Tirupati 178; Calcutta 990)

atha sādhya-vyāpyatvam eva tatra tantram tatra ca bādho na asti iti cet tarhi kūṭa-liṅgād anumitau vahni-vyāpyavattvam eva tantram vahni-vyāpyaṁ ca kiṁcit tatra asty eva । atha kūṭa-liṅge vahni-vyāpya-abhedaḥ pratīyate । tathā ca vahnau kūṭa-liṅga-vyāpaka-abhedo 'pi । anyathā kūṭasya eva vahni-vyāpyatva-apratīteḥ । evaṁ ca kūṭa-liṅga-vyāpako vahnitvena bhāsata iti vahny-anumitir asatyā eva iti cet na । vahni-vyāpya-āloke dhūma-āropāt yatra anumitiḥ tatra asiddhi-bhede 'satyatva-abhāva-āpatteḥ āloka-vyāpake dhūma-vyāpaka-abhedāt ।

Objection: The principle here in this case is just the being pervaded by (i.e. entailing) the probandum. And here there is no defeating (*bādha*, i.e. the fallacy, the "defeated", where it is already known, e.g. that ~*Sa*).

Pūrvapakṣin: Then in the case of inferential knowledge from a misleading inferential sign (e.g. mist), the principle would be just the having of something that is pervaded by fire. And being pervaded by fire would indeed be in some way there.

Objection: Non-difference from that which is pervaded by fire would be cognized with respect to (even) a misleading inferential sign. And so too would non-difference from a pervader of the misleading inferential sign with respect to fire. Otherwise, the misleading (inferential sign) itself would

[7] That is, Tirupati 1982, vol. 2, part 1 (as opposed to our current text, vol. 2, part 2): *Tattvacintāmaṇi*, Anumāna-Khaṇḍa, ed. N.S. Ramanuja Tatacharya, Kendriya Sanskrit Vidyapeetha Series 33, vol. 2, part 1, Tirupati, 1982, p. 338.

not be cognized as pervaded by (as entailing) fire (a thesis controverted by the mist example).

And in this way a pervading of a misleading inferential sign would appear to be fire; thus the inferential knowledge of fire would be simply untrue (i.e. not genuine as not produced by cognition of a genuine prover).

***Pūrvapakṣin*:** No. In cases of (putative) inferential knowledge such as with respect to light which is pervaded by fire (light entails fire), light on which smoke is (erroneously) superimposed, your view faces the difficulty that the knowledge would be untrue if (as we find in these cases) the instance were different from (the fallacy of) the unproven (*asiddhi*). The reason is that there is no difference between a pervading of smoke (entailing fire) and a pervading of light (entailing fire).

***Comments*:** Gaṅgeśa accepts some of the reasoning here, admitting disjunctive provers, e.g. being-smoke-or-light, being pervaded by (and therefore entailing) fire: see in this same chapter of the *Jewel* at the beginning of the *siddhānta* section on "consideration" (Tirupati[8] 367; Calcutta 493). However, I repeat, I do not think he sees the mist case the same way as the *pūrvapakṣin*. This is made clear below, as Gaṅgeśa suggests what is wrong with the view, namely, that knowledge could occur by chance.

Text (Tirupati 179; Calcutta 990)

atha liṅgam anumiti-viṣayaḥ niyamataḥ pakṣa-dharmatā-jñāna-viṣayatvāt vyāpti-jñāna-viṣayatvāt niyamena anumiti-viśeṣaṇa-dhī-viṣayatvāc ca parvatatva-vat sādhya-vac ca । kiṁ ca eka-viśeṣaṇavattvena jñāte viśeṣaṇa-antara-dhī-sāmagrī tatra eva viśiṣṭa-vaiśiṣṭya-jñānam iti dhūma-viśiṣṭa eva vahni-vaiśiṣṭya-anumitir iti । nanv anumitau vyāpakatva-bhāne anumity-avicchedaḥ । na ca phalī-

[8] Again, Tirupati 1982, vol. 2, part 1, p. 367.

bhūta-jñāna-nyūna-viṣayasya eva parāmarśasya anumiti-hetutvam gauravāt । *viṣaya-antara-saṁcārān na anumitir ity api na* । *parāmarśasya carama-kāraṇatvāt pratyakṣa-ādi-sāmagrīto balavattvāc ca iti cet na* । *siddha-sādhana-vicchedāt* । *yady apy evaṁ liṅga-aṁśe 'pramātve 'pi sādhya-pramātvāt kathaṁ tasya asādhakatvam tathā apy uktam asādhakatvam asty eva iti cet astu tāvad evam* । *tathā api daivāt tatra dhūma-sattve kathaṁ tad-aṁśe 'py asatyatā* । *ata eva ārdra-indhana-prabhavo vahnir dhūma-vyāpako na anyaḥ* । *na ca vahnitvena vyāpakatvād anyo 'pi tathā* । *tena vinā api dhūma-sattvāt* । *evaṁ bāṣpe dhūma-bhramāt dhūma-vyāpako vahnir bhāsate sa ca tatra na asty eva iti na sā anumitiḥ satyā iti nirastam* । *daivāt dhūma-sattve satyatvāt* ।

***Objection (by objector-2 to the pūrvapakṣin)*:** The inferential sign by rule is (part of) the (intentional) object of inferential knowledge, *since* it is the object of knowledge of the inferential subject being qualified by the prover property and *since* it is (part of) the object of the thought that causes inferential knowledge in that by rule it is (part of) the object of the knowledge of pervasion, *like* being the mountain (the inferential subject in the stock example) and *like* being the probandum.

Furthermore, the causal complex sufficient to bring about (*sāmagrī*) the thought (the inferential knowledge) of another qualifier (of the inferential subject, namely, the probandum as qualifier, "the mountain is *fiery*"), given that it is (or has been) known as having the one qualifier (namely, the prover, the inferential sign), is in this case (in the case of inferential knowledge) just knowledge of a qualificational complex (*vaiśiṣṭya*) belonging to that which is qualified (*viśiṣṭa*, to wit, the inferential subject). Hence there is inferential knowledge of it as qualified by fire *in regard to* precisely something that is qualified by smoke.

***Objection (by objector-3 to objector-2)*:** With inferential knowledge, there is no discernment that the inferential knowledge is *with regard to* the (prior) knowing that there is a pervader. Nor is the consideration (*parāmarśa*) that is the (immediate) cause of inferential knowledge itself solely the (intentional) object of anything that lacks the character of the knowledge (the inferential knowledge, that is) that is its result! Your view is (by comparison) cumbersome (*gaurava*).

***Reply (by objector-2)*:** It is also wrong to think that inferential knowledge does not originate from transference (of the one) to another (intentional) object. Consideration is the final cause (of inferential knowledge), and the causal complex consisting of perception (of the inferential subject as possessing the prover property) and the rest (the embedding of the knowledge of the prover and of the pervasion) is sufficient because (only) it has the force (to bring it about).

***Pūrvapakṣin*:** Wrong. The discernment would be by means of (the fallacy) "proving what is already known".

***Objection (by objector-2)*:** Let us presume what you say is right. How is your understanding of showing inference failure to apply to the case (e.g. mist misperceived as smoke triggering knowledge of something as fiery which is indeed fiery) where the probandum is known (*pramātva*) although the portion regarding the inferential sign is not known (*apramātva*)?

***Pūrvapakṣin*:** Okay, let what you insinuate be accepted so far as it goes. Nevertheless, given that by chance it could be true (genuine) concerning the smoke (the prover portion), why would it in that very portion be false? (The mist might have been smoke.)

Just for this reason, fire that originates in wet fuel pervades (is entailed by) smoke, not something else.

***Objection*:** There is too something else like that, because, considering fire, there is a pervader.

***Pūrvapakṣin*:** This, too, is wrong. Even without it (whatever it may be) there could be smoke.

Objection: From an error about smoke with respect to mist (where there really is fire), it is fire as a pervader of smoke that appears. And in the example this just does not occur. Therefore, this is not genuine (true) inferential knowledge.

Pūrvapakṣin: This is to be rejected in the fashion explained. By chance it could be true (genuine) concerning the smoke if there really were smoke (thus both smoke and fire at the spot indicated by the mist mistaken for smoke).

Comments: The problem with the *pūrvapakṣin*'s view is that knowledge does not arise by chance, although there may be by chance true belief. Knowledge is not just a cognition that happens to be true but rather one that is produced by a veritable *pramāṇa*, a "knowledge source", perception, inference, analogy, or testimony, according to Nyāya. In my reading, the objection at the end gives the right view and the one Gaṅgeśa wants us to see as right, albeit this comes in a *pūrvapakṣa*.

Next comes the *siddhānta* of the section, text where Gaṅgeśa explicitly expresses his own views, taking himself to speak for the school.

Text (Tirupati 182; Calcutta 992)

ucyate । *sva-jñāna-daśāyāṁ pakṣe sādhya-pratyaya-ajanakatvam asādhakatvam* । *tathā hi viruddhatva-ādi-jñāna-daśā-varti idaṁ pakṣe sādhya-pratyaya-ajanakatvam viruddha-āditvāt* । *pakṣa-viśeṣaṇa-mahimnā tad-daśāyām pakṣe sādhya-pratyaya-ajanakatvam sidhyati* । *bādhita-ādāv api liṅgatva-bhramāt pakṣe sādhya-pratyaya-janakatvam iti na pratiyogy-aprasiddhyā sādhya-aprasiddhiḥ* ।

Gaṅgeśa: We answer. (Showing) inference failure is (D^{10}) (showing) a lack of generation of a notion of a probandum with respect to an inferential subject on the occasion when that is known as that (namely, as a putative inferential subject).

For example, this non-generation of a notion of a probandum with respect to the subject would occur on an occasion when there would be known (any of the fallacies) the contradictory and the rest, since they are (what they are, namely) the contradictory and the others. The non-generation of a notion of the probandum with respect to the subject is proved on such an occasion through a surfeit of qualifiers of the subject.

Also, there is generation of a notion of the probandum with respect to the inferential subject in the case of the defeated and the like, because of an error with respect to the inferential sign (in cases of these fallacies). Thus it is false that the probandum is not well known through the counterpositive being not well known.

Comments: Showing that an inference falls to the fallacy of the defeated (*bādha* or *bādhita*) does not involve a proof of inference failure. It is simply known in advance that ~S*a*, which knowledge blocks inference to S*a*. For example, we would accept no proof to the conclusion that fire is cold because we know in advance that fire is not cold.

Many of the definitions aired in the *pūrvapakṣa* now appear flawed for an additional reason, namely, that even when it is the negation, or counterpositive, of the probandum that is known (~S*a*) because a putative inference falls to the defeated or another fallacy, nevertheless we are in such cases *familiar* with the probandum taken with respect to the inferential subject (to echo the earlier language) even though it is false.

Text (Tirupati 188; Calcutta 994)

yad vā anumiti-pratibandhakatā-avacchedaka-rūpavattvam asādhakatvam । *tathā hi idānīm idam anumiti-pratibandhakatā-avacchedaka-rūpavat anaikāntika-āditvāt jñāna-vat* । *anumiti-pratibandhakatā-avacchedakaṁ ca rūpaṁ jñāne viṣayatayā anaikāntika-āditvam eva* । *na ca sādhya-aviśeṣaḥ upādhi-viṣayasya anumeyatvāt toyatvena pipāsa-upaśamana-samarthatā-avacchedaka-rūpa-paratva-anumāna-vat* ।

(*Gaṅgeśa continues*): Alternatively, (showing) inference failure is (D[11]) (showing) something taking the form of a specifier of what it is to be a blocker of inferential knowledge. For example, this now (i.e. some fallacy or other) has the form of a specifier of what it is to be a blocker of inferential knowledge, *since* it is (an instance of the fallacy) the indecisive or the like, *like* a cognition.

Further, a specifier of what it is to be a blocker of inferential knowledge is something that with respect to the (putative) knowledge is just being (the fallacy) the indecisive or the like in so far as its (intentional) object is concerned. And this is not the absence of a particular probandum, *since* a particular *upādhi* (accident or inferential undercutter) could be inferred, *like* the inference that is about that which specifies the capacity to quench thirst considering water.

***Comments*:** A cognition is "indecisive" considering whether it is true or false, although the default is that at least presentational experiences (*anubhava*, which is one of two broad kinds of occurrent cognition, *jñāna*, the other being remembering, *smaraṇa*) are true or veridical.

The first inference illustrates proving inference failure where any of the fallacies discussed can play the role of vitiator. The second inference suggests that when there is inference failure, the story may not be over, since whether or not there is present an *upādhi*, such as wet fuel in the context of an inference *from* fire *to* smoke, the probandum (smoke), although its prover (fire) would be undercut in an unqualified form, would be present thanks to it *coupled* with the *upādhi* (wet fuel). If a person has a certain disease, water will not quench her thirst. And so for thirst-quenching there has to be fulfilled both the conditions of (a) water, and (b) the thirsty person not having the disease.

Text (Tirupati 189; Calcutta 996)

anye tv anaikāntika-bādhita-viruddheṣv avyāpyaṁ vyāpyatva-asiddhe 'naikāntikatvaṁ sva-rūpa-asiddhi-sat-pratipakṣa-asādhāraṇeṣu daśā-viśeṣe anumiti-pratibandhaka-jñāna-viṣayatvam asādhakatvam । na ca evam anaikāntiko asādhaka iti saha-prayoga-anupapattiḥ । tatra avyāpyatvasya asādhaka-śabda-arthatvāt । asādhakatā-ananugame 'pi ca hetv-ābhāsatvam anugatam eva yasya jñānam anumiti-pratibandhakaṁ tasya hetvābhāsatvād iti ।

(*Gaṅgeśa continues*): But others say the following.

Nyāya faction: (Showing) inference failure is, in the case of the indecisive, the defeated, and the contradictory, (D[12]) (showing) a lack of pervasiveness; for non-establishment of pervasiveness, it is (D[13]) (showing) indecisiveness; for non-establishment by nature (of the inferential subject ruling out the probandum), counterinference, and the unexampled (lack of inductive evidence, *asādhāraṇa*), it is on particular occasions (D[14]) to be the (intentional) object of a cognition that blocks inferential knowledge.

And it is not the case that in this way it would be impossible in the context of a formal reconstruction that the indecisive be the disprover. For, in this case the meaning of the word "disprover" would be the non-pervasiveness.

Moreover, although (showing) inference failure is not a uniform notion, what it is to be a non-genuine prover (*hetvābhāsatva*) is uniform indeed. For, knowledge of something blocks inferential knowledge if it is a *hetvābhāsa*.

Comments: Inference failure cannot be analysed as a single universal or kind, according to the Nyāya faction. Nevertheless, to point out that a putative prover is pseudo-, a *hetv-ābhāsa*, does invariably block inferential knowledge. Surely, Gaṅgeśa is to be taken to agree with this last point although not with the disjunctive view of the Nyāya faction. He has, after all, just given a couple of uniform or unitive definitions of showing inference failure, D[10] and D[11] above.

11

Gaṅgeśa on the Meaning of Verbal Suffixes

Toshihiro Wada

Introduction

THE present paper represents the fourth and final part of my translation with annotation of the "Verbal Suffix Section" (Ākhyātavāda) of the "Language Chapter" (Śabda-Khaṇḍa) of Gaṅgeśa's *Tattvacintāmaṇi* (*TC*). The purpose of this project is to clarify the philosophy of language belonging to the early stage of Navya-Nyāya.[1] The three preceding parts of my translation and annotation are Wada (2007a, 2012, 2013). Apart from them, Wada (2006a, 2014) has analysed Gaṅgeśa's theory of the suffixes of finite verbs.

Part (1) of this paper appeared in 2007. Since then there have been published several important works for my project; I have mentioned them in the introduction of each part. In this paper Diaconescu (2012) should be added to important avenues of research.

The present paper deals with Gaṅgeśa's conclusion. It is not the case that his conclusion completely differs from the

1 Since I regard Udayana as the founder of Navya-Nyāya, the early stage of Navya-Nyāya covers Udayana up to Gaṅgeśa. On the founder of Navya-Nyāya, see Wada (2007b: 9-23), which includes Wada (1999, 2001, 2004).

traditional and new views. At the end of the "Verbal Suffix Section" Gaṅgeśa states only a salient point which differs from those views. He seems to accept whatever points he has not refuted in the previous discussion concerning those views. Wada (2014) clarifies those points which are not mentioned in Gaṅgeśa's final statement but should form his conclusion.

Text, Commentary, and Contents

In translating the "Verbal Suffix Section" I have used the Sanskrit text included in *Tattvacintāmaṇi of Gaṅgeśa Upādhyāya*, 4 vols., edited with *Āloka* of Jayadeva Miśra and *Rahasya* of Mathurānātha, by Kāmākhyānātha Tarkavāgīśa, Vrajajivan Prachyabharati Granthamala 47, Delhi: Chaukhamba Sanskrit Pratishtan, 1990. In this book the "Verbal Suffix Section" is accompanied by Jayadeva's *Āloka* and not by *Rahasya*. I have consulted *Āloka*.

The argument presented in the "Verbal Suffix Section" can be divided as follows.[2] Numbers in brackets refer to page and line numbers of *Tattvacintāmaṇi of Gaṅgeśa Upādhyāya*, 4th vol., 2nd part.[3]

A. Introduction: the presentation of the Nyāya view (pp. 819,1-820,1)

---

[2] Wada (2012: 529) has slightly revised the division of the Sanskrit text presented in Wada (2006a: 73, 2007a: 415). Accordingly, when I have referred to the parts in the section on Basic Concepts in the present paper, I have made use of this revised division of the text.

[3] The Sanskrit text of the Ākhyātavāda is divided according to the parts of the translation. The divided texts are provided in the footnotes to those corresponding parts with the following alterations: *karttr̥* → *kartr̥*, the same treatment for its declensions; *saṅkhyā* → *saṁkhya*, the same treatment for its declensions; *saṅkhyeya* → *saṁkhyeya*, the same treatment for its declensions; *ākāṅkṣ-* → *ākāṁkṣ-*; *tatparyya* → *tātparya*.

B. The Mīmāṁsā View (pp. 820,1-826,13)

C. The Nyāya Refutation (pp. 826,13-830,8)

D. The View of the Author of *Ratnakośa* (pp. 830,9-831,13)

E. The Refutation to the Author of *Ratnakośa* (pp. 831,13-833,1)[4]

F. The Grammarians' Refutation to the Nyāya View (pp. 833,1-834,4)[5]

G. The Nyāya Response to F (pp. 834,4-836,3)

H. The Nyāya View in Detail (pp. 836,3-846,4)

H1-7: The Traditional Nyāya View (pp. 836,4-844,8)

H8: The Navya-Nyāya View (pp. 844,9-845,10)[6]

H9: Gaṅgeśa's Final View (pp. 845,10-846,2)

Part H includes the views of traditional Nyāya[7] and new

---

[4] Since the author of *Ratnakośa* is a Naiyāyika (D. Bhattacharya 1958: 76-78), part E turns out to be a refutation by other Naiyāyikas who hold that a verbal suffix denotes effort. It may not be improper to regard part E as Gaṅgeśa's refutation.

[5] I have hypothetically followed Bhatta (2005: 895) on who the advocate of part F is. Bhatta (2005: 264-65) groups parts F and G together and regards the opponents therein as a Grammarian. To be sure, the opponent in part G is the grammarian because of the indicating sign *iti vaiyākaraṇāḥ*; but the opponent in part F does not show a sure sign by which he can be judged to belong to a particular school. Part F discusses the meaning of verbal suffixes and the three tenses, and this issue is not limited exclusively to the Grammarian school. Part F may function as an introduction to the Grammarians' theory.

[6] This part starts with *navīnās tu* (the new Naiyāyikas, on the other hand), which may suggest that Navya-Nyāya had already been originated in Gaṅgeśa's time. It is not for this reason but for other reasons that I agree that Navya-Nyāya existed before him. It is one thing how Gaṅgeśa sees his own view, and it is another how we describe his view within the context of the history of Indian philosophy. On this issue, see Wada (2007b: 9-23).

[7] It is a problem whether the "traditional view of Nyāya" dealt →

Nyāya as well as Gaṅgeśa's conclusion. The present paper deals with part H.[8]

Basic Concepts[9]

In order to understand the present translation and annotation, it is necessary to have a clear understanding of the concepts of *ākhyāta* (verbal suffix), effort (*yatna, prayatna*), the signifying function of a word (*vṛtti*), verbal understanding (*śābdabodha, śābdajñāna*), and meaning (*artha*). For lack of space, I will give only a brief explanation of them here.

(A) ĀKHYĀTA

The word *ākhyāta* has two meanings: the finite verb and the personal ending of the finite verb (*tiṄ* suffix).[10] Gaṅgeśa's argument with the Mīmāṁsā and Grammarian schools is confined to an analysis of the second of these two meanings. Unless otherwise specified, the suffixes he discusses are those

---

→ with in part H belongs to the Prācīna-Nyāya or not. It may represent the Nyāya view held between the periods of Udayana and Gaṅgeśa. Since I regard Udayana as the founder of Navya-Nyāya, the traditional Nyāya is pre-Gaṅgeśa Navya-Nyāya. On the founder of Navya-Nyāya, see Wada (2007b: 9-23), which includes Wada (1999, 2001, 2004).

8 Wada (2007a) deals with parts A and B; Wada (2012) with parts C, D, and E; Wada (2013) with parts F and G.

9 This section is a reproduction of Wada (2007a: Basic Concepts) with some revisions: fns. 12 and 18 are slightly revised by means of adding the information from Diaconescu (2012); fn. 17 is added here as in Wada (2012: Basic Concepts); (a) *ākhyāta* the second paragraph in Wada (2012: 530) is slightly revised here.

10 On these two meanings, see Joshi (1993: 22). He reports that *Mīmāṁsanyāyaprākaśa* (*MNP*), which was written in the seventeenth century, uses the word in the second sense listed above. But *TC* shows earlier use of the word in this sense. On *tiṄ* suffixes, see Pāṇini's *Aṣṭādhyāyī* (*P*) 3.4.78; Abhyankar and Shukla (1977: 197).

used in the active voice and the present tense. He discusses the meaning of verbal suffixes used in the passive voice in parts F and G of the "Verbal Suffix Section".

Navya-Naiyāyikas, including Gaṅgeśa, hold that a verbal suffix denotes effort, while Mīmāṁsakas of the Bhaṭṭa School[11] hold that it denotes operation (*vyāpāra*), whether internal or external.[12] Internal operation, which Navya-Naiyāyikas regard as effort, occurs in the soul (*ātman*). External operation, which occurs in the body and things, is perceived by the sense-organs. Navya-Naiyāyikas generally call this operation action (*kriyā*). The Grammarians (*pāṇinīya*) argue that a verbal suffix denotes an agent.[13] Navya-Naiyāyikas and Mīmāṁsakas accept Pāṇini's

---

11 The view of the Prābhākara school is briefly referred to and refuted at the end of part C.

12 The operation of Vedic injunctions is not discussed here. However, since the Mīmāṁsakas' method of interpreting sentences in common usage is based on their exegesis of Vedic sentences, we have to consider this exegesis in order to follow their arguments as presented in the "Verbal Suffix Section". On their exegesis, see Edgerton (1929). The verbal suffixes of Vedic injunctions denote the word-efficient-force (*śābdībhāvanā*) which resides in the injunctions themselves. On the "word-efficient-force", see *MNP*, no. 4 and Edgerton (1929: 40). Diaconescu (2012: 47) points out the differences of the Mīmāṁsakas' views on what the term *bhāvanā* means. According to him, Kumārila and Pārthasārathi use it in the sense of operation (*vyāpāra*) or action (*kriyā*), Maṇḍanamiśra and Umbekabhaṭṭa in the sense of operation and effort (*kr̥ti*), and Someśvara or Khaṇḍadeva in the sense of effort. (Diaconescu renders *kr̥ti* as effort, while I have rendered it as resolution. Effort is a rendering of *yatna*, which is used as a synonym for *kr̥ti* in the Nyāya discussion of the meaning of verbal suffixes. Based upon this, Diaconescu seems to render *kr̥ti* as effort.)

13 To be precise, in Pāṇini's grammar a verbal suffix denotes the agent, the object, or – in the case of intransitive roots – action itself. See *P*3.4.69: *laḥ karmaṇi ca bhāve cākarmakebhyaḥ*. Vasu (1977 [1891]: 584) translates this *sūtra* as follows: "The tense-affixes called *la* are used in denoting the object and the agent; and after →

grammar in general, but when they disagree with the grammarians, and with one another, they attempt to prove their own views by analysing common linguistic usage, in this case the usage of the finite verb.

(B) EFFORT (YATNA, PRAYATNA)

Effort, which is regarded as the meaning of a finite verbal suffix by Navya-Naiyāyikas, is one of twenty-four kinds of qualities (*guṇa*s), and we know of its existence in the soul through inference. Nyāya holds that knowledge or cognition (*jñāna*) causes desire (*icchā*), which produces effort, which in turn brings about action.[14] To understand the relation among cognition, desire, and effort, let us consider the case in which we quench our thirst with water. First, we must know that water can remove our thirst and recognize that there is some water within our reach. Second, we must have the desire to take and drink some water. If we have no desire, action does not take place. However, due to certain reasons we do not always take action immediately after we have such a desire. For instance, there may be dead insects in the water and so

→ intransitive verbs, they denote the action as well as the agent". This means that when transitive verbs are used in the active voice, the suffixes denote the agent; when these verbs are used in the passive, the suffixes denote the object. On this issue, see also Cardona (1975: 266).

[14] For the causal relationship among these four, Marui (1987: 145-46 and notes 24, 26) gives two Sanskrit references and their explanation. One is from Udayana's *Nyāyakusumāñjali* (*NKu*) 5.7: *pravr̥ttiḥ kr̥tir evātra sā cecchāto yataś ca sā* । *taj jñānaṁ . . .* ॥, and the other from *Nyāyasiddhāntadīpa* (p. 74,1-4): *pravr̥ttiparavākyaśravaṇāntaraṁ prayojyasya tattadarthasambandhavyāpārānukūlāṁ ceṣṭāṁ paśyaṁs taṭasthaḥ svaceṣṭāyāṁ kr̥teḥ kr̥tau ca cikīrṣāyāś cikīrṣāyāṁ samānādhikaraṇasamaṇaviṣayakajñānasyaivāvadhr̥takaraṇabhāva iti prayojyasyāpi tatkāraṇībhūtaṁ jñānam anumāya tasya jñānasya vākyajanyatāpravr̥ttau janayitavyāyāṁ śabdavyāpāratvam cāvadhārayati.* For a translation of the former passage, see Cowell (1980: 71) and N. Dravid (1996: 433).

on. Hence, we can infer that there must be an intervening factor which is produced by the preceding desire and which brings about the action of drinking. That factor is effort.

Note that effort is often designated as resolution (*kṛti*) in the Navya-Nyāya discussion on the meaning of a verbal suffix. Udayana states in his *Nyāyakusumāñjali* (*NKu*) that resolution is nothing more but effort, a statement quoted by Gaṅgeśa in part B2 of his "Verbal Suffix Section".

(C) THE SIGNIFYING FUNCTION (VṚTTI)

Any meaningful linguistic unit, or morpheme, as well as any word possesses the signifying function and thus can mean something. Navya-Nyāya accepts only two kinds of signifying function: the denotative function (*śakti*) and the indicative function (*lakṣaṇā*).[15] For instance, when we hear the word *śaśin* (the moon) at night, this word first reminds us of the moon in the sky; furthermore it reminds us of a rabbit (*śaśa*). In this case the moon is the direct meaning of the word, and the function pointing to this meaning is called denotative. A rabbit is the indirect meaning of the word, and the function pointing to it is called indicative.

(D) VERBAL UNDERSTANDING (ŚĀBDABODHA, ŚĀBDAJÑĀNA)

The concept of verbal understanding is quite often utilized in analysing the meaning of language units, e.g. a root (*dhātu*),

---

15 Cf. *Nyāyasiddhāntamuktāvalī* (*NSM*), p. 292,3: *vṛttiś ca śaktilakṣaṇānyataraḥ sambandhaḥ*. See also Matilal (1968: 25). The indicative function is defined as the relation with the denoted object/meaning (*NSM* k. 82ab: *lakṣaṇā śakyasambandhas* . . . ।). To explain this definition, when word A denotes meaning B and further indicates the meaning C, the indicative function of A reaches C through B. This function also represents the relation between A and C. The relation between A and B is expressed by "the denoted object" in the definition; the relation between B and C by "the relation" in the definition.

suffix (*pratyaya*), nominal base (*prātipadika*), case-ending (*sUP*), and so on. Since we cannot determine the meaning of an isolated verbal suffix such as *-ti*, we have to deal with a complete word, such as *pacati* ([he] cooks). From *pacati* we obtain a verbal understanding which has some content or structure. Gaṅgeśa and his opponents presuppose that all of this understanding is generated only by the word *pacati*; they attempt to find the correspondence between the constituents of the understanding we obtain on hearing *pacati* and the linguistic constituents, such as the verbal suffix, which make up this word.

There are three competing views of verbal understanding which identify different elements in a sentence as being prominent. According to the first view, the meaning of the noun in the nominative case is predominant (*prathamāntārthamukhyaviśeṣyakaśābdabodha*); according to the second view, the meaning of the verbal suffix is predominant (*ākhyātārthamukhyaviśeṣyakaśābdabodha*); according to the third view the meaning of the root is predominant (*dhātvarthamukhyaviśeṣyakaśābdabodha*).[16] The Nyāya school upholds the first view; the Mīmāṁsā school the second; and the Grammarian school the third.

Take the sentence *caitraḥ pacati* as an example. Let us see what Navya-Nyāya regards as the verbal understanding brought about through hearing this sentence. The word *caitra* denotes a person called Caitra; the case-ending *-ḥ* (*sU*) denotes the number of Caitras; the root *pac* denotes the action of cooking (*pāka*); the suffix *-ti* denotes effort. Effort generates the action of cooking. This relation between effort and cooking

[16] Cf. Rao (1969: 4-34). The expression of verbal understanding may appear to represent its structure, but this is not accepted by some schools of Indian philosophy, i.e. those schools subsumed under the term "Indian Realism", such as Nyāya, Vaiśeṣika, and Mīmāṁsā. This point will be referred to later on under (E).

is not denoted by any meaningful unit of the sentence, but it is understood from the juxtaposition of the two units, *pac* and *-ti*. Similarly, the relation of the effort and Caitra is understood; he (i.e. his *ātman*) possesses effort. Finally, the sentence generates the understanding "Caitra is the possessor of effort conducive to cooking" (*pākānukūlaprayatnavān caitaḥ*).[17]

Mīmāṁsakas, on the other hand, present the following verbal understanding as generated from the same sentence: "There is productive operation conducive to cooking and residing in Caitra" (*caitraniṣṭhā pākānukūlā bhāvanā*). Grammarians give the following analysis: "There is operation conducive to the softening of the cooked substance and occurring in Caitra" (*caitrāśrayakaḥ viklittyanukūlo vyāpāraḥ*). Here I have only briefly illustrated how the three schools analyse verbal understanding.[18]

---

[17] This type of verbal understanding is presented as Udayana's view in *NKu*, p. 531,4: *pākānukūlavartamānaprayatnavān*.

[18] For example, it has not been illustrated how tense and mood are expressed, what the suffix *a* inserted between *pac* and *-ti* denotes, and so forth. For a general illustration of verbal understanding, see Rao (1969: 4-34) and Joshi (1993: 29-36). Cardona (1975) discusses whether or not paraphrase and the analysis of verbal understanding decisively serve to assign partial meanings to the constituents of a sentence or word, such as a root and a suffix. Cardona (1975: 272) remarks that the different schools assign meanings in different ways, based on their particular backgrounds, premises, and aims. Diaconescu (2012: 30, 35, 37) points out a difference between the Nyāya view and the Mīmāṁsā and Grammarians views. The former view takes a preceding meaning element placed in the expression of verbal understanding as the qualifier (*viśeṣaṇa*), and the following element as the qualificand, as stated above. The latter views, on the other hand, respectively take productive operation and operation (or, action) as the qualificands, and all the other meaning elements as their (direct or indirect) qualifiers.

(E) MEANING (ARTHA)

Finally, I would like to call the reader's attention to the word "meaning", which appears throughout my translation. This word does not always stand for "mental representation" in the Indian context. Nyāya, Vaiśeṣika, and Mīmāṁsā hold the view that knowledge or cognition (*jñana*) has no content in itself (*nirākāravāda*) and that recognizing an object means that a cognitive relation occurs between the cognition and the object (*grāhyagrāhakabhāva*). For example, when for these three schools the meaning of the root *pac* is said to be the action of cooking, this does not refer to the understanding of cooking or the concept of cooking but rather refers to the physical action of cooking which takes place in the outer world. Even the expression of verbal understanding (*śābdabodha*) does not represent the structure of understanding or cognition itself but the structure of part of the outer world.

By contrast, the Grammarian school maintains that knowledge has content.[19] For this school the expression of verbal understanding represents the structure of the understanding. This expression also represents the structure of a phenomenon in the outer world as long as the understanding corresponds to this phenomenon. When I am referring to this sense of "meaning" in the course of my translation, I have provided a footnote.

A Translation with Annotation of the Ākhyātavāda of Tattvacintāmaṇi

H. THE NYĀYA VIEW IN DETAIL

H1:[20] The traditional theory [of Nyāya], on the other hand, is

[19] The Vijñānavāda school of Buddhism also takes this position. Gaṅgeśa does not debate with the followers of this school and other Sākāravādins in the "Verbal Suffix Section".

[20] *TC*, vol. 4/2, pp. 836,4-837,1: *sampradayas tu saṁkhyeyamātrasākāṁkṣāpi saṁkhyā bhāvanānvayinaivānveti* →

as follows: even though number has expectancy with regard to all suitable to be counted,[21] the number [denoted by the verbal suffix] is related with the relatum (*anvayin*) of productive operation (*bhāvanā*). This is because [the number and what is suitable to be counted are related with one another] through the relation of being obtained from one and the same meaningful linguistic unit (*pada*). Productive operation, being a kind of operation (*vyāpāra*),[22] requires the unqualified (*śuddha*) meaning[23] of a nominal base (*prātipadika*), and not the object, instrument, and so forth, because they [i.e. the object, instrument, and others] are understood as the possessors of operation on the basis of the second case-ending, and so forth. That is why even the object, and so forth, do not [further] require operation. Therefore, operation is related with what is indicated by [a word associated with] the first [case-ending], since [the meaning of] a nominal base is also required by operation in order that

→ *ekapadopāttatvapratyāsatteḥ. bhāvanā ca vyāpāratvena śuddhaṁ pratipadikārtham ākāṁkṣati na tu karmakaraṇādi dvitīyadinā tasya vyāpāravattvenopasthiteḥ. ata eva karmādy api na vyāpāram ākāṁkṣati. ataḥ prathamānirddiṣṭenaiva bhāvanānvayaḥ prātipadikasyāpi kriyānvayārthaṁ*[(1)] *vyāpārākāṁkṣitatvāt. śuddhaś cāgninā caitras taṇḍulaṁ pacatīty atra kartā caitreṇa pacyate taṇḍula ity atra karma atas tatraiva bhāvanānvaya iti saṁkhyānvayo 'pi tatraiva. tad uktaṁ, yaṁ yaṁ bhāvanānudhāvati taṁ taṁ saṁkhyāpīti sthitir iti.* ([(1)] *TC*, p. 386,10 reads *kriyānvayārtha*, which seems to be a mistake.)

21 Number is a quality (*guṇa*), so it cannot exist without its locus, i.e. a substance (*dravya*) which is countable. "The number existing in the agent" (*kartr̥gatā saṁkhyā*) means the number of the agent.

22 Productive operation is one variety of operation. On this, see Introduction: Basic Concepts: (a) *ākhyāta*.

23 On the specific sense of "meaning", see Basic Concepts: (E) Meaning (*artha*). An unqualified meaning is a meaning or existence which is given no function of action generator (*kāraka*), such as object, instrument, and so forth. On action generators, see Wada (2007a: 421 fn. 31).

[the meaning] be related with action (*kriyā*). The unqualified [meaning of the word associated with the first case-ending] is the agent in the case of *agninā caitras taṇḍulaṁ pacati* ("Caitra cooks rice with fire"), and it is the object in the case of *caitreṇa pacyate taṇḍulaḥ* ("Rice is cooked by Caitra"). Therefore, since it is that [agent, i.e. Caitra,] that is related with productive operation, it is that [agent] that is related with the number [denoted by the verbal suffix *-ti* of *pacati*]. The following is said:

> It is concluded that whatever productive operation chases after, the number also chases after.[24]

H2.1:[25] [Some[26]] will [argue] the following: in the case of *caitras taṇḍulaṁ pacati* ("Caitra cooks rice with fire"), the relation of productive operation with Caitra is possible, because [he is] the locus (*āśraya*) [of productive operation]. In the case of *caitreṇa taṇḍulaḥ pacyate* ("Rice is cooked by Caitra"), productive operation is not related with rice by [the relation of] objectness (*viṣayatā*),[27] because effort has operation conducive to the

---

24 A similar expression appears in *NKu*, p. 537,3-4: *yaṁ yaṁ bhāvanānveti taṁ taṁ saṁkhyāpīti sthiteḥ . . .*

25 *TC*, vol. 4/2, p. 837,1-9: *syād etat caitras taṇḍulaṁ pacatity atra bhāvanānvayaś caitre sambhavati āśrayatvāt, caitreṇa taṇḍulaḥ pacyate ity atra bhāvanānvayas taṇḍulasya na viṣayatayā yatnasya viklittyanukūlavyāpāraviṣayatvāt. viṣayatvenānvaye vā taṇḍulaṁ pacatīty atrāpi taṇḍulasya viṣayatvena bhāvanānvaya iti tadgataiva saṁkhyā syāt nāśrayatayā tatrāvr̥tteś caitre 'pi na yatnānvayaḥ tr̥tīyārthayatnenāvaruddhatvāt ity ananvitaiva tatra bhāvanā. acetane ca bhāvanānvayābhāvāt kathaṁ saṁkhyā-nvayaniyama iti.*

26 They hold that the suffixes of finite verbs, in the active voice or in the passive voice, denote effort or productive operation. This view is also maintained in the answer H2.2 to H.2.1. The Bhāṭṭa school of Mīmāṁsā also holds this view. On the Mīmāṁsā view, see Yoshimizu (2006: 309, 2007, 2012); *Maṇikaṇa*, p. 86,6-7.

27 Objectness is the relation of operation to rice, and not the reverse. A relation in Navya-Nyāya bears upon "direction" unless it is symmetrical. On the Navya-Nyāya concept of relation, see Wada (1990: 66-67, 2007b: 28 fn. 16).

softening [of rice] for [its own] object.[28] Or if [productive operation] is related [with rice] by [the relation of] objectness (*viṣayatva*), rice is related with productive operation as the object even in the case of *taṇḍulaṁ pacati* ("[Caitra] cooks rice"). Hence, it is the number existing in that [rice] that would be [denoted by the verbal suffix *-ti* of *pacati*]. [The relation of productive operation with rice is] not locusness (*āśrayatā*),[29] because [productive operation] does not occur in that [rice]. The relation of effort even with Caitra is impossible, because effort which is the meaning of the third [case-ending][30] has already been related [with him in the case of *caitreṇa taṇḍulaḥ pacyate*]. Hence, productive operation [denoted by the suffix *-te*] remains unrelated in that [case]. How can the rule of the relation of the number be [formulated], since the relation of productive operation cannot subsist in the case of insentient [agents]? [In other words, such a rule cannot be formulated.]

H2.2:[31] [The advocate of the traditional view will answer: This

---

[28] In short, the object of productive operation, or effort, is operation, or action (*kriyā*), and not rice.

[29] Locusness is the relation of a property to its locus, and not the reverse. See also fn. 28.

[30] According to Pāṇini, the third case-ending denotes the agent or the instrument. Cf. *P* 2.3.18: *kartr̥karaṇayos tr̥tīya*. On a translation of this *sūtra*, see Vasu (1977 [1891]: 285). According to the Navya-Naiyāyika, on the other hand, it denotes agentness or instrumentness (*karaṇatva*). Agentness is the state of being possessor of effort (*yatnavattva*), which is identical with effort. On this identification, see Wada (2006b); K. Bhattacharya (2010).

[31] *TC*, vol. 4/2, pp. 837,9-838,8: *na, yatnaviśeṣye saṁkhyānvayāt, caitras taṇḍulaṁ pacatīty atra taṇḍulasya karmatvenānvayāt taṇḍulavr̥ttiphalajanakavyāpārajanakayatnāśrayaś caitra iti pratīyata*[(1)] *iti sa eva viśeṣyaḥ. caitreṇa pacyate taṇḍula ity atra caitravr̥ttiyatnajanyavyāpārajanyaphalāśrayas taṇḍulaṁ pratīyata*[(2)] *iti yatnasya paramparayā taṇḍula eva viśeṣyaḥ. evañ ca yady apy ubhayatraiva caitraḥ kartā taṇḍulaḥ karma tathāpi yatnaviśeṣye saṁkhyānvyaḥ. acetane 'pi ratho grāmaṁ gacchatīty atra* →

is] not correct, because the number [denoted by the verbal suffix] is related to the qualificand[32] (*viśeṣya*) of effort. Since in the case of *caitras taṇḍulaṁ pacati* ("[Caitra] cooks rice") rice is related with objectness (*karmatva*), it is understood that Caitra is the locus of effort producing operation producing the result [i.e. softening] which takes place in rice. Hence, it is he who is the qualificand. Since in the case of *caitreṇa taṇḍulaḥ pacyate* ("Rice is cooked by Caitra") it is understood that rice is the locus of the result [i.e. softening] produced by operation produced by effort which exists in Caitra. Hence, it is rice that is indirectly the qualificand [of effort]. As a result, even though Caitra is the agent and rice is the object in both cases, the number [denoted by the verbal suffix *-ti* of *pacati* or *-te* of *pacyate*] is related with the qualificand of effort. In the case of insentient [agents] too, e.g. in the case of *ratho grāmaṁ gacchati* ("The chariot goes to the village"), it is understood that the chariot is the locus of operation producing the result [i.e. the contact of the chariot with the village] of going which (i.e. result) exists in the village; in the case of *rathena gamyate grāmaḥ* ("The village is approached by the chariot"), [it is understood that] the village is the locus of the result produced by operation which takes place in the chariot. Even in these cases, the number is related with the qualificand.

H3:[33] It should not be argued that if thus [in the cases of *caitras*

→ *grāmavṛttigamanaphalajanakavyāpārāśrayo rathaḥ pratīyate, rathena gamyate grāma ity atra rathavṛttivyāpārajanyaphalāśrayo grāma iti tatrāpi viśeṣye saṁkhyānvayaḥ.* ([(1)] [(2)] *TC*, p. 837,12 reads *pratīyate*, which is a mistake of *saṁdhi*.)

32 The qualificand is that of verbal understanding (*śābdabodha*), which is often called the analysis, the interpretation, or the meaning of the sentence concerned. In the Nyāya system of verbal understanding the meaning of the noun in the nominative case is prominent and is designated as the qualificand. On this, see Basic Concepts: (D) Verbal Understanding.

33 *TC*, vol. 4/2, pp. 838,8-840,4: *na caivaṁ yatnasya vyāpārasya ca viśeṣye saṁkhyānvaye niyāmakam ananugatam iti vācyam.* →

taṇḍulaṁ pacati ("[Caitra] cooks rice") or *ratho grāmaṁ gacchati* ("The chariot goes to the village")] the number is related to the qualificand of effort or operation [respectively], there is no determinant [of the qualificand] common [to both cases].[34] Since the number is related to the qualificand of the object (*viṣaya*) of the speaker's intention (*tātparya*) with reference to the verbal suffix, that [object] is either effort or operation.[35] In the case of *caitreṇa supyate* ("Sleeping is done by Caitra"), Caitra is not the qualificand of productive operation, because the meaning[36] of the third [case-ending], [i.e. productive operation,] has been already associated [with him]. In that

→ *ākhyātatātparyaviṣayasya viśeṣye saṁkhyānvayāt sa ca* (¹*yatno vyāpāro*¹⁾ *vā. caitreṇa supyata ity atra caitro na bhāvanāviśeṣyaḥ tṛtīyārthāvaruddhatvāt. karma ca tatra nāsty evāto dhātvartha eva bhāvanāviśeṣyaḥ phalatvād viṣayatvād veti tatra saṁkhyānvyaḥ. dvivacanabahuvacanayos tatrāsādhutvam eva. tad uktam. "ākṣepalabhye saṁkhyeye nābhidhānasya kalpanā. saṁkhyeyamātralābhe 'pi sākāṁkṣeṇa vyavasthitiḥ" iti. idam eva ca kartuḥ karmaṇaś cākṣepalabhyatvaṁ yad bhāvanāviśeṣyatve sati prathamāntapadopasthāpyatvaṁ na tu saṁkhyāliṅgakānumiti-viṣayatvaṁ anumityā saṁkhyeyamātragatatvena saṁkhyāpratīteḥ.* (⁽¹⁾ *TC*, p. 389,1 reads *yatnāvyāpāro*, which seems to be a mistake.)

34 We have arrived a temporary conclusion that the number denoted by the verbal suffix is related to the qualificand of effort or operation in the verbal understanding. Effort and operation are the qualifiers (*viśeṣaṇa*). In the former case Caitra is treated as the qualificand of effort; in the latter case the village as the qualificand of operation. Now the anticipated objection is: what is the determinant of the qualificands in these two cases? To put it another way, there is no common determinant in those cases.

35 To cover effort and operation in the meaning of the verbal suffix, the proponent introduces the concept of intended object (*tātparyaviṣaya*). In other words, it depends upon the speaker's intention whether the suffix denotes effort or operation. Thus, the common determinant of the qualifier is the state of being the object intended by speaker (*tātparyaviṣayatva*).

36 On the specific sense of "meaning", see Basic Concepts: (E) Meaning (*artha*).

case, the object (*karman*) [of the action of sleeping] is not available at all. Therefore, it is the meaning of the root [*svap*] that is the qualificand of productive operation, since [that meaning is] the result (*phala*) or object (*viṣaya*) [of productive operation].[37] Hence, to that [qualificand], the number is related. [The usage of] dual or plural number in that case is grammatically incorrect (*asādhutvam*) indeed. [To sum up,] the following is said [by Udayana]:

> [We] cannot postulate primary denotative function with reference to what is suitable to be counted and is obtained through implication (*ākṣepa*); it is the conclusion that even if [we] obtain [from the verbal suffix] anything suitable to be counted, [what is the agent or object is determined] by what has expectancy [with reference to resolution].[38]

That the agent and object are obtained by implication (*ākṣepa*) certainly [means] that they are the qualificands of productive operation [in the analysis of verbal understanding] and are recalled from a meaningful linguistic unit (*pada*) ending in the first [case-ending],[39] and does not mean that [the agent and object] are those obtained through inference whose probans

37 The sentence *caitreṇa supyate* ("Sleeping is done by Caitra") will generate the verbal understanding that sleeping is produced by productive operation occurring in Caitra (*caitravṛtti-bhāvanājanyaḥ svāpaḥ*).

38 Cf. *NKu*, k. 5.11:

ākṣepalabhye saṁkhyeye nābhidhānasya kalpanā ।
saṁkhyeyamātralābhe 'pi sākāṁkṣeṇa vyavasthitiḥ ॥

For a translation of this *kārikā*, see Cowell [1980: 76]; Dravid [1996: 455].

39 The Sanskrit expression corresponding to this translation is "*idam eva ca kartuḥ karmaṇaś cākṣepalabhyatvaṁ yad bhāvanāviśeṣyatve sati prathamāntapadopasthāpyatvaṁ . . .*". Grammatically speaking, the first that-clause forms the predicate of the whole sentence because of the usage of *idam* corresponding to the following *yat*; the second clause forms the subject because →

is number, because number is understood by means of inference as existing in all that is suitable to be counted.[40]

H4.1:[41] [Some[42] may object:] Even if productive operation is related to the meaning[43] of a nominal base (*nāma*), the number [denoted by the verbal suffix] is not related with [that meaning]. The reason [for this] is that since the number recalled from the first [case-ending has already been] related [with the meaning], that [number as denoted by the suffix] is not required.[44] It should not be argued that the first [case-ending] does not denote the number [of that recalled from a nominal base] but is for the sake of grammatically correct usage. This is because in the case of *caitra idānīṁ rājā* ("Caitra has now become the king") there being one [of Caitra] is understood

→ of the usage of that *yat*. However, since the meaning of the first that-clause, which is purported by the quoted *kārikā*, should be explained or defined here, I have dealt with it as the subject of the whole sentence.

40 This denied interpretation means that we can infer what the agent or object is from the number denoted by the verbal suffix. To be precise, we cannot determine what the agent or object is only from such a number.

41 *TC*, vol. 4/2, p. 840,4-10: *nanu nāmārthe bhāvanānvaye 'pi na saṁkhyānvayaḥ prathamopasthitasaṁkhyānvayena tasyā nirākāṁkṣatvāt. na ca prathamā na saṁkhyāvācika kin tu prayogasādhur iti vācyam. caitra idānīṁ rājety atra kevalād api ekatvapratīteḥ. anyathā prathamopasthitasaṁkhyā kartr̥karmānvaye saṁkhyā na tiṅartha ity api kalpyeteti cet,*

42 They may be the grammarians.

43 On the specific sense of "meaning", see Basic Concepts: (E) Meaning (*artha*).

44 This objection means: according to the Naiyāyika and the Mīmāṁsaka, in the case of *caitraḥ taṇḍulaṁ pacati* (Caitra cooks rice) the number denoted by the first case-ending (i.e. *-ḥ* or *-s*) has already denoted the number of Caitra, who is the meaning of the nominal base and who possesses productive operation or effort. Hence, it is not required that the verbal suffix *-ti* denote the number of Caitra.

even from the mere [usage[45] of the first case-ending]. Otherwise, if the agent or object is related with the number recalled from the first [case-ending], it would even be postulated that the number [of the agent or object] is not the meaning of the verbal suffix.

H4.2:[46] [The advocate[47] of the traditional view will answer: That is] not correct. This is because one and the same number is denoted by the first [case-ending] and the verbal suffix on account of co-referentiality (*sāmānādhikaraṇya*). For example, in the case [of the expression] *caitro daṇḍī* ("Caitra is the possessor of a stick"), otherwise, even in your view, since Caitra's number is denoted by the verbal suffix, the number denoted by the first [case-ending] would not be related to Caitra. It will be explained [in text H5.2] that in the case of *odanakāmaḥ paceta* ("One who wishes rice gruel should cook") the same method should be adopted even by you, since the agent is not denoted [by the verbal suffix] in that case.

H5.1:[48] [The Grammarian would object:] the agent is also

---

[45] This usage means a sentence which does not involve a verb.

[46] *TC*, vol. 4/2, pp. 840,10-841,5: *na, ekaiva hi saṁkhyā prathamākhyātābhyām abhidhīyate* [(1)]*sāmānādhikaraṇyānurodhāt yathā caitro daṇḍīti atra, anyathā tvanmate 'py ākhyātena caitrasaṁkhyābhidhānāt prathamāvācyasaṁkhyānvayaś caitre na syāt. odanakāmaḥ pacetety atra tvayāpy eṣaiva rītir avagantavyā tatra kartur avācyatvād iti vakṣyate.* ([(1)] *TC*, p. 341.1 reads *samānādhikaraṇyā-*, which seems to be a mistake.)

[47] Bhatta [2005: 902] identifies this Naiyāyika with Gaṅgeśa as in texts C1 and C2.2; but he gives no reason for his identification. My own reason for identifying this Naiyāyika with Gaṅgeśa is that since the views presented in those texts are not refuted in Gaṅgeśa's conclusion, we can conjecture that Gaṅgeśa claims H4.2.

[48] *TC*, vol. 4/2, p. 841,5-8: *atha kartāpy ākhyātavācyaḥ caitraḥ pacatīti* [(1)]*samānādhikaraṇyāt anyathā nāmākhyātayor bhinnapravr̥ttinimittakatve 'py ekatra vr̥ttyabhāve sāmānādhikaraṇyaṁ na syād iti cet.* ([(1)] *TC*, p. 341.1 reads *samānādhikaraṇyāt*, which seems to be a mistake.)

denoted by the verbal suffix, because [the nominal base (*nāma*) expressive of the agent and the suffix have] co-referentiality (*sāmānādhikaraṇya*) in the case of *caitraḥ pacati* ("Caitra cooks"). Otherwise, if the nominal base and the verbal suffix do not possess signifying function (*vṛtti*)[49] with reference to one [thing] even in the case of their having different grounds for using a word (*pravṛttinimitta*),[50] there could not be co-referentiality [in any case].

H5.2:[51] [The advocate[52] of the traditional view would reply: That is] not correct. That is because verbal co-referentiality[53]

---

49 In the present case this function is the denotative function. On the signifying function, see Basic Concepts: (C) The Signifying Function.

50 The ground for using a word, for example, in the case of the word "go" (cow), is cowness, which resides only in all cows. Let us take up the sentence *caitras taṇḍulaṁ pacati* ("[Caitra] cooks rice"). The ground for using the nominal base *caitra* is Caitra-ness (*caitratva*), and according to the Grammarians, the ground for using the verbal suffix *-ti* of *pacati* is agentness (*kartṛtva*). Thus, the grounds in the case of *caitra* and the suffix *-ti* differ, but both *caitra* and the suffix denote one and the same entity, i.e. Caitra who is the agent of cooking.

51 *TC*, vol. 4/2, pp. 841,8-842,9: *na, nīlaḥ paṭaś caitraḥ pacati pacyate taṇḍula ityādau nāmnor nāmākhyātayor vā ekasaṁkhyāvācakatvam eva hi śābdasāmānādhikaraṇyaṁ na tu bhinnapravṛtti-nimittasyaikatrārthe vṛttir gauravāt odanakāmaḥ pacetetyādau vybhicārāc ca. vidhyākhyātasya hi kṛtiśaktasya nāmasāmānā-dhikaraṇyaṁ*[(1)] *tayor ekasaṁkhyābhidhāyakatvāt na tv ekakartṛvācakatvena. tatrāpi kartur vācyatve tasyeṣṭasā-dhanatvabodhane apravṛttis tasyāsādhyatvāt. ayogyatayā kartāraṁ vihāya kṛtiviṣaye pāke pākaviṣayakṛtau veṣṭasādhanatānvaye kartur ananvayād apratīteś ca nābhidheyatvam.* ([(1)] *TC*, p. 842,1 reads *-sāmānādhikaraṇvaṁ*, which seems to be a mistake.)

52 See fn. 47.

53 The term "verbal coreferentiality" sounds strange. "Co-referentiality" connotes the function of words or expressions, so "verbal" is apparently superfluous. On the other hand, the Sanskrit term *sāmānādhikaraṇyam* has two meanings: the co- →

(*śābdasāmānādhikaraṇyam*) is nothing more than [the fact] that two nominal bases, or one nominal base and one verbal suffix, denote one and the same number in the cases of *nīlaḥ paṭaḥ* ("The cloth is blue"), *caitraḥ pacati* ("Caitra cooks"), *pacyate taṇḍulaḥ* ("Rice is cooked"), and so forth, and not [because co-referentiality] is not the signifying function of [words having] different grounds for using those words with reference to one thing. The reason [for this] is that [your theory is] cumbersome,[54] and because [your theory] deviates in the case of *odanakāmaḥ paceta* ("One who wishes rice gruel should cook"). The reason [for the deviation of your theory] is that the optative suffix (*vidyākhyāta*) denoting resolution possesses co-referentiality with the nominal base (i.e. *odanakāma*), because they both denote one and the same number, and not because they denote one and the same agent. Even in that case [of the optative suffix], if the agent is denoted [by the suffix], that suffix would not operate to cause an understanding of the "state of being the means for a desired object" (*iṣṭasādhanatva*). This is because that [agent] is not a thing to be accomplished (*sādhya*).[55] If, having

→ referentiality of words and the coexistence of entities. To differentiate the former from the latter, the advocate of H5.2 calls the former *śābdasāmānādhikaraṇyam* (i.e. verbal *sāmānādhikaraṇyam*). The above term is unavoidable unless we provide a common rendering of *sāmānādhikaraṇyam* in the two cases of meaning.

54 On the reason for being cumbersome, see Wada (2006a: 84-85).

55 The optative suffix (*vidhiliṅ*) denotes the state of "being the means for a desired object". The verbal understanding of *odanakāmaḥ paceta* ("One who wishes rice gruel should cook") will be *iṣṭasādhanapākānukūlākṛtimān odanakāmaḥ* ("One who wishes rice gruel possesses resolution conducive to cooking which is the means for a desired object, [*iṣṭha*, i.e. rice gruel]"). This means that one produces the means (*sādhana*, i.e. cooking) of making rice gruel, namely, that the means is to be accomplished (*sādhya*) by the person. In other words, the optative suffix denotes the means →

discarded [the theory that] the agent [is denoted by the verbal suffix] by reason of its being inappropriate, [you] relate the "state of being the means for a desired object" with cooking which is the object of resolution or with resolution which has cooking for the object, [the agent is] not denoted [by the verbal suffix] because the agent[56] remains unrelated [with the meaning of the optative suffix] and because [the agent is] not understood [from any meaningful linguistic unit in the sentence *odanakāmaḥ paceta*].

H6.1:[57] [The Grammarian will argue:] the agent is denoted [by the verbal suffix], because [we can] paraphrase *pacati* ("[He] cooks") as *pākayatnavān* ("[He is] the possessor of effort for cooking").[58]

→ to be accomplished by the person. This conclusion is not guaranteed if the optative suffix denotes the agent, for the agent is not the means to be accomplished. On the Navya-Nyāya concept of the optative suffix, see Marui (1987: 146-47, 1988: 128-29), which elucidates its three meanings in *KĀ*, kk. 146-50; *NSM*, pp. 472,7-490,6: the state of being to be accomplished by resolution (*kṛtisādhyatva*), the state of being the means for the desired thing (*iṣṭasādhanatva*), and the state of being not connected with great harm (*balavadaniṣṭānanubandhitva*). *MK* (p. 76,3) also presents those three meanings. Gaṅgeśa's "Injunction Section" (Vidhivāda) is translated by Jha (1987).

56 This agent is the meaning understood from the suffix *-ta*.

57 *TC*, vol. 4/2, p. 842,9-10: *pacatīty asya pākayatnavān iti vivaraṇāt kartā vācya iti cet.*

58 The opponent insists that even if the Nyāya analysis of the sentence under discussion holds true, it must be concluded that the verbal suffix denotes the agent. As the traditional view tells us, *pāka* (the action of cooking) is obtained from the root *pac*, and *yatnavat* (the possessor of effort) is obtained from the suffix *-ti*. The possessor of effort is nothing more than an agent. Thus, the suffix must denote the agent.

H6.2:[59] [the advocate[60] of the traditional view would reply: that is] not correct. The reason [for this] is that even if [we can obtain] the paraphrase of a compound such as a *dvandva*, and the like, on the basis of analysis (*vigraha*), [the compound possesses] no primary denotative function with reference to [its] analysed meaning, and as a result [your determination about the meaning of the verbal suffix depending upon the paraphrase] deviates [in the case of compounds];[61] or that when the agent is ascertained not to be denoted [by the verbal suffix] by reason of its being obtained from the other [linguistic unit, i.e. *odanakāma*], paraphrase [simply] informs [us] of the object of speaker's intention; or that [your way of thinking] is based on the wrong cognition [that the verbal suffix possesses] the primary denotative function with reference to the agent. Truly speaking, if in the case of *pacati* ("[He] cooks") the possessor of effort is denoted [by the verbal suffix], the meaning of the root, which is the object (*viṣaya*) [of effort] or that which is to be accomplished (*sādhya*) [by effort], would not be related with resolution. The reasons [for this] are that if [resolution] recalled

[59] *TC*, vol. 4/2, pp. 842,10-843,14: *na, dvandvādisamāsasya vigraheṇa vivaraṇe 'pi vigrahārthe śaktyabhāvena vyabhicārāt kartur anyalabhyatvenāvācyatvasthitau vivaraṇasya tātparya-viṣayajñāpakatvāt kartṛśaktibhramamūlatvād vā. vastutaḥ pacatīty atra yatnavataḥ śakyatve dhātvarthasya viṣayatvena sādhyatvena vā kṛtāv anvayo na syād itarapadārthaviśeṣaṇatayopasthite padārthaikadeśe itarapadārthasyānanvayāt. rājapuruṣam ānayety atra rājña ivānayane padārthe padārthānvayasya*[(1)] *vyutpattisiddhatvāt. yatnasyāśrayānvitatvenopasthitasyetarānākāṁkṣatvāt. pākayatnavator anvaye ca yatnavatsādhyaḥ pākaḥ pākajanako yatnavān iti dhīḥ syāt na tu pākayatnayor viṣayaviṣayibhāvadhīḥ. pākakartā ity atrāpi na pākasya kṛtāv anvayadhīḥ kṛter apadārthatvāt. kiṁ tu kṛtyaśrayaḥ pākajanaka iti pratītiḥ. ata evāpacaty api pācakapadaprayogāt vuṇaḥ kṛtiyogyatā vacyeti nirastam. pākasya kṛtāv ananvayaprasaṅgād iti tatra pācakapadaṁ gauṇam eva.* ([(1)] *TC*, p. 843,5 reads *padārthānvayasya*, which seems to be a mistake.)

[60] See fn. 47.

[61] On a *dvandva* compound analysis, see Wada (2007a: 419 fn. 20).

as the qualifier of the meaning of the meaningful linguistic unit (i.e. *yatnavat*) other [than *yatna*] is part of the meaning of [that] unit, the meaning of the other unit (i.e. *pāka*) cannot be related [with that part],[62] that as in the case of *rājapuruṣam ānaya* ("Bring a subject of the king") in which [there is no relation] of the king with [the action of] bringing (*ānayana*), it is established by [our] learning that the [whole] meaning of a meaningful linguistic unit is related to the [whole] meaning of another unit, and that effort recalled as related to [its own] locus (*āśraya*) does not require the other [meaning, i.e. cooking].[63] Then, [as the opponent argues,] if cooking and the possessor of effort are related, [there] would be an understanding that cooking is to be accomplished by the possessor of effort or that the possessor of effort produces cooking, and no understanding of the object and object–possessor relationship[64] between cooking and effort. Even in the case of *pākakartā* (the agent of cooking) there would be no understanding of the relation of cooking with resolution,[65] because resolution is not the meaning of the meaningful

[62] According to the opponent, the paraphrase of *pacati* by analysis is *pākayatnavān* (the possessor of effort for cooking), and here *pāka* (cooking), the meaning of the root, appears to function as the qualifier of *yatna* (effort), which is part of the meanings obtained from the suffix *-ti*. The Naiyāyika's rule is that the whole meaning obtained from one meaningful linguistic unit should be related to the whole meaning obtained from the other unit. According to this rule, the root meaning cannot be related to the part of the meaning of the suffix, effort. Hence, the above paraphrase does not hold good.

[63] Effort is one of the qualities (*guṇa*). A quality requires a locus; otherwise it does not exist.

[64] The object corresponds to effect; the object-possessor, to cause, so this relationship is, in reality, a cause and effect relationship.

[65] The advocate anticipates that the grammarian further paraphrases *pacati* ([he] cooks) as *pākakartā* (the agent of cooking) instead of *pākayatnavān* (the possessor of effort for cooking). In the former paraphrase effort or resolution is not directly denoted by the unit *kartṛ*.

linguistic unit [i.e. *kartā*]. Instead, [from the paraphrase *pākakartā* (the agent of cooking) we have] an understanding that the locus of resolution produces cooking.[66] That is why it is ruled out that because of the usage of the word *pācaka* (cook) even at the time of no cooking, the *vuṇ* suffix[67] denotes ability (*yogyatā*) to be related with resolution. The reason [for this] is that [the above interpretation of the suffix] would lead [us] to the wrong outcome that cooking is not related with resolution.[68] Therefore, the word *pācaka* [used] in that case [of no cooking] is really of a secondary usage (*gauṇa*).

H7.1:[69] [The Grammarian will object:] the agent and object are denoted by L-suffixes. Therefore, when the agent or object is not denoted [by the suffix], a case-ending [denoting] the agent or object prescribed by the rules following the heading rule

---

66 To establish a relationship between cooking and effort (or resolution), effort has to enter into the understanding or analysis of *pacati*.

67 The term *vuṇ* seems to be used for *ṇvul*. This is conjectured from *Agnipurāṇa* 359,6cd: *vuṇtr̥cau sarvadhātubhyo bhāvako bhavitā*. √*pac* + *ṇvul* → *pac* + *vu* (P7.2.115) → *pāc* + *aka* (P7.1.1) → *pācaka*. On this formation, see Vasu (1977[1891]: 399). The term *vu* is the general term for the suffixes *vuK*, *vuC*, *vuÑ*, and *vuN*.

68 According to the opponent, the word *pācaka* is paraphrased as the root *pac* plus the suffix *-aka*; the suffix denotes the ability to be related with resolution. Then, we would have an understanding of the ability to be related with resolution conducive to cooking. This understanding indicates that cooking is related with resolution which is part of the meaning of the suffix. However, it cannot be accepted that we have such an understanding, because of the above-mentioned rule that the whole meaning of a meaningful linguistic unit be related to the whole meaning of another unit.

69 *TC*, vol. 4/2, pp. 843,14-844,5: *nanu kartr̥karmaṇī lakāravācye tenābhihite kartari karmaṇi cānabhihitādhikārīyā kartr̥karmavibhaktir na bhavati kin tu prathamaiva lakāreṇa tayor anabhidhāne ca caitreṇa pacati taṇḍulaṁ caitraḥ pacyate odanam*[(1)] *ityādy api syād iti cet.* ([(1)] *TC*, p. 843,4 reads *ādenam*, which seems to be a mistake.)

anabhihite ("If not expressed")[70] will not appear, but only the first [case-ending will result]. If both of them are not denoted by L-suffixes, there would result even [the wrong expressions] **caitreṇa pacati taṇḍulaḥ* and **caitraḥ pacyate odanam*.[71]

[70] That the verbal suffix denotes the agent or object is prescribed by *P* 3.4.69: *laḥ karmaṇi ca bhāve cākarmakebhyaḥ*. "The tense-affixes called 'la' are used in denoting the object and the agent; after intransitive verbs, they denote the action as well as the agent" (tr. Vasu (1977 [1891]: 584)). This rule is governed by the heading rule *P* 2.3.1: *anabhihite* "If [the object or agent is] not expressed". On this governing rule, see Joshi (1976: 3-5).

[71] Generally speaking, if the Grammarian's view is not accepted, ungrammatical sentences will result as follows. If the verbal suffix does not denote the agent in an active voice sentence such as (a) *caitraḥ taṇḍulaṁ pacati* ("Caitra cooks rice"), the third case-ending must be introduced after *caitra*. Then, the sentence would be (a1) **caitreṇa taṇḍulam pacati*. In addition, if the suffix does not denote the object in a passive voice sentence such as (b) *caitreṇa odanaḥ pacyate* ("Rice gruel is cooked by Caitra"), the second case-ending must be introduced after *odana*. Then, the sentence would be (b1) **caitreṇa odanam pacyate*. However, Gaṅgeśa provides two examples different from (a1) and (b1): (1) **caitreṇa pacati taṇḍulaṁ*, and (2) **caitraḥ pacyate odanam*, so we can conjecture that he ascribes to a different way of thinking from that of the Grammarian. Here it is supposed to be a principle that the verbal suffix *-ti* or *-te* denotes either the agent or object. Let us take up sentence (a). If the verbal suffix *-ti* does not denote the agent, it must denote the object. Then, the agent must be denoted by the third case-ending, and this ending is introduced after *caitra*. As a result *caitreṇa* is formed. Since the suffix denotes the object, the second case-ending denoting the object does not need to be introduced after *taṇḍula*. Consequently the first case-ending is introduced, and *taṇḍulaḥ* is formed. Thus, sentence (1) results, but it is grammatically incorrect. Next, let us take up sentence (b). If the verbal suffix *-te* does not denote the object, it must denote the agent. Then, the object must be denoted by the second case-ending, and this ending is introduced after *odana*. As a result *odanam* is formed. Since the suffix denotes the agent, the third case-ending denoting the agent does not need to be introduced after *caitra*. Consequently the first case-ending is introduced, and *caitraḥ* is formed. Thus, sentence (2) results, but it is also grammatically incorrect.

H7.2:[72] [The advocate of the traditional view will answer: That is] not correct. The reasons [for this] are that only by [understanding that] denoting or not by denoting the number existing in the agent or object, [we] can apply grammatical operations (*kārya*) [of the rules] based on [whether something is] denoted or not-denoted, and that such expressions [as provided in text H7.1 with asterisks] are not grammatically correct. When correctness [of an expression is known], grammar [can be established] indeed. And it is not the case that by following grammar, correctness [is established]. The reason [for this] is that [if the above is not accepted,] *grāmagāma*[73] (a person who goes to the village) [which is a grammatically correct but unusable expression] would be an appropriate usage.

H8:[74] The New Naiyāyikas, on the other hand, [will argue the following]. [We have] an understanding that a case-ending causes an understanding of the number existing in the meaning

[72] *TC*, vol. 4/2, p. 844,5-8: *na, kartṛkarmagatasaṁkhyābhidhānānabhidhānābhyām* [(1)]*evābhihitānabhihitakāryopapatteḥ tādṛśaprayogasyāsādhutvāc ca. sādhutve hi saty anuśāsanaṁ na tv anuśāsanānurodhena sādhutvam grāmagāmādau sādhutvāpatteḥ.* ([(1)] *TC*, p. 844,6 reads *evāhitānabhihita-*, which seems to be a mistake.)

[73] √*gam* + *aṆ* (*P* 3.2.1) → *gāma*. *P* 3.2.1: *karmaṇy aṆ* (tr. Vasu (1977 [1891]: 407): The affix *aṆ* comes after a verbal root when the object (or whatever sort it may be), is in composition with it (as an *upapada*).

[74] *TC*, vol. 4/2, pp. 844,9-845,10: *navīnās tu supaḥ prakṛtyarthagatasvārthasaṁkhyābodhakatvaṁ tiṅaḥ prathamāntapadārthagatasaṁkhyābodhakatvam iti vyutpattir eva vyutpattiś ca tatsvabhāvatvaṁ tac ca phalonneyam. prathamāntapadārthaḥ kartā karma vā. ata eva caitreṇa supyate ity atra prathamāntapadābhāvān na saṁkhyānvayaḥ. na ca dhātvarthe saṁkhyānvayaḥ, svāpasya dvitvabahutve 'pi dvivacanabahuvacanayor abhāvāt supyata ity eva prayogaḥ syāt. ata eva svāpamātrāvagamāt ākhyātārthayatnasaṁkhyayor ananvaye ākhyātaṁ prayogamātre sādhv iti tiṅaṁ vinā dhātoḥ kevalasyāsādhutvāt. ato na saṁkhyānurodhena kartṛkarmaṇī lakāravācye.*

of the base (*prakṛti*), which (number) is the meaning of [the case-ending] itself,[75] and that the verbal suffix causes an understanding of the number existing in the meaning[76] of a word (*pada*) ending in the first [case-ending]. Understanding [of this kind] is the state of possessing the nature of them [i.e. a case-ending and a verbal suffix], and that [nature] is to be inferred from the result [i.e. verbal understanding]. The meaning of a word ending in the first [case-ending] is either the agent or object. That is why in the case of *caitreṇa supyate* ("Caitra sleeps") the number [denoted by the verbal suffix *-te*] is not related [with any other meaning], since there is no word ending in the first [case-ending]. Furthermore, the number [denoted by the suffix] is not related with the meaning of the root [*svap*]. Since dual and plural numbers are impossible even in case of two or three times of sleeping being possible, only the expression *supyate* is available. It follows from this that only sleeping is understood [from the expression *supyate*], and hence that when the effort and the number, i.e. the meanings of the verbal suffix, are not related [with any other meaning], [to use] the verbal suffix is grammatically correct only for the sake of expression. [This is concluded,] because [to use] a mere root without a verbal suffix is not grammatically correct. Therefore, by following the theory of the numbers [being denoted by the word ending in the first case-ending and the verbal suffix, it is concluded that] the agent and object are not denoted by the verbal suffix.

---

75 According to *P* 2.3.46: *prātipadikārthaliṅgaprimāṇavacanamātre prathamā*, the first case-ending can denote the meaning of the base. Vasu (1977 [1891]: 295) translates this *sūtra* as follows: "Where the sense is that of the Nominal-stem (I.2.45) or of gender only, or measure only or number only, the first case-affix is employed."

76 On the specific sense of "meaning", see Basic Concepts: (E) Meaning (*artha*).

H9:[77] We, on the other hand, claim as follows: In the cases of *caitreṇa pacyate taṇḍulaḥ* ("Rice is cooked by Caitra") and *rathena gamyate grāmaḥ* ("The village is reached by the chariot"), rice and the village would be understood as the objects; they both [i.e. rice and the village] possess objectness (*karmatva*), i.e. the state of possessing result of action (*kriyā*) inhering in the other [i.e. Caitra in the former case and the chariot in the latter]; it is that [objectness] that is denoted by the verbal suffix [*-te* of *pacyate* and *gamyate,* respectively]. The reason [for this] is that objectness is not obtained from [any other meaningful linguistic unit] other than [the suffix *-te* in the above two cases] unlike in the case of *taṇḍulaṁ pacati* ("[Caitra] cooks rice") [in which objectness is obtained] from the second [case-ending]. Therefore, like agentness (*kartr̥tva*)[78] objectness is also denoted by L-suffixes, because the loci of them, i.e. [the entities called] the agent and the object [respectively], are obtained from the other [meaningful linguistic units].[79]

---

77 *TC, vol. 4/2, pp. 845,10-846,4: vayan tu brūhaḥ. caitreṇa pacyate taṇḍulaḥ rathena gamyate grāma ity atra taṇḍulagrāmau karmaṇī pratīyete asti ca tayoḥ parasamavetakriyāphalaśālitvaṁ karmatvaṁ tac cākhyātavācyam eva. taṇḍulaṁ pacatīty atra dvitīyāta ivānyataḥ karmatvālābhāt. tasmāt kartr̥tvavatkarmatvam api lakāravācyaṁ taddharmiṇoḥ kartr̥karmaṇor anyata eva lābhād iti. iti śrīmadgaṅgeśopādhyāyaviracite tattvacintāmaṇau śabdākhyaturīyakhaṇḍe ākhyātavādaḥ.*

78 Agent is the possessor of effort (*yatnavat*); agentness is the "state of possessing effort (*yatnavattva*)", which is nothing more than effort (*yatna*). On this, see Wada (2006b); K. Bhattacharya (2010).

79 If the verbal suffix denotes agentness or objectness, their locus, i.e. the agent or the object, is obtained from the word ending in the first case-ending. This means that the suffix does not need to denote the agent or object. In the case of *caitraḥ taṇḍulaṁ pacati* ("Caitra cooks rice"), the verbal suffix *-ti* denotes effort, or agentness. The suffix does not need to denote objectness, because the second case-ending *-am* denotes objectness. The locus of agentness is understood from the fact that the number denoted by the verbal suffix is identical with the number →

Here ends the "Verbal Suffix Section" (Ākhyātavāda) in the Fourth Book (*khaṇḍa*) named "Language" (Śabda) of *Tattvacintāmaṇi* composed by Revered Gaṅgeśa Upādhyāya.

(*the end*)

Acknowledgements

This research was supported by a Grant-in-Aid for Scientific Research (C) by the Japan Society for the Promotion of Science, Tokyo. I wish to thank Dr Charles Pain for correcting my English, and Dr Toshiya Unebe and Dr Bhagyalata Pataskar for answering my questions about Pāṇini's grammar.

References

PRIMARY SOURCES

Agnipurāṇa, edited by Baladeva Upādhyāya, Kashi Sanskrit Series 30, Varanasi: The Chowkhamba Sanskrit Series Office, 1966.

KĀ: *Kārikāvalī* or *Bhāṣāpariccheda* of Viśvanātha Pañcānana, edited with *NSM*. See *NSM*.

Maṇikaṇa, in Sarma 1977.

MNP: *Mīmāṁsānyāyaprakāśa*, edited in Edgerton [1929].

NKu: *The Nyāyakusumāñjali of Śrī Udayanācārya* with Four Commentaries: the *Bodhanī* of Varadarāja, the *Prakāśa* of Vardhamāna, the *Prakāśikā* of Mecha Thakkura, and the Makaranda of Rucidatta, ed. Padmaprasada Upadhyaya and

→ denoted by the case-ending -*s* or -*ḥ* of *caitraḥ*; in other words, it is known that agentness resides with the number denoted by that case-ending in the meaning of the word associated with the case-ending, i.e. *caitraḥ*. Similarly in the case of *caitreṇa taṇḍulaḥ pacyate* ("Rice is cooked by Caitra") the verbal suffix -*te* denotes objectness. This suffix does not need to denote agentness, because the third case-ending denotes agentness. The locus of objectness is understood from the fact that number denoted by the suffix is identical with the number denoted by the case-ending; in other words, it is known that objectness resides with the number denoted by that case-ending in the meaning of the word associated with the case-ending, i.e. *taṇḍulaḥ*.

Dhundhiraja Shastri, Kashi Sanskrit Series 30, Varanasi: Chowkhamba Sanskrit Series Office, 1957.

Nyāyasiddhāntadīpa of Śaśadhara, ed. B.K. Matilal with the Ṭippana of Guṇaratnasūri, L.D. Series 56, Ahmedabad: L.D. Institute, 1976.

NSM: *Nyāyasiddhāntamuktāvalī* of Viśvanātha Pañcānana, ed. Narayancharan Shastri and Swetvaikuntha Shastri, Kashi Saskrit Series 212, Varanasi: Chowkhamba Sanskrit Series Office, 1972.

P: *Aṣṭādhyāyī* or *Pāṇinisūtra*, edited in Vasu [1977 (1891)].

TC: *Tattvacintāmaṇi of Gaṅgeśa Upādhyāya*, 4 vols., ed. Kāmākhyānātha Tarkavāgīśa, Vrajajivan Prachyabharati Granthamala 47, Delhi: Chaukhamba Sanskrit Pratishthan, 1990.

SECONDARY SOURCES

Abhyankar, Kashinath Vasudev and J.M. Shukla, 1977, *A Dictionary of Sanskrit Grammar*, Gaekwad's Oriental Series 134, Baroda: Oriental Institute.

Bhatta, V.P., 2005, *Word: The Śabdakhaṇḍa of the Tattvacintāmaṇi*, 2 vols., Delhi: Eastern Book Linkers.

Bhattacharya, Dineshchandra, 1958, *History of Navya-Nyāya in Mithilā*, Mithilā Institute Series 3, Studies 2, Darbhanga: Mithilā Institute of Post-Graduate Studies and Research in Sanskrit Learning.

Bhattacharya, Kamaleswar, 2010, "On the Two Questions of the New Logic of India", in Andrew Schumann (ed.), *Logic in Religious Discourse*, Frankfurt: Ontos Verlag, pp. 34-43.

Cardona, George, 1975, "Paraphrase and Sentence Analysis: Some Indian Views", *Journal of Indian Philosophy*, **3**: 259-81.

Cowell, E.B., 1980 (1864), *Kusumāñjali*, Varanasi: Bharat Bharati.

Diaconescu, Bogdan, 2012, *Debating Verbal Cognition: The Theory of the Principal Qualificand (mukhyaviśeṣya) in Classical Indian Thought*, Delhi: Motilal Banarsidass.

Dravid, N.S., 1996, *Nyāyakusumāñjali of Udayana*, vol. 1, New Delhi: Indian Council of Philosophical Research.

Edgerton, Franklin, 1929, *The Mīmāṁsā Nyāya Prakāśa or Āpadevī: A Treatise of the Mīmāṁsā System by Āpadeva*, New Haven/London: Yale University Press.

Jha, V.N., 1987, *The Philosophy of Injunction*, Delhi: Pratibha Prakashan.

Joshi, S.D., 1993 (1960), "Kauṇḍ Bhaṭṭa on the Meaning of Sanskrit Verbs (1)", *Nagoya Studies in Indian Culture and Buddhism: Saṁbhāṣā*, **14**: 1-39. (Reproduction of the author's Ph.D. dissertation submitted to Harvard University in 1960.)

Joshi, S.D. and Roodbergen, 1976, *Patañjali's Vyākaraṇa-Mahābhāṣya Anabhihitāhnika (P2.3.1-2.3.17)*, Publications of the Centre of Advanced Study in Sanskrit Class C No. 11, Poona: University of Poona.

Marui, Hiroshi, 1987, "Meireibun no Imi wo Tou Giron" (The Meaning of Injunctions: the Navya-Nyāya Argument), in: *Ga no Shisō* (Indian and Buddhist Studies: Prof. Jikido Takasaki Felicitation Volume), Tokyo: Shunjūsha, pp. 139-54 (in Japanese).

———, 1988, "Meirei Kinō no Ronriteki Kaimei" (Logical Analysis of the Function of the Vedic Vidhi: With Special reference to the Nyāya Theories of *Vidhi*), *Tohōgaku* (Eastern Studies), **76**: 123-34 (in Japanese).

Matilal, Bimal Krishna, 1968, *The Navya-Nyāya Doctrine of Negation*, Harvard Oriental Series 40, Cambridge, MA: Harvard University Press.

Rao, Veluri Subba, 1969, *The Philosophy of a Sentence and Its Parts*, New Delhi: Munshiram Manoharlal.

Sarma, Sreekrishna, 1977, *Maṇikaṇa: A Navya-Nyāya Manual*, The Adyar Library Series 48, Madras: The Adyar Library and Research Centre.

Vasu, Śrīśa Chandra, 1977(1891), *The Aṣṭādhyayī of Pāṇini*, 2 vols., Delhi/Varanasi/Patna: Motilal Banarsidass.

Wada, Toshihiro, 1990, *Invariable Concomitance in Navya-Nyāya*, Sri Garib Dass Oriental Series 101, Delhi: Sri Satguru Publications.

———, 1999, "Shin Niyāya Gakuha no Kigen to Bunseki Hōhō" (The Origin of Navya-Nyāya and the Position of this School in the History of Indian Logic), *Indo-Shisōshi Kenkyu* (Studies in the History of Indian Thought), **11**: 15-41 (in Japanese).

———, 2001, "The Analytical Method of Navya-Nyāya", *Journal of Indian Philosophy*, **29**: 519-30.

———, 2004, "The Origin of Navya-Nyāya and Its Place Within the History of Indian Logic", in S. Hino and T. Wada (eds.), *Three Mountains and Seven Rivers: Professor Musashi Tachikawa's Felicitation Volume*, Delhi: Motilal Banarsidass, pp. 439-62.

———, 2006a, "A Navya-Nyāya Presupposition in Determining the Meaning of Words", in M. Hattori (ed.), *Acta Asiatica: Bulletin of the Institute of Eastern Culture (Word and Meaning in Indian Philosophy)*, **90**: 71-91.

———, 2006b, "A Rule of Substitution in Navya-Nyāya: *x-vat-tva* and *x*", in M. Banerjee, U. Jha, T. Wada, N. Kulkarni, and A. Mishra (eds.), *Nyāya-Vasiṣṭha: Felicitation Volume of Prof. V.N. Jha*, Kolkata: Sanskrit Pustak Bhandar, pp. 356-69.

———, 2007a, "Gaṅgeśa on the Meaning of Verbal Suffixes (1)", in K. Preisendanz (ed.), *Expanding and Merging Horizons: Contributions to South Asian and Cross-Cultural Studies in Commemoration of Wilhelm Halbfass*, Vienna: The Austrian Academy of Sciences, pp. 415-29.

———, 2007b, *The Analytical Method of Navya-Nyāya*, Gonda Indological Studies 14, Groningen: Egbert Forsten Publishing.

———, 2012, "Gaṅgeśa on the Meaning of Verbal Suffixes (2)", in C. Watanabe, M. Desmarais, and Y. Honda (eds.), *Saṁskṛta-Sādhutā: Goodness of Sanskrit: Studies in Honour of Professor Ashok N. Aklujkar*, New Delhi: D.K. Printworld, pp. 528-44.

———, 2013, "Gaṅgeśa on the Meaning of Verbal Suffixes (3)", *Nagoya Studies in Indian Culture and Buddhism: Saṁbhāṣā*, **30**: 1-14.

———, 2014, "Gaṅgeśa's Theory on the Meaning of Verbal Suffixes", in K. Bhattacharya (ed.), Papers from the *15th World Sanskrit Conference: Nagoya Studies in Indian Culture and Buddhism: Saṁbhāṣā*, **31**: 61-75.

Yoshimizu, Kiyotaka, 2006, "Kumārira niyoru Teidōshi Setsuji no Hyōji Riron nitsuite" (Kumārila, on the Denotation of a Verbal Suffix), *Indotetsugaku Bukkyogaku* (Hokkaido Journal of Indological and Buddhist Studies), **21**: 298-315 (in Japanese).

———, 2007, "Teidōshi no Kāraka Hyōji Ronshō to Kumārira niyoru sono Hihan nitsute" (Kumārila's Criticism on the Denotation of a Kāraka by a Finite Verb), *Ronshū* (Studies in Religions East and West) **34**: 486-506 (in Japanese).

———, 2012, "Tradition and Reflection in Kumārila's Last Stand Against the Grammarians' Theories of Verbal Denotation", in C. Watanabe, M. Desmarais, and Y. Honda (eds.), *Saṁskṛta-Sādhutā: Goodness of Sanskrit: Studies in Honour of Professor Ashok N. Aklujkar*, New Delhi: D.K. Printworld, pp. 552-86.

12

On the Concept of Ayutasiddha in the Definition of Inherence

Katsunori Hirano

Introduction

AMONG the categories which the Vaiśeṣika enumerates, the sixth category, inherence (*samavāya*), is a relation together with conjunction (*saṁyoga*) conceived as a quality (*guṇa*). According to the Vaiśeṣika, the relation of inherence is real as well as the related entities. And it is established: (i) between substance (*dravya*) and quality, activity (*karman*), universal (*sāmānya*), and particular (*viśeṣa*); (ii) between universal and its substratum (substance, quality, and activity); and (iii) between the whole (*avayavin*) and its parts (*avayava*s). *Padārthadharmasaṁgraha* (*PDhS*) by Praśastāpada (*c.* 550–600),[1] which reconstructed Vaiśeṣika's teaching and was regarded as an authoritative text, together with *Vaiśeṣikasūtra*, defines inherence as follows:

> That which is the relation, being a cause of the idea "[this is] here (this is in that)", between entities that do not exist separately, which [stand as] the superstratum and the substratum, is inherence.[2]

---

1 On the dates of authors referred in this paper, see Potter (ed.) (1995a [1970], 1995b [1977]).

2 On the translation of inherence's definition in *PDhS*, Jha (1982 [1915]: 32) translates it as: "Inherence is the relationship →

(*PDhS*, no.9: *ayutasiddhānām ādhāryādhārabhūtānāṁ yaḥ sambandha ihapratyayahetuḥ sa samavāyaḥ*)

As the definition says, the state of entities between which inherence is established is described with two parts. One is "entities that do not exist separately (*ayutasiddha*)" and the other is "entities that [stand as] the superstratum and the substratum (*ādhāryādhārabhūta*)". The aim of this paper is to explore a little further into the conception of *ayutasiddha*, which is often translated into "inseparable",[3] in order to understand a new aspect of inherence from the viewpoint of the state of relata of inherence, referring to the commentaries on *PDhS*, *Vyomavatī* (*Vy*) of Vyomaśiva (*c.* 900-960), *Nyāyakandalī* (*NK*)

→ subsisting among things that are inseparable, standing to one another in the character of the container and the contained, – such relationship being the basis of the idea that 'this is in that'." Hirano (2009: 46) translates the inherence's definition in *PDhS* into: "The relation, which is a cause of the idea '[this is] here (this is in that)', between entities that are incapable of existing separately [and] that stand as the superstratum and the substratum, is inherence." In this paper, the translation has been modified based on the understanding that the word, *ādhāryādhārabhūtānāṁ*, modifies the word, *ayutasiddhānām*. Regarding the role of *-bhūta* as making attributive substantive in the compound, see Whitney (1997 [1924]: 493) and Tubb and Boose (2007: 167-68).

[3] Regarding the English equivalent for *ayutasiddha*, Jha (1982 [1915]: 32) and Ui (1917: 176 fn. 3) suggest, "things that are inseparable". D.N. Shastri (1976 [1964]: 380), Potter (ed.) (1995 [1997]: 283), and Bhattacharya (1994: 18) suggest, "inseparable"; Kannu (1992: 201), "inseparable things"; Halbfass (1993 [1992]: 147), "relata that are [. . .] incapable of existing separately"; B. Shastri (1993: 116), "inseparably connected"; and Kumar (2012: 34). "Two objects which are inseparable." Moreover, Jha (1982 [1915]: 35 n. 3) explains the word *ayutasiddha* as follows: the word *ayutasiddha* means that which is *known* (*siddha*) as *not separate* (*a-yuta*) – the word *yuta* being derived from the root *yu* to separate.

of Śrīdhara (*c*. 950–1000), and *Kiraṇāvalī* (*Kir*) of Udayana (*c*. 1050–1100).[4]

Yutasiddhi in *Padārthadharmasaṁgraha* and Its Commentaries

The conception of *ayutasiddha* can be literally translated into "entities that do not exist separately. Although *PDhS* itself does not explain this, the commentaries on *PDhS* do interpret it through the denial of the conception of *yutasiddha* in which *yutasiddhi* (separate existence) exists, so that to clarify the conception of *ayutasiddha* we should start from the investigation of *yutasiddhi*.

PDhS defines *yutasiddhi* in the chapter of disjunction (*vibhāga*) as follows:

> As to transient entities, on the other hand, separate existence [in two entities] means inhering [of the two entities or either of the two] in separate (*yuta*) loci. Since the sense of touch and the body [. . .] inhere in separate loci, conjunction with each other is established.[5]

According to the Vaiśeṣika theory, the sense of touch inheres in the atoms of air (*vāyu*) and the body inheres in the atoms of earth (*pr̥thivī*) which are separate from the atoms of air, so that separate existence is proved in the sense of touch and the body. As D.N. Shastri (1976 [1964]: 393-94) points out, however, the definition of *yutasiddhi* in *PDhS* is logically defective because the word "separate" (*yuta*) is used in the

---

[4] Although Mitra (1997: 220-23) has already considered inherence from the analysis of the concept of *ayutasiddha*, this paper explores more closely the same subject, referring to the materials he does not use.

[5] *PDhS*, nos. 191-92: *anityānāṁ tu yuteṣv āśrayeṣu samavāyo yutasiddhir iti. tvagindriyaśarīrayoḥ . . . yuteṣv āśrayeṣu samavāyo 'stīti paraspareṇa saṁyogaḥ siddhaḥ.*

definition of *yutasiddhi*[6] and the definition comes to apply to the case of a whole and its parts, where *yutasiddhi* is not proved.

The commentaries on *PDhS* show an interpretation of *yutasiddhi* (separate existence), which avoids the two defective points. First, *Vy* gives an interpretation of *yutasiddhi* in the chapter of disjunction as follows:

> As to transient entities, on the other hand, separate existence means inhering [of the two entities] in separate [or] different loci. [Objection:] Even so, separate existence would be in the parts and their whole, since [both] are inherent in separate loci. To be more explicit, since a whole subsists in the parts and the parts subsist in their parts, [the parts and their whole are] inherent in separate loci. [Reply:] This is not right, because the meaning [of *yutasiddhi*] is not understood at all. As a cloth is inherent in a different locus with exclusion of a pot and its locus, and a pot [is inherent in a different locus] with exclusion of a cloth and its locus, a whole is not inherent in a different locus with exclusion of the parts. Therefore, there is not separate existence [in the parts and their whole].[7]

Moreover, *Vy* mentions *yutasiddhi* in the same chapter:

---

[6] *PDhS* (no. 180) also shows the definition of *yutasiddhi* in the chapter of conjunction: *sā punar dvayor anyatarasya vā . . . pṛthagāśrayāśrayitvaṁ ceti.* (Moreover, it (separate existence) means [. . .] and the sate of residing of two [entities] or either of the two in different loci.) It must be noted here that Praśastapāda uses not the word *yuta* but *pṛthak*. Accordingly, we could not say that Praśastapāda had no awareness of the defective point.

[7] *Vy*, vol. II, 85,20-25: *anityānān tu yuteṣu pṛthagbhūteṣv āśrayeṣu samavāyo yutasiddhir iti. nanv evam api avayavāvayavinor yutāśrayasamavāyād yutasiddhiḥ syāt. tathā hi, avayavī avayaveṣu vartate avayavāś ca svāvayaveṣv iti yutāśrayasamavāyaḥ. na, abhiprāyāparijñānāt. yadā [yathā] ghaṭatadāśrayavyatirekeṇa āśrayāntare samavāyaḥ paṭasya, paṭatadāśrayavyatirekeṇa ghaṭasya naivam avayavino 'vayavavyatirekeṇa āśrayāntare samavāyaḥ, tasmān na yutasiddhiḥ.*

> The sense of touch and the body [. . .] have a separate existence, because both are inherent in their own locus only apart from each other.[8]

According to the objection, a whole and its parts are inherent in separate loci. For instance, a pot resides in its pot-shards and the pot-shards reside in their parts, i.e. clay. For the Vaiśeṣika, however, separate existence is not established in both of them. Vyomaśiva, therefore, amends the definition of *yutasiddhi* in *PDhS* by adding a word *itaretarāśrayaparihāreṇa* (apart from each other). The word can avoid the case of a whole and its parts since a whole (a pot) never exists apart from its parts (its pot-shards). Moreover, he uses the word *āśray<u>āntara</u>* (different locus) or *<u>svā</u>śraya* (its own locus) in his interpretation instead of *yuta*.

Second, *NK* mentions *yutasiddhi* in the chapter of disjunction:

> As to transient entities, separate existence means inhering of two [relata] or either of the two in a locus other than [a locus of the other] apart from each other.[9]

---

[8] *Vy*, vol. II, 86,7-10: *tvagindriyaśarīrayor . . . yutasiddhiḥ, tayor itaretarāśrayaparihāreṇa svāśrayeṣv eva samavāyāt*.

[9] *NK*, 160,11-12: *dvayor anyatarasya vā parasparaparihāreṇān-yatrāśraye samavāyo yutasiddhir anityānāṁ*. For this part, D.N. Shastri (1976 [1964]: 393-94) gives an explanation: "separability in the case of non-eternals is the *inherence* of one (of the related objects) in a different substratum of such a kind as excludes (even indirectly) the subsistence of the other therefrom. In the example of threads and cloth, although they subsist in their different substrata, as stated above, one of them (threads) subsist in its parts, viz. the fibres of cotton, from which (indirect) subsistence of cloth cannot be excluded." His explanation implies that the word *parasparaparihāreṇa* indicates the exclusion of subsistence of one relata in the locus of the other. However, my understanding of *parasparaparihāreṇa* is the exclusion of mutual subsistence, i.e. both relata are not loci of each other and exist in isolation leaving one another. The reason why I do not →

In the citation from *NK*, Śrīdhara shows a case of separate existence, i.e. inherence, of either of the two relata in a locus other than a locus of the other apart from each other. Such separate existence is between ether (*ākāśa*) and the flying bird since ether as eternal substance does not have a locus, whereas, the flying bird has a locus as its parts of the body.[10]

Moreover, *NK* also adduces the following argument in the chapter of inherence's definition to explain *yutasiddhi*:

> Separate existence (*yutasiddhi*) [means] different existence, different residence [in space], [or] the state, possessed by both of two relata, of residing in different loci apart from each other. It (separate existence) is not present between two entities that do not exist separately. The relation between those [two entities] is inherence. For instance, [there is inherence] between the threads and the cloth. Even if the threads inhere in a locus other than the cloth (i.e. the fibers of cotton, *aṁśus*), still both [the threads and the cloth] do not have the state of residing in different loci apart from each other, since the cloth resides in the threads only.[11] On the other hand, where both of two relata reside in distinct loci apart from each other,

---

→ accept his opinion is that a pot and its colour, which are regarded as *ayutasiddha* in the Vaiśeṣika theory, cannot be explained by his opinion. They subsist in their different substrata. A pot subsists in its pot-shards, and colour of the pot subsists in the pot. The point is that the subsistence of the pot's colour is or must be excluded from the pot-shards, since the colours of a whole and that of its parts are regarded as different in the Vaiśeṣika theory.

10 "Moreover, the [flying] bird as the other entity of a [flying] bird and ether, resides in a different locus." (*NK*, 160,13: *śakunyākāśayoś cānyatarasya śakuneḥ pr̥thagāśrayāśrayitvam*.)

11 *Ṭippaṇa* (p. 47,14; p. 48,9) of Naracandrasūri (*c.* 1210), which is a commentary on *NK*, comments on the words *paṭasya tantuṣv eva* as follows: *tantupaṭayor hi pr̥thagāśrayāśrayitvam asti tantūnāṁ svāvayavasamavetatvāt paṭasya tu tantusamavetatvāt paraṁ* →

> there is a separate existence [between the two relata]: for instance, between the sense of touch and the body. Indeed, the body dwells in the different locus, its own parts, apart from the sense of touch [. . .].[12]

Śrīdhara has put forward, more or less, the argument of Vyomaśiva with different words in order to avoid two logical defective points in the definition of *yutasiddhi* in *PDhS*: first, by adding a word *parasparaparihāreṇa* (apart from each other) in order to exclude the case of a whole and its parts. Second, he uses words *pṛthagāśrayāśrayitva* (the state of residing in a different locus), *vyatiriktāśrayāśrayitva* (the state of residing in a distinct locus), *pṛthagāśraya* (different locus), and *anyatrāśraya* (locus other than [a locus of the other]) in his interpretation instead of *yuta*.

Third, Udayana mentions in the chapter of disjunction in *Kir*:

> Separate existence means inhering of substances and so on in the different loci apart from each other.[13]

→ *parasparaparihāro nāsti paṭasya tantuṣv eva samavetatvāt.* (Indeed the threads and the cloth have the state of residing in different loci since the threads are inherent in their own parts and the cloth is inherent in its threads. However, (they) do not have [the state of being] "apart from each other" since the cloth is inherent in the threads only.)

12 *NK*, 14,9-16: *yutasiddhiḥ pṛthaksiddhiḥ pṛthagavasthitir ubhayor api sambandhinoḥ parasparaparihāreṇa pṛthagāśrayāśrayitvaṁ sā yayor nāsti tāv ayutasiddhau tayoḥ sambandhaḥ samavāyaḥ yathā tantupaṭayoḥ. yady api tantavaḥ paṭavyatiriktāśraye samavayanti tathāpy ubhayoḥ parasparaparihāreṇa pṛthagāśrayāśrayitvaṁ nāsti paṭasya tantuṣv evāśrayitvāt. yatra tu dvayor api sambandhinoḥ. parasparaparihāreṇa vyatiriktāśrayāśrayitvaṁ tatra yutasiddhiḥ yathā tvagindriyaśarīrayoḥ śarīraṁ hi tvagindriyaparihāreṇa pṛthagāśraye svāvayave samāśritaṁ . . . .* On the explanation of this part, see Bhattacharya (1994: 19).

13 *Kir*, 157,21-22: *parasparaparihāreṇa dravyādīnāṁ teṣu pṛthagbhūteṣv āśrayeṣu samavāyo yutasiddhir ity arthaḥ.*

According to these commentaries on *PDhS*, the meaning of *yutasiddhi*, as the case of transient entities, is understood as "inherence of entities (or one of them) in loci other than a locus of the other apart from each other". The interpretation by the commentaries commonly eludes the two logical defects in the definition of *yutasiddhi* in *PDhS*.

Ayutasiddha in the Commentaries on *PDhS*

As already stated, *PDhS* does not define *ayutasiddha*.[14] It is laid down by the denial of *yutasiddha* in the commentaries on *PDhS*. *Vy* says in the chapter of inherence's definition as follows:

> Those in which the separate existence (*yutasiddhi*) that is going to be stated later[15] exists are entities that exist separately (*yutasiddha*). And by denial of them (the entities that exist separately), the entities that do not exist separately (*ayutasiddha*) occur. [Then, inherence subsists] between them (the entities that do not exist separately).[16]

NK also offers a simple account for *ayutasiddha* through negation of *yutasiddhi*:

> [. . .] but [the word] *ayutasiddhānām* means "between entities

---

14 Regarding the concept of *ayutasiddha*, see B. Shastri (1993: 117-20).

15 Tubb and Boose (2007: 228) explain that "*vakṣyamāṇa* may mean 'to be stated by the *mūlakāra*'". My translation of this portion is dependent on their explanation. In fact, Praśastapāda, being the *mūlakāra*, mentions the concept of separate existence (*yutasiddhi*) in the chapter of disjunction (*vibhāga*) of *PDhS* (no. 190-93). Note that there is a possibility that *vakṣyamāṇa* may refer to the commentator's own work, see Tubb and Boose (2007: 230).

16 *Vy*, vol. I, 26,2-3: *yutasiddhir vakṣyamāṇā, sā vidyate yeṣāṁ te yutasiddhās tanniṣedhena cāyutasiddhās teṣām iti.*

that do not reside in different loci apart from each other".[17]

According to *Vy*, those in which *yutasiddhi* exists are *yutasiddha*, i.e. entities (or one of them) that inhere in loci other than a locus of the other apart from each other, and *ayutasiddha* is defined negatively by such entities (*yutasiddha*). To put the matter simply, *ayutasiddha* is defined as entities that do *not* have the state of inhering in loci other than a locus of the other apart from each other. Here we could assume three cases of the meaning of *ayutasiddha* from the point where negative prefix *a-* of *a-yutasiddha* qualifies in the conception of *yutasiddha*,[18] i.e. entities (relata) that inhere in loci other than a locus of the other apart from each other. In the first case, the negative prefix qualifies "other than". In the second case it refers to "apart from each other", and in the third case it does both.

In the first case, *ayutasiddha* means entities that inhere in the *same* locus, apart from each other. In the second, it means entities that inhere in loci other than a locus of the other *without* being apart from the other. In the third, it means entities that inhere in the *same* locus *without* being apart from each other.

For the first case, we can show examples from *Vy*, i.e. "largeness (*mahattva*) in ether (*ākāśa*) and the articulated word 'largeness' (*mahattvaśabda*) for largeness in ether", under the relation of the denoted and the denoter (*vācyavācakabhāva*).[19]

---

[17] *NK*, 15,8-9: . . . *kiṁ tv ayutasiddhānām iti parasparaparihāreṇa pr̥thagāśrayānāśritānām ity arthaḥ.*

[18] Here I do not mean to inquire which negative prefix *a-* of *ayutasiddha* qualifies *yuta* or *siddha* in the word *ayutasiddha*. I mean to inquire where it qualifies with regard to meaning. Regarding the argument of the former, see *NK* (pp. 14,25-15,11) and Hirano (2012: 94-96).

[19] *Vy*, vol. I, 26,5-7: *tathā hy ākāśamahattvam ākāśe samavetaṁ mahattvaśabdavācyam ity ākāśamahattvatacchabdayor vācyavācakabhāvaḥ sambandho na ca yutasiddhir vibhinnāśrayasamavāyit-* →

As well, there is "desire (*icchā*) in a soul and consciousness of desire (*icchālambanavijñāna*) in the soul", under the relation of an object and the cognition of the object (*viṣayaviṣayibhāva*).[20] According to the Vaiśeṣika theory, "largeness" in ether and the articulated word "largeness" are qualities, and both of them inhere in the same locus, i.e. ether. The relation of the denoted and the denoter is found between "largeness" and the articulated word "largeness" and both relata are regarded as entities that inhere in the same locus apart from each other. With regard to the example of desire and consciousness of desire, both are qualities, and both inhere in the same locus, i.e. soul. The relation of an object and the cognition of the object is found between them, and both relata are regarded as entities that inhere in the same locus apart from each other.[21]

For the second case, a whole and its parts are applicable. For instance, a cloth as a whole and its threads as its parts are regarded as the entities that inhere in loci other than a locus

→ *vābhāvāt. tathā hy ākāśamahattvam ākāśe samavetaṁ tadvācakaś ca śabdas tatraivety ayutasiddhatvam.* Regarding the explanation and translation of this portion, see Hirano (2012: 32-33, 74-76).

20 *Vy*, vol. I, 26,8-9: *evam icchādyālambanaṁ vijñānam ātmani samavetam icchādayaś ca tatraivety ayutasiddhatve saty eṣāṁ viṣayaviṣayibhāva. . . .* Regarding the explanation and translation of this portion, see Hirano (2012: 32-33, 74-76).

21 We can take as an example for the first case *ayutasiddha* from *NK*. "[. . .] that which is the relation of merit (*dharma*) and pleasure (*sukha*), which has a character of the relationship of cause and effect, would also come to be inherence since there is no separate existence between those two [merit and pleasure] that are residing in the same soul." (*NK*, 14,19-20 . . . *dharmasya sukhasya ca yaḥ kāryakāraṇabhāvalakṣaṇaḥ sambandhaḥ so 'pi samavāyaḥ prāpnoti tayor ātmaikāśritayor yutasiddhyabhāvāt.*) Regarding the translation and explanation of the portion, see Hirano (2012: 91-92). Based on the same example in *NK*, Mitra (1997: 222) points out that "it does not follow that all relations holding between inseparable pairs are *samavāya*".

of the other without being apart from the other. The cloth inheres in its threads and the threads inhere in its cotton fibres. Therefore, the cloth and its threads inhere or reside in different loci. But the cloth does not exist apart from its parts. Accordingly, both the cloth and its threads are entities that inhere in different loci without being apart from the other.

In the third case of *ayutasiddha*, entities are understood to inhere in the *same* locus *without* being apart from each other. However, there is no conclusive proof to make an example for such entities as in the third *ayutasiddha* in accordance with the Vaiśeṣika ontology. At least, such examples as the third case of *ayutasiddha* are not found in the arguments of *yutasiddhi* and *ayutasiddha* in the commentaries on *PDhS*.

Conclusion

To know the state of entities in which inherence is established will lead us to know the conception of inherence itself. *Ayutasiddha*, which is one of the definitions of inherence, could be literally translated into "entities that do not exist separately". As to transient entities, however, the state of *ayutasiddha* which consists in the direct negation of *yutasiddha* or in the indirect negation of *yutasiddhi* (separate existence), is not one but diverse. It depends on where it is denied by negative prefix in the conception of *yutasiddha*: entities or one of them that inhere in loci other than a locus of the other apart from each other.

Among the three states of *ayutasiddha*, each of which shows different world structure, inherence is proved in the entities that inhere in loci other than a locus of the other *without* being apart from the other.[22] Therefore, such entities are often

---

22 *Ayutasiddha* is a part of the definition of *inherence* in *PDhS* and is interpreted by *Vy* and *NK* as entities that do not have the state of *inhering* in different loci apart from each other. Accordingly, we can point out a logical defective point where the defined property →

translated and explained with the words, "inseparable entities".[23] If it were so by a reason why one entity never exists apart from the other (independently of the other),[24] "inseparable entities" is not proper for the entities inhere in the *same* locus, apart from each other. It will thus appear that all cases of *ayutasiddha* are not regarded as "inseparable entities", and the relation between entities in the state of *ayutasiddha* is not always inherence.

Acknowledgement

I would like to thank Dr. Matthew Pelowski for correcting my English.

References

PRIMARY SOURCES

Kiraṇāvalī (*Kir*) of Udayana, in *Praśastapādabhāṣyam with the Commentary Kiraṇāvalī of Udayanācārya*, ed. J.S. Jetly, Gaekwad's Oriental Series 154, Vadodara: Oriental Institute, Reprint, 1991.

Nyāyakandalī (O) of Śrīdhara, in *Nyāyakandalī Being a Commentary on Praśastapādabhāṣya, with Three Sub-commentaries*, ed. J.S. Jetly and Vasant G. Parikh, Gaekwad's Oriental Series 174, Vadodara: Oriental Institute, 1991.

NK: *Nyāyakandalī* (S).

Nyāyakandalī (S) of Śrīdhara, in *the Praśastapāda Bhāṣya with Commentary Nyāyakandalī of Śrīdhara*, ed. Vindhyesvari Prasad Dvivedin, Sri Garib Dass Oriental Series 13, Delhi: Sri Satguru Publications, 1984.

Padārthadharmasaṁgraha (*PDhS*) of Praśastapāda, in Bronkhorst and Ramseier (1994).

Ṭippaṇa of Naracandrasūri, see *Nyāyakandalī* (O).

→ (inherence) is included in the interpretation of the definition of inherence. On this point, see Hirano (2011).

[23] See n. 3.

[24] See D.N. Shatri (1976 [1964]: 379-80), B. Shastri (1993: 120), and Bhattacharya (1994: 18).

Vyomavatī (*Vy*) of Vyomaśiva, in *Vyomavatī of Vyomaśivācārya*, ed. with the *Praśastapādabhāṣya* by Gaurinath Sastri, 2 vols., M.M. Śivakumāraśāstrī-granthamālā 6, Varanasi: Sampurnanand Sanskrit University, 1983, 1984.

SECONDARY LITERATURE

Bhattacharya, Tushar Kanti, 1994, *Samavāya and the Nyāya-Vaiśeṣika Realism*, Calcutta: Sanskrit Pustak Bhandar.

Bronkhorst, Johannes and Yves Ramseier, 1994, *Word Index to the Praśastapādabhāṣya: A Complete Word Index to the Printed Editions of the Praśastapādabhāṣya*, Delhi: Motilal Banarsidass.

Halbfass, Wilhelm, 1993 (1992), *On Being and What There Is*, Sri Garib Dass Oriental Series 168, 1st Indian edn., Delhi: Sri Satguru Publications.

Hirano, Katsunori, 2011, "Vaishesika Gakuha no *samavāya* to *ayutasiddha*" (on *samavāya* and *ayutasiddha* in the Vaiśeṣika), *Journal of Indian and Buddhist Studies*, **60**(1): 315-20 (in Japanese).

———, 2012, *Nyāya-Vaiśeṣika Philosophy and Text Science*, Delhi: Motilal Banarsidass.

Jha, Gaṅgāṇātha, 1982 (1915), *Padārthadharmasaṁgraha of Praśastapāda, with the Nyāyakandalī of Śrīdhara* (English Translation), Chaukhambha Oriental Studies 4, repr., Varanasi/ Delhi: Chaukhambha Orientalia.

Kumar, Shashiprabha, 2013, *Classical Vaiśeṣika in Indian Philosophy: On Knowing and What Is to Be Known*, London and New York: Routledge.

Mitra, Madhabendra Nath, 1997, "Samavāya and the Relation of Predication", in Sukharanjan Saha (ed.), *Essays in Indian Philosophy*, Calcutta: Jadavpur University and New Delhi: Allied Publishers, pp. 213-32.

Potter, K.H. (ed.), 1995a (1970), *Encyclopedia of Indian Philosophies*, vol. I: *Bibliography*, 3rd rev. edn., Delhi: Motilal Banarsidass.

———, 1995b (1977), *Encyclopedia of Indian Philosophies*, vol. II: *Indian Metaphysics and Epistemology: The Tradition of Nyāya-Vaiśeṣika up to Gaṅgeśa*, repr., Delhi: Motilal Banarsidass.

Shastri, Biswanarayan, 1993, *Samavāya Foundation of Nyāya-Vaiśeṣika Philosophy*, Delhi: Sharada Publishing House.

Shastri, Dharmendra Nath, 1976 (1964), *The Philosophy of Nyāya-*

Vaiśeṣika and Its Conflict with the Buddhist Dignāga School: Critique of Indian Realism, repr., Delhi/Varanasi: Bharatiya Vidya Prakashan.

Tubb, G.A. and E.R. Boose, 2007, *Scholastic Sanskrit: A Manual for Students*, New York: The American Institute of Buddhist Studies at Columbia University.

Whitney, W.D., 1997 (1924), *Sanskrit Grammar*, Delhi: Motilal Banarsidass.

13

Mantric Effect, Effervescent Devatās, Noetic Supplications, and Apūrva in the Mīmāṁsā

Purushottama Bilimoria

Is what the Pūrva-Mīmāṁsakas are preoccupied with tantamount to what in pre-modern and modern parlance we call "prayer" and "worship"? If not, what else is significant about its conceptualization and hermeneutic praxis as read in the post-modern moment of subreption? Has it something to say to us late-moderns? Has it some "gift" for the perplexed post-modern world read in hindsight *as if* in a moment of transgressive bafflement? Or are we, *after*-Mīmāṁsā, as Heidegger in a moment of deep lament and (in)finite resignation put it, "Too late for the gods, too early for God"? I nuance this question in the background of comments such as that by the late Wilhelm Halbfass, that the Pūrva-Mīmāṁsā, in its exegetical defence of the Vedic sacrificial *dharma* as the principal purpose of inquiry into language into the period of the classical philosophical systems, carried with it "a set of pre-Upaniṣadic notions and ways of thinking which may appear obsolete in the new atmosphere".[1]

---

[1] Halbfass, "Karma, Apūrva, and 'Natural' Causes: Observations on the Growth and Limits of the Theory of Saṁsāra", in Wendy Doniger O'Flaherty (ed.), *Karma and Rebirth in Classical Indian* →

Let us start with *ṛta*, the Vedic concept of normative ordering that corresponds in likeness to the cosmic order, "that world" (*āmuṣmika*) "three-fourths" of which remain hidden or unmanifest from the purview of "this worldly" reality (*aihika, bhū*). As we know from *Ṛgveda*, "the cycles of day and night, the succession of the seasons, and the cycles of birth, growth, and decay and regeneration all proceed from *ṛta*".[2] *Ṛta*, then, embodies the rhythm of existence and the dynamic onto-cosmological principle of all movements and transformations, within and without. To maintain and sustain the order *in toto* all beings are obliged to act in harmony and accord with the originary *ṛta*. *Yajña* is the ritual embodiment of *ṛta*. In time, the requisite actions, pre-eminently sacrificial, came to be constellated under the overarching normative concept of *dharma*, that which "holds together, supports, and sustains" the structuration of existence, the universe as an independent whole, and grounds the moral and social actions of the people to adhere to the Vedic wisdom. To that extent *dharma* does have an ethical dimension that emphasizes knowing one's place in the world; there is also a performative element to *dharma* – as there is for the concept of *Li* in Confucian thought – which bears out in the practice of rites and rituals. But of course, the acts themselves, as the many *yajña*s, can be rather complex and with varied significations and rules governing their proper performance. This calls for interpretation or hermeneutics so that there is an unmistakable understanding of the purpose and time, and place and the most effective discharge of the duty-like performatives: *itikartavyatā* (procedure).

→ *Traditions*, Berkeley, Los Angeles, London: University of California Press, and Chicago: University of Chicago Press, 1980, pp. 268-302, esp. p. 273.

2 John Koller, "From Ṛta to Dharma" in Bimal K. Matilal and P. Bilimoria (eds.), *Sanskrit and Related Studies*, Delhi: Indian Book Centre, 1990, p. 84.

And so Jaimini (400–200 BCE) sets about systematizing the thinking on the art of sacrifice and its attendant *dharma* significations: just what does it mean to say "one must perform sacrifice with the Citrā ritual on such and such a moon-night phase"? What is the power behind its efficacy when the act is properly executed, etc.? And what is the *topoi* or true signification of the deity (*devatā*) invoked? In other words, in what grammatical taxonomy does *devatā* that gets a mention in the injunction (*vidhi*) or in the accompanying *mantra* reside or hide, and what indeed is its ontological status? Is its reference internal (noetic/psychological) or is it external (ontic/ontological), or is merely in the word? Uncovering the deeper contours of the ritual geography requires as much an epistemological if not simply the linguistic-hermeneutical excavation of the epistemé of *dharma*. The Vedas are believed to be composed of *vākya*s (discrete sentences) (not exactly equivalent but the approximation should do for our purposes); in fact, they are referred to as *codanā*s, which are *vidhi* (injunctive statements), close to what we in modern times call, imperatives, not unlike prudential commands, sometimes expressed in conditional forms, e.g. if you desire *X* you should do *Y*.

Indeed, inasmuch as *dharma* embeds the definitional matrix of *yajña*: hence *athāto dharma jijñāsā* (now, therefore, the enquiry into *dharma*), and the opening salvo in Jaimini's *Mīmāṁsā-Sūtra* regales us with: *codanālakṣaṇo 'rtho dharma*? (now, therefore, the definition of injunction/duty). Jaimini believed that such an enquiry can only proceed not with ratiocination but a decisive investigation into the function of language as a valid *pramāṇa* (means of knowing) and hence the entire meaning of the Vedic utterances or basic sentences can be summed up in this cryptic proposition. The enquiry is as much into the procedural workings of language as it is in the principal rhetorical term of enquiry, namely, *dharma*.

Dharma is defined by that which is known as *codanā*, and *codanā* (as later commentators like Śabara explain) refers to a particular kind of the imperative sentence (*vidhi*), "the ought" that incites one toward action,[3] that is indicative of *dharma*. Secular imperative sentence just would not do (although the *pramāṇa*-hermeneutical epistemography applies by extension as much to its testimonial iteration as well, since all discourses are compoundedly composed of sentences *qua vākya*); the necessary condition is that it be a ritual imperative, and the sufficient condition is that it be Vedic and *apauruṣeya* (trans-personal) or *alaukika* expression (otherwise it would not be a *pramā*). Later commentators were concerned to bring out the nuance of *artha* – the purpose or the goal of ritual – in this formulaic definition of *dharma* by extending its scope beyond the simple linguistic metonymy to that of moral praxis. As the *Arthasaṁgraha*, states: "*dharma* is sacrifice, etc."[4] (or *yāga*). The "etc." includes chanting (*japa*), austerity (*tapas*), and charity (*dāna*). But since not all sacrifices are desirable (in fact, some are positively undesirable), the same author adds: "*dharma* must be a desirable matter which serves some purpose (*prayojanavadārtho dharma*)".[5] A second definition along the same lines of the just preceding ones runs as follows: "*dharma* is that from which well-being (*abhyudaya*) and the highest good (*niḥśreyasa*) come about".[6] The soteriological significance of *nihśreyasa* is particularly underscored by Śabara, one of the first commentators on the *Mīmāṁsā-Sūtra*. An answer to the question "what is

---

[3] *codanā iti hi kriyāyāḥ pravartakaṁ vavanamāhuḥ* । – Laugākaṣī Bhāskara, *Arthasaṁgraha*, ed. A.B. Gajendragadkar and R.D. Karmarkar, Delhi: Motilal Banarsidass, 1998.

[4] *yāgadireva dharmaḥ* । – ibid.

[5] *prayojanavadārtho dharma iti* ।

[6] *yato 'bhyudayaniḥśreyasasiddhiḥ* । – Kaṇāda, *Vaiśeṣikasūtra*.

dharma?" – which abandons the project of defining it – is this: "*dharma* is that which the cultivated persons (*āryāḥ*) praise when it is done, and *adharma* is that which they condemn when it is done".[7]

This is how Mohanty represents the common structure regarding "incitement to action" – a structure, he says, that is accepted by all thinkers in the Indian tradition:

Knowledge →	desire →	will to →	motor effect →	the action
(*jñāna*)	(*cikīrṣā*)	(*pravṛtti*)	(*ceṣṭā*)	(*kārya*)

Knowledge produces desire, desire produces the will-to-do, this in turn produces actual motor effort, the consequence of which is the action as a completed performance.[8]

Let me switch for a moment to Saussurean deconstructionist language and explain some of the terms and process involved here. The *signifier* (represented by Sr, with its *liñ* + *dhātu* [action-verbal form]) is linked to the subtle medium of "phonemes" (*varṇa*s = sound-letters) which in turn as a collective (morpheme) is recalled/illuminated (*abhivyaṅgya*) by the traces (*saṁskāras*) left behind by the sound-image (*dhvani*) or, secondarily, by the graphic image (*lipi*) and other modes of materiality which awaken the meanings by this supplementary process (by first arousing *śābdībhāvanā*, impulse for *śabda*, the literal grasping). *Varṇasamūhaḥ* (combination of "sound-letters") gives us

[7] *yam tu āryāḥ kriyamānam praṣansanti sa dharmaḥ yam garhante so 'dharmaḥ – Āpastamba-Dharmasūtra* | 1.30.7

[8] J.N. Mohanty, "Dharma, Imperatives, and Tradition: Toward an Indian Theory of Moral Action", in P. Bilimoria, J. Prabhu and Renuka Sharma (eds.), *Indian Ethics Classical and Contemporary Challenges*, vol. I, New Delhi: Oxford University Press, 2008, pp. 57-78, esp. p. 60.

words related to their respective semantic contents; combination of words (and related word-meanings) in a syntactical order gives us sentences (*vākya*, the unit of which is a *yajuṣ*); and the combination of sentences produces text. Since the syntactical formation yields sentence-meaning (*ekavākyārtha*), requiring for its fulfilment various conditions, grammatical rules, metaphorical transfiguration, intentional re-arrangement, and so on.

Furthermore, it is the overall signified (in a more composite expression) that governs the performative function of speech. Curiously, one does not have to be kept waiting for the textual cipher: an urge or impulse (*bhāvanā*) towards a potential signified (the purpose, or end – *artha* – as in *puruṣārtha*s, though not restricted to the generic foursome, it could be a specified object of desire) may be enough to propel one to action (*ārthībhāvanā*). And if we agree to return to *artha* the magical sense, incantational potency of *mantra*s, then we move it away from "concept" or the *idea* as the pure signified, the intelligible within spoken sign, and we then have a system of signs-rhythms, silences, gestures, noises – which is not exhausted by logical speech or rational discourse. But I am straying here, for I want to return to the linguistic ramifications of this position, not its anti-metaphysical ruses as such, apart from the agnosticism implied in the paradoxical transcendentalism of *apūrva*.

To illustrate this remark via an illustration, suppose we take the injunctive expression (*vidhi*) "whosoever desires *svarga* [heaven] should perform an *agniṣṭoma* ritual for Agni (*agniṣṭomayāgaṁ yajeta agnaye svargakāmaḥ*)". Without concerning ourselves with the syntax, we notice here a string of signs, which breaks up into the signifiers, basically, as the *liṅ* + *dhātu*, *kāraka* (which is neutral in the instrumental case), etc. the dative *agnaye*, and the signifieds *qua kāma* as the twofold *bhāvanā*s or impulses (efficiencies), namely, the "performative task" *yāga* and *phala* (*svarga*, in this instance, but it could be cows, rains, sons, and another longed for). More technically, the injunctive suffix conveys *śābdībhāvanā*, also called *pravartanā* or *preraṇā* (directing, imploring, impelling). It prompts one as to what is to be done. The inducement itself is called *ārthībhāvanā*, i.e. *pravṛtti*, that evokes gnostic or *intellectus* episode, i.e. a particular noetic imaginary. *Yāga* is its *karaṇa* (instrument) and *svarga* its *bhāvya*; and *apūrva*, the withheld cumulative social security in the person, or with Internal Revenue Services, ITO, over which the gods of the Oval wage wars on the perceived *asuraloka*s.

However, *phala* (outcome), is not actually observed or is not forthcoming in the sacrifice itself, for it is the outcome, albeit in deferral traces in some possible world. What this implies is that the two complementary *bhāvanā*s in turn become signifiers portending a third signified: namely, *apūrva*, the "hitherto unprecedented" efficiency (efficacy as *potentiate*), this is the "transcendental signified", which remains *adṛṣṭārtha* (literally, "unseen effect"), its presentation is thus postponed, and its signifier is crossed-out, seamlessly.

A word on the "transcendental" and the "instrumental" case. *Apūrva*, however, is "transcendental" (but not in a *kūṭastha*, absolute or unchanging sense) only in a provisional and operational (*taṭastha*) sense, for its significance is not so much in being *adṛṣṭatva* or even *astitva* (is-ness) as in being a mysterious result "which has nothing before it" (literally what *apūrva* means), or being without a preceding instance, i.e. in its novelty and prior unknownness or elusiveness (it has no prāmāṇic-generatable *jñātatā*), and so also in its near-empirical givenness for it retains the phenomenality of the *almost certain phala* (result/effect) – a reality that is productive of itself *qua auto-poesies*, or what David Lewis called the enigma of elusive knowledge strung mid-way between the possible and the actual world – *antarikṣa*. It is by a certain feat of what Kant had called in the aesthetic of the sublime "*subreption*", "a clandestine metalepsis" in Gayatri Chakravorty Spivak's terms, in which there is isolation of a moment of transgression or bafflement in a text, that entails the substitution of an "effect for a cause".[9] What is important therefore, when the facticity of the transgressive sign – the self-erasing signifier – is realized, is the "effect" not the cause as such (for there is no other or transcendental signified as an "extra effect" – hence my choice or coinage of the neologism, "*mantric effect*"). Here the cause is of no real effect or *consequence*, or that the cause is in the effect, the antecedent, itself as by the law of *satkāryavāda,* just as for the Mīmāṁsā epistemology the conditions of the validity ("truth-bearing" effect) of a cognition (*jñāna*) is constitutively given or inherent in the conditions and causes for the possibility of the cognition itself (by their thesis of the little understood *svataḥprāmāṇyavāda*).

Elsewhere, in the Chinese tradition, by a parity of distant analogy, *Ziran* in Daoist thought follows its own course, in a state that is dynamic, but its truth remains hidden. Furthermore, *apūrva* will erase its smoky traces the moment the entitative *phala* has found maturity or manifestation, is born or issued. Hence, once again, the result or substantive *phala* in this actual world functions as the signifier for the deferred but now-imminent signified, namely, *svarga,* and which too, like its polar signifier, *devatā* – even though the latter signifier is usually in the dative – has no ultimate or absolute ontological status in the Mīmāṁsā episteme, whose (*svarga*'s) significance possibly extends to no more than beyond an inner state of happiness (comparable to Aristotle's ideal of *eudemonia*) in this lifetime or in another birth, or

[9] Gayatri Chakravorty Spivak, *A Critique of Postcolonial Reason: Toward a History of the Vanishing Present,* Cambridge: Harvard University Press, 1999, pp. xiii and 98.

something to be consumed, and so its self-identity is eroded. And of course, *apūrva* can be compromised or annulled by taking a wrong step — *bhāda* — in the sacrifice or some specific code and prescribed performative rule is not followed to the tee. What is interesting is that *apūrva,* which has no sign for it in the expression itself, and so it cannot achieve reference to itself, self-reflexively or otherwise, remains yet the "hidden" (*avyakta*), unmanifest and "not yet visible"; still, it does succeed in achieving signification, though at the upper split level, i.e. as the pure signified. We will notice that the loci of this significance, indeed of the overall signification, is the *vacana* (the utterance itself), not the *vācaka* (the utterer, or speaker) (there need be none), given that in the theory the utterance has its own syntagmatic and metonymic force, coupled with the *mantra* (about which more shortly). The hearer's intention (*bhāvanā*), induced here, is more important than any reference, directly or implicitly, to that of the *auctor, "author"*. Hence the jurisprudential impersonality of the interpretive or hermeneutic process, with two overall implications: (i) that the Mīmāṁsā eschews any attempt to forge a direct, unmediated link between textuality and ritual, or word and action (the empty third space is kept on hold via the mediation of the transcendental signified, *apūrva as the "mantric effect"*), and (ii) it eschews any role of an intermediary personal agency, be that of a *devatā* (another out-of-this-world hearer or witness) or the utterer (but for his interlocutory help, *purohita* (the priest), *yajamāna* (the sponsoring patron), and such functionaries.

Devatā and Mantra

Having elucidated *dharma, vidhi, phala,* and *apūrva,* we now move to the other three Sg/Sd here, viz. *devatā, mantra,* and *arthavāda.*

I have been long worried about the status and role of *devatā* in this ritual soteriology, and why the familiar ideas like the "Lord" (*Īśvara*), and "yogic perception" (*yogī-pratyakṣa*), are marginalized in the Mīmāṁsā discourse? What price, one might wonder, the preoccupation with the efficacy of Vedic rituals? Halbfass gives us an interesting clue – his concern is with tracing the genealogy of the theory of *karma*'s causality in Indian thought; nevertheless, the ramifications for us are profound:

> [T]he efficiency of the Vedic rituals entails its own special and "trans-karmic" (or rather "proto-karmic") causality . . ..

And here Halbfass couldn't resist recourse to the concept of *apūrva*, which he describes *à la* Kumārila as "that particular "potency" which gathers and stores the efficacy of the Vedic rituals and makes it possible for transitory sacrificial performances to have lasting effects in distant future."[10]

The inference for the facticity of *apūrva* is based on *arthāpatti* "circumstantial inference", or "negative implication",[11] and yet the instrumentality of the Vedic action in respect of the causal efficiency is never deferred to a personal agency, such as a *devatā* or *Īśvara*, whose names may well be invoked, but as "*nominens*": "the rectification of names"; various auxiliary actions also contribute to specific units of *apūrva* to yield the final and comprehensive *apūrva* of the complete sacrifice, which in turn (as we saw earlier) corresponds to the unity and totality of the result, for example, *svarga*.[12] But is it not that in popular Vedic understanding it is the gods who collect the

---

[10] Halbfass, 1980, op. cit., p. 274 (from Kumārila's *apūrvādhikaraṇa* in *Tantravārttika*, see n. 11).

[11] This *prāmāṇika* view of Kumārila is discussed at length in a rejoinder to grammarians and Buddhists by Toshiya Unebe in his paper "'Apūrva','Devatā', and 'Svarga': Arguments on Words Denoting Imperceptible Objects", *Journal of Indian Philosophy*, 2011, (**39**): 535-52.

[12] Ibid., p. 276.

essential offerings (*dāna, tyāgavastu*) in the sacrifice in the invisible realms and safeguard the marked potency therein for their fructification in a time appropriate by their own cosmic clock? Śaṅkara in his *Bhāṣya* defends the proposition that several gods are able to descend at the same time (wherever their prior temporal location or attendance elsewhere) to the site of a sacrifice, which makes Śaṅkara a perfect modal logician: arguing for an indivisible and indefeasible temporal instantiation in a spatial singularity of varied possible worlds.

That might be so, but Kumārila Bhaṭṭa rejects this proposition and ultimately resorts to *ātman* (soul) of the initiator or sponsoring patron of the sacrifice – although, as Halbfass quickly clarifies, *apūrva* remains for him a potency (*yogyatā*) generated by, and in a sense belonging to, not the sacrificing person, but the principal sacrifice (*pradhāna karman*) itself (*ālayayajña*). "The causal potencies created and left behind by the sacrificial acts remain present as traces or dispositions (*saṁskāra*) in the person who performed them; according to Kumārila, there is no other possible substratum in which they could inhere"; these are Kumārila's exact words: *yadi svasamavetā-eva śaktir iṣyeta karmaṇām, tadvināśe tato na syāt, kartr̥sthā tu na naśyati.*[13] All other placement or markers of agency as it were vanish with the self-efficacious action. (This modality may not extend to non-Vedic, or secular, actions; but that is not our concern here.)

Halbfass sums up this insight in a rather crisp passage (and for such insightful articulation he, like Frits Staal, will be well remembered in the scholastic circles for long):

> There seems to be a basic assumption that if Vedic rites, including all subsidiary acts, are performed in strict

---

[13] Kumārila's *Tantravārttika* and *Ṭupṭīkā*, ed. Kashinath Vasudeva Abhyankar and Gangesa Sastri Joshi, 4 vols., 2nd edn., Poona: ASS (1927) 1970-74, p. 369; Halbfass, p. 277 n. 32.

> accordance with the Vedic rules, they will not fail to produce their proper results. Sacrificial, "apūrvic" causality seems to operate within a finite and well-defined set of conditions, a kind of closed system, in which it seems to be secure from outside interference: in bringing about its assigned result, the power of sacrifice, that is, *apūrva*, will prevail over other possible influences, including those which might arise from the general karmic status of the sacrificer.[14]

And he continues with these final remarks:

> The sacrificer gestures to the official act of initiating the sacrifice (*utsarga*); the actual performances themselves may be left to the "paid agents". "I give to the sacrifice in order that it may give back."[15]

Hence the question of personal authorship (as much of the sacrifice at hand) and responsibility is less important here:

> what produces *apūrva* is rather the impersonal power of the sacrifice itself, which is only unleashed, activated during the actual performance of the sacrifice. *Apūrva* may be stored and coordinated by the soul [as food in a camel]; yet it is not merely and not even primarily a quality or subordinate ingredient of the soul; it is and remains the effect and the stored power of the sacrifice. — Ibid.

In the accompanying footnote Halbfass comments: "the *puruṣa* is not the *sādhana* (material means) of the result to be effected, *sādhya*."

In more phenomenological terms, the sponsor of the sacrifice is addressed by something external to him (the ritual efficacy, *kārya*): he is even appealed to, by the imagery of the *devatās*, and he finds himself always in the dative case, the

[14] Kumārila's *Tantravārttika* and *Ṭupṭīkā*, p. 277.

[15] Ibid., p. 282.

grammatical case of someone being spoken to by another. Husserl's technical term for this relation between phenomenon and knower (subject) is *Gegebenheit* (givenness); and in a pregnant phrase in his *Idea of Phenomenology* he wrote that absolute *givenness* is a final term. . . .[16] My discovery here is that the true "*dative*" – note its alliteration with *devatā* – is the subject-knower-doer, by the law of divine anti-gravitational negativation.

There is a question whether the taxonomic analysis applies to all "ought" injunctions, i.e. categorical imperatives, or largely to "optional" ones (*kāmyakarman*), conditional/ prudential imperatives, of the kind "if you so desire . . ." or "it might be prudent to . . ."? For Prabhākara (the elder colleague to Kumārila), *apūrva* is not of the same concern as the core of the Vedic injunctions; it is not about the instrumentality or even the desire motivating the undertaking (*iṣṭasādhanatā*, nor *iṣṭakāmanā*), but rather about the entitlement (*adhikāra*) and intent of performing it as a matter of "duty" (*kāryatā: "this is my task"*), which carries its own purpose (*prayojana*) or goal (*bhāvya*). The Prābhākaras align the significance of the Vedic injunction, which to them is the acme of "verbal testimony" or *śabdapramāṇa* (the pre-eminence of language as an exclusive and *sui generis* means of knowing), to three aspects: (i) *niyoga*, i.e. the directive; (ii) *kārya*, the noetic structure of what is to be accomplished; and (iii) *apūrva* – which they identify with *kārya* itself, which according to Śālikanātha is the import of the injunction in Jaimini's *Codanāsūtra*. And he invoked one Bādari as stating that *kārya* produces the result, i.e. *svarga*. Supplemental to this is *kriyā*, the physical event, the actual act of performing the *yāga*. *Kriyā* does not produce the

[16] Paul J. Griffiths, *The Vice of Curiosity: An Essay on Intellectual Appetite*, Winnipeg, Manitoba: Canadian Mennonite University, 2006, p. 37.

result as such. *Yāga* is both the subject and instrument of *kārya;* but "*yāga*" *qua* "*kriyā*" is a temporal event, it vanishes with the smoke. What remains is *kārya,* when accomplished, in the self of *niyojya.* That you might desire heaven (*svarga*) merely entitles or qualifies you to take the initiative (*niyoga*); thereafter, it is the "work of sacrifice" (compare Luce Irigaray's "work of gifting", or Derrida's "work of mourning") as *kāryatājñāna* not *kriyā; svarga* is of secondary importance, a spin-off as it were. *Apūrvabhāvanā* and *phalabhāvanā* are coterminous terms in this theory, because they reject the two other polar-*bhāvanā* theory, *ārthī,* and *śābdī,* of Kumārila's. Hence the concept of *kārya* or efficacy performs an important limiting function on the Vedic fixation with ritual propriety, and thereby goes a considerable way to de-legitimizing desire and *devatā*-based *yāga,* and permits only the *niyoga*-type.

K.T. Pandurangi explains:

> The *kārya* is more an ethical concept than a ritualistic concept. Even if taken as a ritualistic concept, it has to be taken out of [the] empirical level and has to be looked upon as [having] a mystical or transcendental value. Achieving such mystical efficacy of Vedic rituals is the goal of performing Vedic rituals. The other benefits are by-products.[17]

This echoes the Confucian dictum that *Li* (arguably a cognate of *kārya* as "rite") must be internalized, for it is not simply rituals which, if acted out correctly, ensures that a person is benevolent and human (*ren*). It must become an internal act, a noetic supplication indeed. Mencius saw *Li* as an internal aspect much more than a rite of action. *Li* becomes internalized, integrated as part of the person, so much so that the rites are acted out without thought: rather, they are

---

[17] K.T. Pandurangi, *Prakaraṇapañcikā* [= *PPK*] *of Śālikanātha Miśra,* with an exposition in English, ICPR, 2004, pp. xvi-xvii.

manifested in every part of life.[18]

> To return to the observance of rites through overcoming the self, then the whole empire would consider benevolence to be his. However the practice of benevolence depends on oneself, and not on others.[19]

Like the virtue of water, it is not acting with passivity, but not acting with a certain outcome in mind, a way that lets one's *ātmā* unfold, there is no bifurcation between subject and object, no awareness of "agent" performing the act as being distinct from an objective action being committed, yet an awareness of everything being equally itself and other. There is an intellectual release from the "womb of darkness", but not one that ends in a catatonic-zombied-out *apavarga* state (as in Nyāya soteriology) which is still in the realm of desire. Disordered desire must need be checked and bracketed out, for an undeconstructed desire is the function of the self, and this self's consciousness, as Sartre reminded us, is produced by the perception of the self through the perspective of the other.[20]

The second issue that arises concerns why some rites, e.g. the Citrā ceremony, do not yield cattle immediately. It is obvious to any good theorist of rituals, such as Mary Douglas

---

18 See, Alan K.L. Chan, "Confucian Ethics and the Critique of Ideology", *Asian Philosophy,* vol. 10, no. 3, 2000, pp. 245-61, esp. p. 246; cf. A.T. Nuyen, "Confucianism and the Idea of Equality", *Asian Philosophy,* vol. 11, no. 2, 2001, pp. 61-71, esp. pp. 61-63. Also, Julia Ching, "Human Rights: A Valid Chinese Concept", in *Confucianism and Human Rights,* ed. De Bary and Tu, Columbia University Press, 1998, pp. 67-83, esp. pp. 76-77.

19 D.C. Lau (tr.), *Confucius: The Analects* (Lun Yu), London: Penguin, 1999, Book XII.

20 Jean-Paul Sartre, "The Look", in *Being and Nothingness: A Phenomenological Essay on Ontology,* New York: Washington Square Press, 1996, pp. 340-43.

for example, that the true meaning of ritual is symbolic and its function is intellectual. She argues that the fertility rites of primitive societies are performed not to produce crops – as earlier theories had supposed – but to give order to life by demarcating seasons. As she says:

> Of course the Dinka hope . . . that the rain ritual will (magically) cause rain, healing rituals (magically) avert death, harvest rituals (magically) produce crops. But instrumental efficacy is not the only kind of efficacy to derive from the symbolic action. The other kind is achieved in the action itself, in the assertion it makes. . . .[21]

Durkheim and other social scientists believed that ritual was a way in which people worshipped society; others that rituals provide a conduit to historical connections, the reliving of legends, of *illo tempore*, the originary beginnings, as well as the performance of the ethical knowledge of the larger cosmology.

The practice and observance of rituals, *altarity*, then, with its supplementary supplications in the recitation of the accompanying *mantras*,[22] enable the accumulation of divine "credit chits" (that my colleague M.K. Sridhar has called *apūrvakārya*) and through its empowering force, or "benediction", some good, or the *Good* (*śreyasa*), is realized in the ever-transforming earthly *alterity* (the sense of being poised as the other; oneself as other, and the other as oneself). Or perhaps (crossing now the Oriental border) as Confucius had put it:

---

21 Mary Douglas, *Purity and Danger: Collected Works, An Analysis of Concept of Pollution and Taboo*, Routledge, 2003, p. 69.

22 Harvey Alper (ed.), *Understanding Mantras*, Albany, NY: SUNY Press, 1989; J. Gonda, "The Indian Mantra", *Oriens* (1963), **16**: 244-97.

> Submitting to ritual is Good; if (a ruler) could for one day himself submit to ritual, everyone under Heaven would respond to his Good-ness.[23]

It induces piety, which the Confucians quickly translate for its beneficence (*ren*, humanity) in filial and wider governance relations, etc.

I wish now to move on to the remaining ontological issues that I am attempting to track. And so a final word on *devatā*: I would call it the case of the elusive *dative* (the subject to whom some *x* is directed or given over: *agnaye, devāya, nārāyaṇāya, gaṅgei*), for it is subsidiary to the substantive nominative and the connected, though, unmarked instrumental case, which we have located in *kārya*. That is all there is to the deity: an effervescently and effusively egregious, and only just efficacious, symbol that has no substantive signified beyond its moment of iteration. Hence, divinity, gods, the idea of authorship, human beings and their craving, and the external world are simply *qualia* (*gauṇa*, substanceless properties, attributes, aspects) that are judged against another benchmark that has as its signified the sacrificial whole and *dharma*, the transcendental sum of all right rituals, ritual relations, and cosmic structuration and ordering of the universe as well as all right actions and practices. Even the gods have to conform to this "law of the One"; there is an interesting narration in *Aitareya Brāhmaṇa*, where *yajña* as food fled from the gods; the gods panicked and said: "The *yajña* as food hath left us; this *yajña*, food, let us search for." [But] "How shall we search?" Answer: by the *Brahman* and meters or metrical forms (*chandas*). They consecrated the Brāhmaṇa with the meters; for him they

23 *Analects* XII: 1 (Ames, "Yin and Yang", in Antonio S. Cua (ed.), *The Encyclopedia of Chinese Philosophy*, New York and London: Routledge, 2003, pp. 846-47; and *Heaven Doesn't Speak*, ABC Encounter, radio program, 6 August 2006.

performed the *yajña* up to the end; they also performed the joint offerings to the wives (of the gods). It seems, the unity of Brāhmaṇa (as *mantra*) with the meters defines *yajña* and yields food as much for the gods, not otherwise, nor the converse.[24] The gods, knowing that they are not entitled or qualified to perform sacrifice, except perhaps the primordially primeval one, depend upon human performance and "gifting" to their chosen deities.

The Prābhākaran commentator, Śālikanātha, categorically refutes the view that *yāga* is of the nature of worship of deities. He finds no authority for such claims. Further, he avers that *devatā*s have no form and therefore cannot comprehend worship offered to them. This rules out the possibility of their grace. *Devatā*s are *gauṇa* in the sacrifice.[25] To introduce notions of future life, or a divine being or beings who might influence this world (*lokasaṁsāra*) from an invisible world beyond, is a mere speculation. The Prābhākaras echo what Confucius was teaching over at the other end of the Silk Road.

"Until you are able to serve humanity, how can you serve gods?" (*Analects* 11.11) And as the late and respected *ācārya* Frits Staal adroitly noted, the rendering of gods as "mental forces", which elsewhere smacks of excessive symbolism (as in the Alexandrian interpretation of the Homeric pantheon), is in Hinduism quite natural[26] – or at least in the Mīmāṁsā and lately in the Ārya Samāj's aniconic *homa*graphy.

---

24 N.N. Bhattacharyya, *Ancient Indian Rituals and Their Social Content*, Delhi: Manohar, 1996, pp. 119-20.

25 In K.T. Pandurangi translation of *PPK*, p. 413: *nanu yāgādi-kriyā devatāḥ-ārādhana upāyabhūta satī kāryatā ucyatām . . . sā tat-pratyāsatti-dvareṇa kā 'āntarepi phalam janayitumalam-eva; devatā phaladānasamarthā karmabhiḥ ārādhyate; sā ārarādhitā prasīdati* ।

26 Frits Staal, *Exploring Mysticism*, US/London: Penguin Books, 1975, p. 194.

And, Finally, What of Mantras?

The recent literature on *mantras* in the Mīmāṁsā is extensive: Staal (following Lèvi Strauss and Louis Renou), Daya Krishna, Pattabhirama Shastri, K.T. Pandurangi, and John Taber among others have been engaged in the disputations. I will report on few of the salient points from this debate in concluding this discussion, but I begin with the Bhāṭṭas. For Kumārila *mantras* appear to have the same grammatical function as the rest of the Vedic sentences, albeit in a more formulaic form uttered in the context of a ritual. But do they really have any *meaning*, do they refer to anything in particular? What meaning does a *mantra* such as "Aditi is heaven, aditi is the atmosphere", "*Agner vrata*"; do they carry any signification? The consensus among the Mīmāṁsakas seems to be that, although *mantras* embed meaning, linguistically speaking (even as part of an elaborate speech-act), they belong to the *arthavat* "useful" or *arthavāda* category, to whit, auxiliary, or subsidiary effectations in the procedure, and they have an explanatory role as well, in that they register the name-place for each *sāmagrī* (sacrificial ingredient) and their elemental correspondence, plus their significance in the procedure that is largely and substantially one of *tyāga* (giving up), *dāna* (gifting), and for this one may need imaginary *atithi/arghya* (*atithi devo bhavaḥ* – guest is god). Nevertheless, *mantras* fall outside the *sādhana-sādhya-itikartavyatā* matrix.

Hence, according to Śabara, "*mantras* serve to bring to light the *subsidiary* parts of the sacrifice as it is being performed".[27] Derived as it is from the root *man*, to think, it alludes to "the bringing to mind" (*manasā*; *noesis*) *-tra*, from *trāṇa*, releasing the noetic supplication as the ostensive "*mantric effect*", the particular *devatā* as efficacious name-place marker

---

[27] I.2.32, I.50; John Taber, "Are Mantras Speech-Acts?", in Alper, 1989, p. 149.

of the intended potency to be generated in the procedure. (Recall that the as-yet-unmanifest *mantric effect* is the *apūrva*, which more properly is the *yāga-* or *yājñic-effect*). *Mantras* then bear a deferred signification rather than any direct indicative signification, drawing on "mythologic and symbolic" associations in the mind. Again, the deities they name or stamp the sacrifice with, Agni, Vāyu, Aditi, Indra, et al., are granted pseudo-existence, a momentary effervescence in the wider imaginary of what might pick out the divinities of light (*divya*) had the Mīmāṁsā any inkling towards the onto-theos (or theism of any variety and persuasion, notwithstanding later emendations by the converted "Uttara-Mīmāṁsakas"). My scholastic *paṇḍit* in Varanasi once asked me what is "e-mail login"? I replied to the effect that

> what *mantras* are to the Mīmāṁsakas exactly as you have explained them to me, so *mantras* are like the login name and passwords we use for logging into our cyberspace internet accounts (the smoky realms): they have no role in what we do after and the directives we might follow once the core messages are downloaded in the inbox or outbox!

Giving it a yet different spin, Taber argues that *mantras* have an illocutionary force, of an Austinian speech-act kind: e.g. as when the Army's Chief of Staff or the Prime Minister proclaims, smashing a bottle of champagne against the Agni missile:

> Today, I have much pleasure in launching Agni II, India's newest defence invention and symbol of deterrence to our neighbouring states.

The expression embeds mere platitudes, or it names a trajectory and the procedure-as-it-unfolds, or yet to be actualized fully; for Agni II's *itikartavyatā* is complete only when it is launched across the skies toward an intended "enemy" target, even if pre-emptively. And the new nationalist *mantra*: "Hindu-Chin bhai-bhai; Hindu–Muslim bye-bye". I think the illustration serves a point; *mantras* have no epistemic status, and as such they yield no real knowledge, because they are not part of *pramāṇa* (epistemic platform) as such, but only a subsidiary part of *śābdībhāvanā*: inciting gnostic or *intellectus*, i.e. a particular noetic imaginary. It is also called *pravartanā* or *preraṇā*. This knowningness evokes *ārthībhāvanā*, i.e. *pravṛtti* of what is to be done, which is also conveyed by the injunctive suffix. *Yāga* is its *karaṇa,* instrumental force, and *svarga* its *bhāvya;* and *apūrva,* the withheld cumulative invested-credit in the person or wherever the performative is intentionally coming from. *Mantras* are generative of their own "intentionality" and are reflective of the Heideggerean adage that "language speaks", "language precedes speech", and "language is the house of being" (and we might add for the present subreptive account, "of non-being").

But Taber brings in his own criticism at this point, suggesting that for all its sophisticated understanding of the functioning of language, as a theory of *mantric* utterance it is woefully inadequate. He argues that the variety and complexity of *mantric* forms are hardly explained by saying that they serve as reminders [For] [A]s mere reminders, they would do better with a simpler structure and thinner content. In Sanskrit literature, a certain class of texts is clearly designated to serve a mnemonic function, *sūtras*, but *mantras* hardly have that character. Why should there be references to gods in *mantras*? And, why to particular gods in some *mantras*, to other ones in others? The Mīmāṁsā makes only the lamest effort to account for such things, invariably taking references to deities to be mere *arthavādas* – and it does that only when forced to.

> Indeed, it would seem that the Mīmāṁsā is not really interested in explaining *mantras* at all but only in eliminating

> them as potential source of doubt about the rationality of the Veda.[28]

Vedic *mantra*s had to await later commentators such as Sāyaṇa for a semblance of semantic grace to be restored to their fledging figurative and furtive life.

I agree with Taber, but I would qualify his gripe with two alternative suggestions. One, that at least under the Prābhākara theory of sentence-meaning, which is *anvitābhidhānavāda* (context-principle) (a more syntactically-oriented theory), no word or part conveys separate or partite meaning; the whole arises in interconnectedness of the parts, less the parts, which could even play a symbolic or metonymic role. And this procedural *vāda* is extended to Vedic *yajuṣ* as well, which is what Jaimini takes to be a ritual "sentence" (*vākya*), not as in our ordinary linguistic usage. A sentence, as one knows, in Sanskrit is a big-long affair; more so in its ritualistic form in Vaidika-*vācya*. Why then go chasing after the partite *mantra*s, when the whole is not quite the sum of the parts?

The second suggestion comes via Frits Staal. For all his polemic, back in the 1980s, about the meaninglessness of *mantra*s (whence he compared them to "bird-songs"), Staal makes a valid observation that *mantra*s are really pre-semantic tropes that none-the-less have a particular form in natural language, which is more important than their meaning. The "form" is based on what J.G. Frazer called "laws of similarity" which we find in the general principle governing Vedic ritual, viz. that there should be a one-to-one correspondence (*sadṛśya*) between *mantra*s and rites (*ekamantrāṇi karmāṇi*).[29] *Kātyāyana*

---

[28] I.2.32, I.50; John Taber, "Are Mantras Speech-Acts", in Alper, 1989, p. 153 (Taber in Alper 1989).

[29] Frits Staal "Mantras and Bird Song" 1985a, p. 5; "Vedic Mantras" in Apler 1989, pp. 72-73; *Āpastamba-Śrauta-Sūtra* 24.1.28; also in P.V. Kane, *History of Dharmaśāstra,* vol. II, part I, chapter XXIX, pp. 976-1008.

Śrauta-Sūtra 1.3.1, for example, defines *mantras* as *ṛc, yajuṣ, sāman, nigada*, which comprise all that is different from Brāhmaṇa and Saṁhitā. Staal notes:

> In the Mīmāṁsā, *mantras* are similarly defined and their formal character and difference from language are similarly stressed (e.g. the order of words [*karma*] in *mantras* is fixed, as in Sanskrit within compounds, or in English, and unlike word order in ordinary Sanskrit which is free).[30]

So *sāmans* are *mantras*, like the *bīja-mantras* of Tantrism;[31] they may contain meaningless sounds, but their sheer form lends significance to the syntactical structure and function of the rite being enunciated.[32]

Historical Locution

I wish to conclude with a historical observation on the overall project of the de-mantrification, the de-deification and especially the impersonalization of Vedic sacrifice, and its authority in toe, in the hands of the Pūrva-Mīmāṁsakas. This would be my reasoning.

Consider the impending impersonality of the Upaniṣads, gods replaced by a neuter *Brahman*, the platform for authorless authority, again impersonally grounded, hence rituals have to be in a pre-poned sense impersonally serviced: no middle or intermediary agency is permissible for that is an impossibility in the iteration of the spokenless word. I would even venture to suggest that the Supreme Principle of Existence is rendered *apauruṣeya* – applying the charactertistic

---

30 Frits Staal, op. cit., p. 11.

31 See Gavin Flood, *The Tantric Body: The Secret Tradition of Hindu Religion*, UK: IB Taurus, 2006.

32 See also, Guy L. Beck, *Sonic Theology Hinduism and Sacred Sound*, Delhi: Motilal Banarsidass, 1995.

of *apauruṣeyatva* beyond the concern with language and the pre-eminence of Śruti as the divinely sacred language of being and non-being; there is a song I recorded in India once which speaks of the Divine having taken *apauruṣeya-rūpa* (impersonal formless) rather than *Brahman* having taken *pauruṣeya-rūpa,* the personal form as in *Saguṇa-Brahman,* or *Īśvara* in onto-theo-logos parlance. This is complete in the doyen of Uttara-Mīmāṁsā, Bādarāyaṇa, followed more ardently and radically, I suggest, by Śaṅkara: not even Śruti really matters (although its *sui-generis* sanctity is retained as the *pramāṇa* in lieu of personal authority for which *Īśvara,* he feared, might be brought in via the "secondary definition" to which he relegates *Saguṇa-Brahman* [*Brahman* qualified or with qualities]): the only *pramā* is ultimately *Brahman,* all else, the self and the world, are *mithyā.* Sheldon Pollock argues that the Mīmāṁsā are on the apologetic track of denying history, the historicality of the uneven temperaments and arrangements, such as the caste-based social structuration and the implied exclusion of the śūdra from the performative acts (Vedic rituals and Sanskrit as the dead language of the gods), and of women too to a large extent. As Taber rightly points out, the Mīmāṁsā probably evolved at a time when the traditional sacrificial lore was becoming less known.[33] I would add a corollary to that: we have to look ahead, not to history but the future-to-be from the moment a little before the classical philosophical turn in India, with Buddhism and Jainism increasingly competing with Vedic ritualism with their own pre-*karuṇā*-version of an impersonal *karma* (doing) theory. It is about denying *pauruṣeyatva* of all possible authority and procedure, and the results thereto. No decent secular Constitution puts the heavens or the gods or God above its authority (except in Pakistan or other theocratic

---

[33] Op. cit. (in Harvey Alper 1989), p. 146.

nation states): this adage might serve as a heuristic here, for again it is the Mīmāṁsā's rule of interpretation, the veritable hermeneutics, that becomes the basis of interpretive rules for the Śrauta-Śāstras and especially the Dharma-Śāstras, in matters Śāstric and secular to boot, and it survived the colonial legalistic re-structuring, and continues to be invoked and utilized in juridical matters in the Indian courts to this day. That's a legacy not to be forgotten. Perhaps, fast-forwarding the social-political clock of the future-to-be to the contemporary/contemporaneous/modern times, the Mīmāṁsā were a peculiar, indeed idiosyncratic progenitors of the secular (in the way Gandhi understood "secularity": the in-between personal and impersonal; and Charles Taylor returns us to this seculocution in his massive "The Secular Age", 2009). On the more ritualistic and soteriological side, it is curiously interesting that the Ārya Samājī or rather its founder, Dayanand Saraswati revived a deity-less *havi* or *homa* as they call their own orthopraxis based on Vedic Saṁhitās and *mantras*, and Dayanand, like the Mīmāṁsā, eschewed the idea of final, irreversible liberation (*mokṣa*), recognizing only temporary "paradises" or states of bliss (*svarga* as multi-tiered *ānandalokas*, *sukr̥tasyalokas*, world of pious works; to the Paurāṇics, it is *devayāna, pitr̥yāna*).[34]

Would I, then, be a Mīmāṁsaka in the post-modern/post-colonial/post-secular – and all-post times (for here the most impossible appropriation is "faith" or *śraddhā*)? Yes, albeit, qualifiedly, an Apūrva-Mīmāṁsaka (not, that is, Pūrva or Karma-Mīmāṁsaka). (I have never been a faithful Uttara-Mīmāṁsaka; and confessedly have been something of an apostate among Naiyāyikas because they made spurious arguments for the existence of *Īśvara*, for which one doesn't need Gadādhara or Śiromaṇi's' Navya-logic to refute the

[34] Halbfass, op. cit., fn. 21, p. 273.

fallacies retained, Kumārila, the Buddhists and Kant's Hume did that better for me, and I followed suit.)[35]

[35] P. Bilimoria, "Nyāya and Navya-Nyāya" (that also discusses Parimal Patil's excellent reconstruction of the Buddhist refutations of the Nyāya arguments), in *Brill Encyclopedia of Hinduism* (ed. Jacobsen, Narayana, et al.), vol. 4, *Philosophy*, Leiden: E.J. Brill, 2011, pp. 657-71. See the following works by me: "The Idea of Authorless Revelation (Apauruṣeya)", in *Indian Philosophy of Religion*, ed. Roy W. Perrett, Dordrecht: Martinus Nijhoff/Kluwer Academic Publishers, 1989, pp. 143-66; "Hindu Doubts About God: Towards a Mīmāṁsā Deconstruction", in *International Philosophical Quarterly* (Fordham, NY) December 1990, vol. 30, no. 4, pp. 481-99; "Authorless Voice, Tradition and Authority in the Mimamsa: Reflections of Crosscultural Hermeneutics", Nagoya Studies in Indian Culture and Buddhism, *Sambhasa* (1995), **16**: 137-60.

P. Bilimoria, 2000, "J.N. Mohanty's Critique of Word as a Means of Knowing and 'Authorless Tradition'", in Bina Gupta (ed.), *The Empirical and the Transcendental: A Fusion of Horizons*, pp. 199-218, USA [B1]: Rowman & Littlefield Publishers.

Śabdapramāṇa: Word and Knowledge, Dordrecht: Kluwer Academic Publishers, 1988, and feature review thereof by Stephen H. Phillips, *Philosophy East and West*, **45**(2): pp. 273-80; the book with Phillip's commentary is now re-issued as *Śabdapramāṇa: Testimony in Indian Philosophy*, New Delhi: DK Printworld, 2011.

14

Translation as the Cultural Space of Tibetan

Lokesh Chandra

TRANSLATION is the dream space of a language at a critical moment of unknowing when it seeks to endow its words with the immensity and heights of expression, in quest of a new world of higher thought, a dynamized centre for intellection to discover new universes of ideas and new material evolution. From a dialect, it becomes a language of sophistication, a concordance of values and materiality. Let us take an example. Latin literature began as translation from the Greek, that largely conditioned its development. Roman writers absorbed and transfigured the borrowed elements. Whereas the Greeks excelled in abstraction, the Romans had an unusually concrete vision. Their ideal was a blend of culture and kindliness. Cicero, the statesman, orator, poet, critic, and philosopher, developed the Latin language to express abstract and complicated thought with clarity. Alexander the Great had taken Indian scholars to Pergamum, which became a home of learning as well as the eagle's nest of his treasures. It became the earliest home of Greek grammar, and grammatical terms like genitive, accusative, and aorist are its permanent contributions to the grammars of European languages. The generative principles of Sanskrit grammar became the linguistic plenum of Latin vocabulary. From simple words related to our biologic needs (like go, sleep, walk, talk *ad infinitum*) was a qualitative leap to a new vocabulary of learning like alphabet, book, lesson, vowels, consonants, going on to abstract concepts. A simple Latin root like *spec* (to see) (from Sanskrit *spaś*) gave rise to a few hundred new words: a-spec-t, circum-spect, con-spectus, in-spect, intro-spect, per-spect-ive, pro-spec-t, re-spec-t, retro-spec-t, su-spec-t, and so on. These processes are referred to by the Tibetan Emperor Khri Lde.sroṅ.btsan in his foreword to the Bam.po.gñis.pa who speaks of the importance of Vyākaraṇa, the correlation of Tibetan and Sanskrit syntax, as well as the prefixes *pari*, *sam*, and *upa* to be translated in an appropriate manner as *yoṅs-su* (entirely), *yaṅ.dag.pa* (truly), or *ñe.ba* (proximately).

The emperor also cautioned:

> But in cases where meaning is not augmented [by them] and there is no need for a surplus of words, use a designation that accords with the meaning.

Buddhism has been a major formative linguistic component of many Asian languages, both extinct and extant, like Khotanese, Parthian, Tokharian, and Sogdian which became victims of historical processes; or the dynamic Chinese, Korean, Japanese, Cambodian, Thai, Laotian, and Simhalese that are alive and creative media in their countries.

Gold and Sūtras

The contacts of Sanskrit and Tibetan begin with Emperor Lha.tho.tho.ri who received a casket containing the *Kāraṇḍavyūha*, *sūtras*, *dhāraṇīs* and a golden *stūpa* from India in AC 373. The *Kāraṇḍavyūha* is the original scripture of *oṁ maṇipadme hūṁ*. The Tibetan state prospered and the *sūtras* and *stūpa* became a great blessing. This was during the reign of the Gupta emperor Samudragupta. His name means "who defends the seas" like the song "Britannia rules the waves" during the imperial glory of the UK. The Gupta emperors brought an economic and cultural renaissance and a political and strategic deterrant by their international relations in trade and academics. Śrīgupta the founder of the Gupta dynasty realized the importance of transoceanic trade with China and built the Chīna-vihāra near Nālandā for Chinese monks to come in later years. Samudragupta must have known that Tibet is rich in gold. The mausoleum of the previous 13th Dalai Lama is embellished with lavish quantum of gold which was extracted by traditional methods. Kālidāsa speaks of Alakā, the city of Kubera, in the Himalayas in *Meghadūta* 2.7. Alakā is explained by the commentator as Kubera-nagarī. It reminds us of the golden land of Tibet. Kālidāsa lived during the reign of Kumāragupta (r. 415-55) in whose honour he composed the *Kumārasambhava*. Kumāragupta I started the construction of a monastery at Nālandā by building the first convent at the request of Rājavaṁśa, a monk of Uttarāpatha or north-west India, probably of Bactria. All the *stūpa*s and monasteries of the north-west regions of India were destroyed by the Hūṇas. Sung-yun who visited Gandhāra in AC 520 speaks of the devastation of the Hūṇas. The famous Chinese pilgrim Hsüan-tsang says that 1,600 *stūpa*s and monasteries were razed to the ground by the Hūṇas.

The Gupta emperors were constantly engaged in fighting the Hūṇas and it was but natural that a monk of the north-west request Emperor Kumāragupta I to establish a university at Nālandā in the distant east so that Buddhist learning continues unhampered by political turmoil and prospers in peace and freedom. The Bactrians have played a major role in the spread and sophistication of Buddhism. They and the Tibetan monks were commanded by Emperor Khri Lde.sroṅ.btsan at his court to prepare a catalogue of the Tibetan translations and to collect all the neologisms in Tibetan deriving from Sanskrit, as a preparation for the final redaction of *Mahāvyutpatti*. The epic of Gesar from the Latin Caesar and the majestic headgears of the Lamaist hierarchs could go back to the Bactrians who had contacts with the West.

The contacts of India and Tibet continued in border trade and major commercial undertakings in the precious metals. The Yarlung dynasty revered *sūtras* that had come to the palace of Lha.tho.tho.ri, which were a blessing for the prosperity and happiness of the palace and the people, in the trade avenues it had opened up. There was no one to read *sūtras*, or to pronounce *dhāraṇīs*. They were venerated for 250 years but left the desire to comprehend them alive.

Tibetan Impirium, Script, and Literary Language

Sroṅ.brtsan.sgam.po united the Tibetan clans in his powerful state, shifted the capital from the Yarlung Valley to the more central Ra.sa "City of Goats" which became Lhasa "City of Gods". From goats to gods was the mighty ascension to a new order of a powerful central authority. It needed a communication system to reach the remote distances of a sprawling country. For this, the Emperor sent Thon.mi Sambhoṭa with sixteen companions to study in India, create a script, and work out a grammar for a standard language. As the tradition goes, Sambhoṭa wrote eight works on grammar, which refer to its model of *Aṣṭādhyāyī* of Pāṇini in eight chapters. The long tradition of transferring the linguistic culture of Sanskrit into Tibetan had begun. The two queens of Sroṅ.brstan were Buddhists and had brought holy icons from Nepal and China whence they came. Script and sacred images of Buddhism must have been accompanied by *sūtras* whose translation was an imperative under the sagacious policies of Emperor Sroṅ.brstan. Now Tibet was on the way to an alphabetic civilization.

The Early Translations

Emperor Khri.sroṅ.lde.brtsan was actively promoting Buddhism and he laid the foundations of the first monastery of Bsam.yas in about AC 779 to train Tibetan monks. He invited Śāntarakṣita and Padmasambhava to make the country well disposed to Buddhism. Śāntarakṣita was a great philosopher, and Padmasambhava started the interiorization of local deities into Buddhism as guardians of the faith. Initiation of monks and tradition of translations of scriptures began in right earnest and by AC 800 a large number had been translated by various lotsavas, as can be seen from the Ldan.dkar catalogue. The immense philosophical literature had to have a common terminology and the next emperor took up this task. About AC 792 a debate between Indian and Chinese monks was held as to whether Indian or Chinese teachings should be followed. The Indian scholar Kamalaśīla won over the Chinese Hoshang. Tibet was at war with China and this weighed in favour of Kamalaśīla. Henceforth only Sanskrit texts were rendered into Tibetan. Some of these early translations have survived in Tun-huang which was under Tibetan control during AC 781–848. While these translations are more literal, the revised versions are clearer, more precise and easier to understand.

Here is a stanza from *Saddharma-puṇḍarīka-Sūtra* in Sanskrit, and its early Tibetan translation from a Khotanese manuscript and the revised Tibetan version. The last quarter of the Sanskrit has not been understood by the translators. The Sanskrit original means: "O Lord (Vināyaka) tell the name of that universe (*lokadhātu*)". The early translation has wrongly understood the last quarter and rendered it as "lord of the universe". The genetive *lokadhātor* goes with *nāma* and means "name of the universe". It does not pertain to Lord (Vināyaka) which is the vocative: "O Lord". The revised version has followed the earlier version and did not consult the Sanskrit original. But the revised version in Kanjur (the Narthang edition) has the appropriate Tibetan syntax and a better idiomatic style in accord with the genius of the language.

न ह्येते जातु अस्माभिर् दृष्टपूर्वाः कदाचन ।
आख्याहि नो तस्य नाम लोकधातोर्विनायक ॥

— *Saddharma-puṇḍarīka-Sūtra* 14.28

Khotanese manuscript

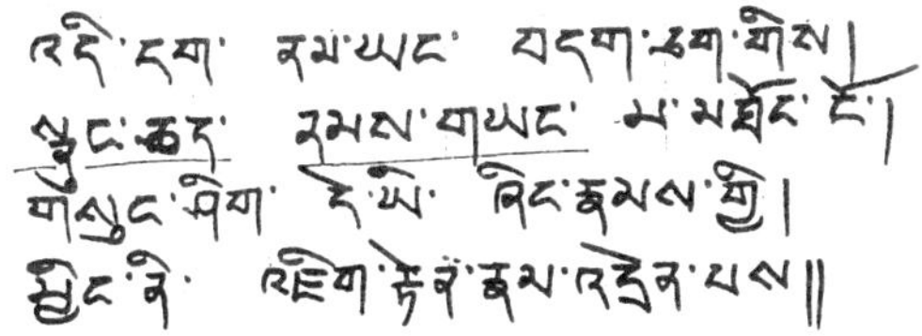

– Nils Simonsson, *Indo-Tibetische Studien*, 1957: 89
(Sven Hedin expedition 1927-33
Ethnographic Museum, Stockholm)

Narthang edition

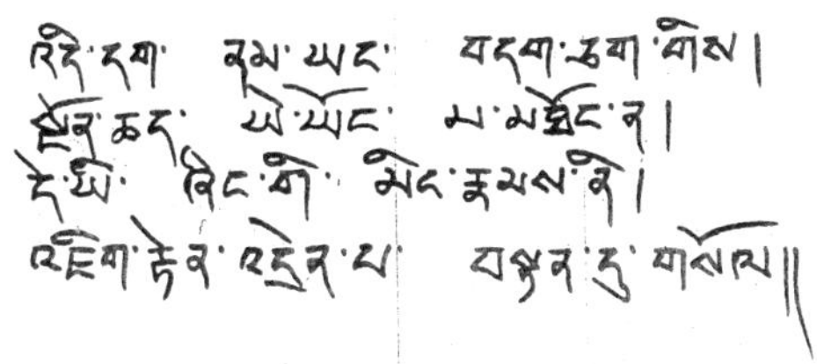

Standardization of Terms

In about AC 800 Emperor Khri.lde.sroṅ.brtsan came to the throne. He convened an assembly to discuss military matters, and to receive tributes. He commanded the Bactrian and Tibetan preceptors to catalogue the texts translated, and to list all the Tibetan coinages of Sanskrit terms. In AC 814 the Sanskrit–Tibetan lexicon of Buddhist terms *Mahāvyutpatti* was compiled from various texts. The emperor himself wrote the introduction to its complimentary text in two chapters: Bam.po gñis.pa to explain the coining of neologisms as well as the technique of translation. He made the following points:

1. In his father's time many terms were not in accord with the doctrine or with Vyākaraṇa (he uses the Sanskrit term). Hence in the new effort the terms will be in accord with the original text, with the conventions established according to Vyākaraṇa, and the appropriate translation of the plain language.

2. The challenges of syntax in the two languages have to be crossed over by deviating from the order in the original "according to what is easy".
3. In the case of homonyms, Sanskrit loan words should be used. Gautama means phrase, direction, earth, light, *vajra*, cow, and heaven, use a noun in accord with the context.
4. In the names of countries, flowers, plants and the like prefix the word with country or flower according to whatever is named, e.g. yul wā.rā.ṇa.si to specify that Varanasi is a place.
5. Put numbers in the Tibetan way: "one thousand two hundred fifty" and not "twelve hundred monks with a half".
6. Translate prefixes like *pari* by semantically appropriate *yoṅs.su* "entirely". When the meaning is not augmented by them, there is no need of the surplus element.
7. Honorific and rank-ordered terms to be used only for Buddhas.
8. No person is to correct or form neologisms hereafter. The translators were explicitly forbidden to coin new terms. When it was unavoidable, they were directed to report to a special commission attached to the Royal Palace (Padma.dkar.po's *Annals* 102b-103b).

These rules promulgated by Emperor Khri.lde.sroṅ.brtsan in AC 826 have been followed ever since. New coinages of proper names in Tibetan were however common in later times: Mñan.yod for Śrāvastī. The Bam.po gñis.pa is an unparalleled source of principles of translation into Tibetan, and deserves an English translation with extensive annotations.

Creation of a new Tibetan literary language may be illustrated by:

śes	"to know"
śes.rab	"prajñā" (rab = pra)
ye-śes	"jñāna"
ye, ye.nas	"completely"
ye.rdzogs	"perfectly".

From a nomadic dialect, Tibetan arose to a unique world status as the second major classical language after Sanskrit in profundity of expression, clarity of thought, and the power of subtle reasoning. The major classical languages are: Sanskrit, Tibetan, Greek, Latin, Arabic, and Chinese. Once Prof. Baldanzhapov of Buryatia said: "One has to be a *bodhisattva* to master Tibetan." The lotsavas or Tibetan masters, who translated Sanskrit *sūtra*s into Tibetan along with Indian masters, are celebrated in a marriage song as "jewels granting all wishes", that follows:

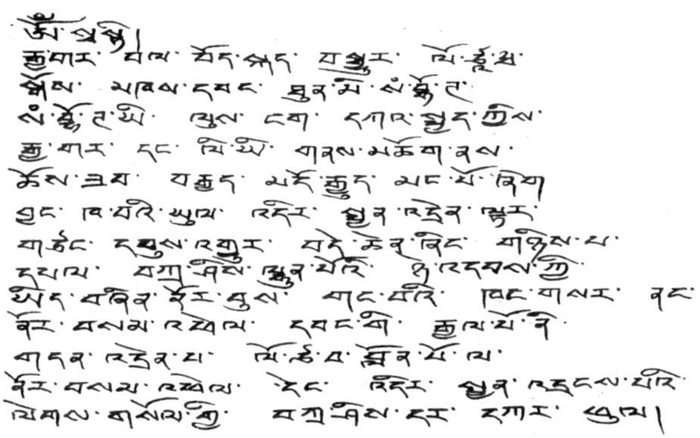

(The party of the bridegroom)

Oṁ svasti
The Lotsavas, the translators of Tibet, India and Nepal
And specially the lord of the learned men, Thonmi Sambhoṭa,
With hardships of body and speech like those of Sambhoṭa,
From the holy places of India and Khotan
Introduced here, into this northern Country of the Snow

The eight deep doctrines and many Sūtras and Tantras.
In the same way, in the proximity of the blessed Tashilhunpo
Which is a second Sukhāvatī in the middle of Tsang,
Inside this new house full of jewels granting every wish
You like the minister Lotsava (Sambhoṭa) have brought
This powerful king of the jewels granting all sorts of wishes.
We offer this white auspicious scarf (to you)
With our thanks for having brought here this jewel granting all sorts of wishes.

— G. Tucci, *Tibetan Folk Songs*, 1966: 37, 57-58

Refinement of Tibetan Literary Culture

With the standardization of the Tibetan philosophical, ritual, mathematical, astronomical, and other terms in the Sūtras and Tantras, the vast Buddhist corpus was translated into Tibetan. In the twelfth-century Sa.skya Paṇḍita (1182–1251, Kapstein, p. 777) introduced the ideals of literary learning as intellectual excellence. He must have been fluent in Sanskrit to be able to read a Sanskrit text like the *Sarasvatī-kaṇṭhābharaṇa*. He studied the grammars of kalāpa and cāndra, kāvyas, metrics, science of poetic ornament (alaṁkāraśāstra), synonymics, dramas, āyurveda, technical sciences (śilpaśāstra), astronomy, and introduced a comprehensive programme of classical study to the Tibetan world. His exposition of the *rasa* theory has endured in Tibet till today. His "Eight Ego Poem" reflects his historic contribution:

I am the grammarian. I am the dialectician.
Among vanquishers of sophists, peerless am I.
I am learned in metrics. I stand alone in poetics.
In explaining synonymics, unrivaled am I.
I know celestial calculations. In exo- and esoteric science
I have a discerning intellect equaled by none.
Who can this be? Sa.skya alone!
Other scholars are my reflected forms.

The earliest Japanese collection of poctry *Manyoshu* speaks of Japan as "the country where word-souls (*koto-dama*) flourish". The words and ideas of Buddhism have been oneiric sensitivity and summon us: "follow me to the spring and find its secret". The translations from Tibetan would be a glimmer of eternity descending upon the beauty of our world.

Transgression, Translation and Transcreation

The above three levels of rendering remind us of the high onus on our intellect to convey "the fragrance of the blue lotus" in the words of the Tibetan *Rāmāyaṇa*. Higher language has to be different from common speech in forms of expression that have to produce aesthetic suggestion and ascend to transcension. A text on meditation was translated into English, in which the yogic term *kumbhaka* was rendered as "pot meditation". It simply means "retention of the breath within". This misleading rendering is a transgression, even if it is literal. Translation conveys the meaning of words but misses the waves that shape reveries. Transcreation animates the image within and we become flowering beings. Miranda Shaw has translated a stanza from the *Citta-guhya-dohā* from the Derge Tanjur in a manner that becomes expanding consciousness:

Who speaks the sound of an echo?
Who paints the image in a mirror?
Where are the spectacles in a dream?
Nowhere at all —
That's the nature of mind.

— Miranda Shaw, *Passionate Enlightenment*, p. 90

Its Tibetan original is cited from the Thugs.kyi gsaṅ.ba glur.blaṅs.pa zhes.bya.ba, sDe-dge 2443, fol. 70a2-3:

brag ciḥi sgra ḥdi su.yis smras ।
me.loṅ gzugs.brñan su.yis bris ।
rmi.lam ltad.mo gaṅ.du gyis ।
gaṅ.na aṅ med.do sems.kyi ṅaṅ ॥

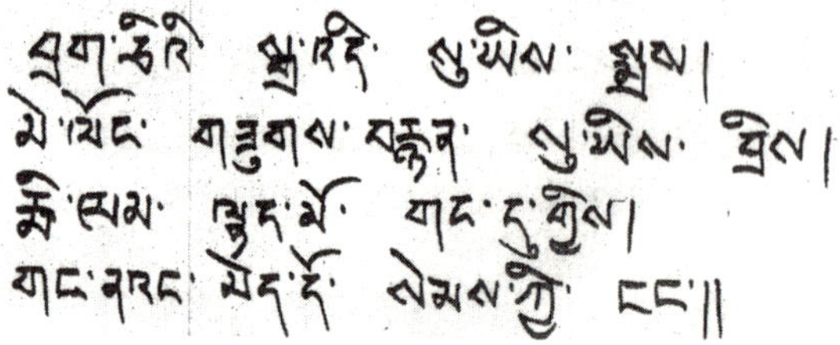

— चित्तगुह्यदोहा by a Ḍākinī

A limp and listless translation loses the very structure and spirit. It has to be the shadow *en passant* in an effortless innocence to restructure the haunting light and music of words. Failing this, its translator sinks into oblivion.

15

Sanskrit and Tamil Interrelation

S. Revathy

THE two greatest and most formative components of culture in India are Sanskrit and Draviḍian. By the range and variety of its secular, philosophic, and religious literature, and its adaptability to all intellectual needs and its immensely rich vocabulary, Sanskrit stands in the same position to India as Greek and Latin did to Europe and America for many centuries. The literature of Tamil (and to a lesser degree of the other Draviḍian tongues, Telugu, Kannada and Malayalam) is almost as ancient, and as extensive as that of Sanskrit but here again the literary language needs simplification. Telugu, Kannada and Malayalam languages owe at least as much to Sanskrit as to the Draviḍian elements in every aspect.

From ancient times, the Tamil and Sanskrit tongues have lived in friendly commensality. *Tolkāppiyam* is the earliest extant work in Tamil literature and is usually assigned to the third century BCE. Its preface asserts that the author utilized the Grammar of Indra (*Aindram*) and was a disciple of Agastya who himself is reputed to have composed several works on literature, music, and drama (*iyal, isai nāṭkam*). Tolkāppiar is in fact described as *aindiaram niṛaindavar* meaning thereby that he was proficient in Sanskrit. From that day down to Thāyumānavar and Rāmaliṅga Swāmigaḷ, the two streams of national culture have flown side by side.

Nadiyuṇḍa kaḍalenaccamayattaiyuṇḍa parajñāna vānandavoḷiyē. sings Thāyumānavar about the *malaivaḷarkādali*, and his style and message are deft combinations of the two cultural influences.

The Śaiva Siddhānta system of philosophy is one of the typical manifestations of the Tamil genius and it may be noted that the early Śaiva Siddhānta works, called Āgamas, were written in Sanskrit and very great antiquity is claimed for some of them. The early Śaiva Siddhāntins who were Tamilians by birth decided to use Sanskrit, not on account of any lack of love for Tamil, but because they loved truth and worked for its propagation among the different nationalities. In any case, we find the philosophical terms used in the Śaiva Siddhānta are Sanskrit words, although the specific doctrines and their exposition are largely a product of the Tamilian intellect. The Tamil language will benefit and not suffer; if it incorporates and assimilates not only Sanskrit but other foreign words, images, and thoughts; and the same remark applies to Sanskrit. In fact it has been stated that the word *āgama* itself may be construed as implying that the system "came from" or was derived from another culture.

The great Vaiṣṇavite reformers have translated and adopted in Tamil, the Vedas and other scriptures, and even created a mixed language wherein Sanskrit and Tamil have been combined to create not only marvellous religious poetry but a flexible composite tongue that is spoken by young and old.

Addressing the convocation of the Vikram University at Ujjain in 1961, the late Sir C.P. Rāmaswāmi Iyer observed:

> It is obvious that some of the prejudice and much of the propaganda against Hindi in the non-Hindi localities of India will disappear or at all events be minimized, by the cultivation of Sanskrit; because it is an undoubted fact that all over India and even in places where non-Sanskritic

> languages like Tamil are spoken, not a little of the vocabulary and much of the ideology and basic philosophical and religious concepts is bound up with Sanskrit. This will be evident from a perusal of the Tamil and Telugu classics through the centuries.

Sanskrit, the oldest surviving member of the Indo-European family of languages, is our priceless heritage. Its contribution to world literatures is well known to scholars as rich and varied. Its impact on Indian languages is an undisputed fact. While almost all the languages spoken in north India are derivatives of Sanskrit, its influence on the major south Indian languages, viz. Tamil, Kannada, Telugu, and Malayalam is quite profound and interesting. The south Indian languages belong to a different linguistic family, viz. the Draviḍian. Yet because of centuries of coexistence, both ideas and expressions have been imbibed by these languages from Sanskrit. Even in the earliest corpus of Tamil poetry, the influence of Sanskrit can be seen by an impartial observer. The Tamil grammarian Senāvaraiyar in his commentary on *Tolkāppiyam* observes that Sanskrit is the common language of all parts of India. But it is in the three major south Indian languages that the influence of Sanskrit has to be seen and enjoyed. In Telugu and Kannada its influence reaches a very high degree; but in Malayalam, it reaches a point of saturation. In fact, a literary genre called *Maṇipravāḷa* (*Gem and Coral*) flourished in Malayalam using a mixed diction of Sanskrit-cum-Malayalam. The same style was cultivated extensively in Tamil in the Śrī Vaiṣṇava religious writings. We shall elaborate on this point a little later.

In the field of aesthetics the Tamil grammatical tradition expounded in *Tolkāppiyam* includes within itself the theories on rhetorics and aesthetics; the Sanskrit tradition has its base in *Nāṭyaśāstra* which deals with the theories of dramatic art, rhetorics, etc. elaborately. Both these works are similar in many respects yet being independent. While the *rasa*s are eight for both; both deal with only four *alaṁkāras*. Both treat of the two types of *śṛṅgāra* and the types of *nāyikās*. While *Nāṭyaśāstra* deals with poetics in detail, *Tolkāppiyam* includes it under the section on *Poruḷ* while elaborating on *Akattiṇai* and *Purattiṇai*. The critical literature in Tamil, after *Tolkāppiyam* has as its basis, the five motives – *ezhuttu, sol, poruḷ, yāppu* and *aṇr*. The works that discuss in detail the *Aṇiyiyal* are mostly based on *Kāvyādarśa* of Daṇḍin (seventh century CE). Although such works have developed between twelfth and sixteenth century CE, they do not seem to have been influenced by Ānandavardhana and Kṣemendra. There are four major works on *Aṇiyiyal*: (i) *Daṇḍiyalaṁkāram* which was written on the basis of Daṇḍin's *Kāvyādarśa* (as the name implies) by an unknown author and unknown date. The text is divided into *poduviyal poruḷaṇiyiyal* and *sollaṇiyiyal* with about 125 aphorisms. Of these, thirty-five aphorisms describe *aṇis*. (ii) *Vīrasōzhiyam* was composed by Buddhamitra during eleventh century CE in the name of king Vīra Rājendra Coḷa (CE 1063-70). Of the 184 verses in *Kaṭṭaḷaikalitthurai*, forty-one are devoted to *aṇi*. It is the only such work written by a Buddhist. The author claims *Kāvyādarśa* as his model. (iii) *Māranalaṁkāra* of Tirukkurugai Perumāḷ Kavirāyar of sixteenth century CE was again modelled on *Daṇḍiyalaṁkāram*. It also follows the tradition set by *Tolkāppiyam Tonnūlviḷakkam* of Vīramāmunivar of CE 1730 has 370 verses. The author has followed both the traditions of Sanskrit and Tamil rhetorics. *Muthuviḷakkam* and *Ilakkama Viḷakkam* of the same period have no new ideas. Mampazhakkani Siṅganāvalar has translated into Tamil the *Rasamañjarī* of Bhānudatta. In recent times, the texts *Dhvanyāloka, Daśarūpaka, Aucityavicāracarcā,* and *Kuvalayānanda* have been translated into Tamil. Thus it could be seen that the Tamil tradition has its rhetorical and aesthetic theories drawn from the Sanskrit tradition.

Tamil is considered by the scholars as the forerunner of the cultivated languages of south India. It has retained its vigour and youthfulness with an abundant vocabulary to express even modern ideas. W.D. Whitney in his book *The Life and Growth of Language* says that Tamil is a finer language to think and speak in, than any European tongue. On the basis of certain words found in Vedas some scholars think that Tamil, the Draviḍian tongue, might have had an impact on Sanskrit. It is said that the word *Arici* in Tamil was introduced into the European language as Rice even as early as King Solomon's time (about tenth century BCE.). The word *paḷḷi*, which means a small village, occurs in Sanskrit as well as in Tamil, Telugu, and Kannada. It must have had its origin in Draviḍian language since the word *paḷḷi* is common in south India. C.W. Dāmodaran Piḷḷai derives *tamizh* from *tami* (lonely) and according to him *tamizh* means Peerless. In *Priṅgaḷandai* X.580, a Tamil lexicon, it is explained that *tamizh* means sweetness and mercy. *Inimaiyum niṛamaiyum tamizh enavāgum.*

But the influence of Sanskrit, an Āryan language, on Tamil was very much pronounced in some of the great works of the period between CE 1100 and 1750. *Vālmīki Rāmāyaṇa*, the revival of Śaivism, and the movement of Vaiṣṇavism which emphasized *bhakti* were principally responsible for this influence of Sanskrit. During the period after CE 1850, however, the unearthing of the Saṅgam and other ancient works from private possessions and their printing gave a new impetus to the development of modern Tamil. The credit goes to *U.vē. Sāminatha Iyer* whose masterly editions with copious notes deserve special mention. The rise of the national poet Subramanya Bharathi in Tamil Nadu was a contributory factor to the growth of patriotic feelings among Tamils. The advent of Bharathi ushered an era of literary renaissance in Tamil Nadu.

After the arrival of the Āryans in India, Sanskrit influenced almost all the languages in the subcontinent. On account of the intercultural intercourse among the various sections of the Indian people, there has been integration of languages, values, norms, and traditions. K.M. Munshi, the founder of the Bharatiya Vidya Bhavan, writes about the impact of the two cultures, viz. the Āryan and the Draviḍian, as follows:

> The impact of the two cultures took place in north India where the two races first came in contact during the Vedic and the post-Vedic periods. There is a strong Draviḍian element even in the Vedic Sanskrit, and a marked "Draviḍization" of the spirit of the Āryan languages. There is an equally powerful infusion of Draviḍian elements in Āryan religion, ritual and thought, mythology, and legendary history, all indicating that the fusion took place in the plains of north India.

Rāmāyaṇa and *Mahābhārata* have been, over the years, rendered in all Indian languages. Vālmīki's original work and Kālidāsa's abridged adaptation which are in Sanskrit and Kamban's work in an elaborate form in Tamil may have the same base, that is, the life and mission of Rāma. But each has its uniqueness, especially so in the case of Kamban who employs a different language from Vālmīki and Kālidāsa; a language that has a genius and poetic tradition of its own.

Let me give some examples as to how Kamban has been influenced by Kālidāsa. In the opening verse of his *Raghuvaṁśa* Kālidāsa writes:

> क्व सूर्यप्रभवो वंशः ? क्व चाल्पविषया मतिः ।
> तितीर्षुर्दुस्तरं मोहात् उडुपेनास्मि सागरम् ॥
>
> अथवा कृतवाग्द्वारे वंशेऽस्मिन् पूर्वसूरिभिः ।
> मणौ वज्रसमुत्कीर्णे सूत्रस्येवास्ति मे गतिः ॥

> Whither is the Solar dynasty which emanated from the Sun God? Whither is my small intellect? I am attempting to cross the ocean with the aid of a barge, out of love (for poetry). Or shall I say that my attempt at this great (literary) adventure in exploring into the great Epic of Solar dynasty (created by Vālmīki) is akin to driving a thread through the hole in a gemstone which had been drilled into by diamond?

Kamban's opening verse echoes the similar idea:

noytin noyya sol nūṛkaluṛṛēn-enai
vaita vainn marāmaram ēzhtuḷai
eyta eytavaṛku eytiya mākkatai
seyta seytavan sol ninṛa tēyattē

See another similar instance from Vālmīki, Kālidāsa and Kamban. Vālmīki writes:

सोऽहं विश्रममिच्छामि रामं कृत्वा प्रजाहिते

"Therefore I wish to retire after handing over the kingdom to Rāma", said Daśaratha.

Kālidāsa writes the same with a metaphor

तं कर्णमूलमागत्य रामे श्रीर्न्यस्यतामिति ।
कैकेयीशङ्कयेवाह पलितच्छद्मना जरा ॥

As if out of fear for Kaikeyī, old age in the form of grey hair, appeared near Daśaratha's temple region, and secretly whispered in his ears, "Hand over the kingdom to Rāma".

Kamban is influenced more by Kālidāsa than Vālmīki that he writes very much similar to Kālidāsa:

mannanē! avaniyai maganukku īnduni
panna orundavam puri paruvam īduena
kanna mūlattinil kazhaṛa vandena
min enak karumai pōy veḷuttatu ōr mayir

Old age in the form of grey hair by losing its darkness and shining like lightning, appeared near Daśaratha's ears and secretly whispered to him, "Hand over the kingdom to your son and you retire to forest for penance".

The story of *Rāmāyaṇa,* as is but natural, was adopted by all the Āḷvārs to a greater or lesser extent in accordance with their own outpourings which have been collected in

Nālāyiraprabandham, i.e. a compilation of 4,000 hymns and is known as *Draviḍopaniṣad.* All the Āḷvārs took Rāma and Kṛṣṇa as the incarnations of Viṣṇu and were engrossed in devotion to them. A later commentator Peria Vāchān Piḷḷai has brought out a *Rāmāyaṇa* by name *Pāśurappaḍi Rāmāyaṇa* consisting of lines and words from *Nālāyiraprabandham* only.

Even the great epic *Mahābhārata,* which contains many didactic hymns, has influenced the great Tamil classic *Tirukkuraḷ* by Tiruvaḷḷuvar. Referring to temperance in speech *Tirukkuraḷ* says:

tīyināl suṭṭa puṇ uṭṭāṛum āṛadī
nāvināl suṭṭa vaḍu

and

yāgāvārāyinum nākākka kāvākkāl
sōkāppar sollizhukkuppaṭṭu

Bhagavad-Gītā conveys a similar idea in the verse:

अनुद्वेगकरं वाक्यं सत्यं प्रियहितं च यत्।
स्वाध्यायाभ्यसनं चैव वाङ्मयं तप उच्यते ॥

– *Bhagavad-Gītā* XV.17

Further, two of the Purāṇas, *Bhāgavata* on the side of Viṣṇu and *Sūtasaṁhitā* described as part of the *Skanda Purāṇa* on the side of Śiva, bear unmistakable evidences of south Indian nativity. The two epics were done into Tamil very early, a Tamil Bhārata going to the Saṅgam age itself. The Purāṇic mythology, and the religious and cultural milieu are already reflected in the Saṅgam works, particularly in *Paripāḍal.* The account of the sixty-three Śaiva saints by Sundaramūrti, one of them, who belonged to the later Pallava times is referred to as a Purāṇa. *Yāpperunkala Vṛtti* (prosody) cites a work called *Purāṇasāgara* in *veṇbā* meter; the text and the gloss are both by Jain writers. There is a lengthy article titled "A Tamil Version of the Purāṇas" by the late V. Rāghavan in his commemoration volume.

Mention was made earlier about the *Maṇipravāḷa* style. The earliest definition of *Maṇipravāḷa* in Tamil states that if there is an intermixture of Sanskrit syllables in Tamil writing, it is called *Vīraviyal,* and that if there happens to be an intermixture of Sanskrit words, it is called *Maṇipravāḷa.* However, in later times, the term *Maṇipravāḷa* is applied to the Tamil prose literature of the Vaiṣṇavas and Jains which came into existence between the twelfth and fifteenth centuries. One might wonder why this particular style was used by the Vaiṣṇava *ācārya*s. To understand this we must explore the intricacies of the development of Ubhayavedānta and its relation to *Maṇipravāḷa.* Ubhayavedānta, as the acknowledgement of a twofold scriptural tradition, also implies the acknowledgement of two religious languages – Tamil and Sanskrit – as parallel religious languages in the writings of the Āḷvārs. Although the Āḷvārs sang their praises of the Lord in Tamil, their mother tongue, they considered themselves part of the Vedic tradition. Since scripture was to be made available to all Śrī Vaiṣṇavas, it was the responsibility of the *ācārya*s to instruct the diverse people of the Śrī Vaiṣṇava community in the Ubhayavedānta as well as the teachings of the *ācārya*s themselves. To accomplish this task they needed a medium of instruction that would be intelligible both to the ordinary devotees and to the intelligentsia of the community, to those who knew only their mother tongue – Tamil – as well as to those who understood Sanskrit. Being adept in both the languages, the *ācārya*s themselves, were masters of both the languages and so were qualified to interpret to the devotees, the teachings of the Upaniṣads as well as the Tamil hymns of the Āḷvārs. While interpreting the Upaniṣads and philosophical works they often used Sanskrit words and phrases. These words were thought of as technical terms in the sense that exact meaning which the *ācārya*s had in view could be conveyed – or at least they thought that it could be conveyed only by using those Sanskrit terms. Consequently there developed a variety of prose, basically Tamil in structure and vocabulary but including many Sanskrit terms and phrases, which came to be called *Maṇipravāḷa*. The most prominent characteristic of *Maṇipravāḷa* is that it is a situational language as it developed in specific circumstances to expound Ubhayavedānta to a diverse religious community whose mother tongue was Tamil and was used in specific context (religious instructions) involving the larger tasks of writings – *vyākhyāna*s and *sampradāya grantha*s – i.e. works concerning the tradition like *rahasyatrayasāra.*

Now in *Maṇipravāḷa* which is a mixture of Sanskrit and Tamil words, the way the words are mixed and in the form they are used differed from writer to writer according to his own scholarship and capacity to essay a different style. For example, Piḷḷān the first Śrī Vaiṣṇava to use the *Maṇipravāḷa* prose, used long compound sentences. When he uses Sanskrit words he provides Tamil endings. Next, Nāñjiyār avoided long compound sentences in favour of simple sentences. Vaḍakkuttiruvīdi Piḷḷai and Peria Vāchān Piḷḷai use more Tamil vocabulary 2:1 while Piḷḷai Lokācārya used still more Tamil vocabulary 3:1 and introduced the *sūtra* style into *Maṇipravāḷa* prose. Vedānta Deśika reverted to a Sanskrit dominated Tamil prose (3:2) although he wrote works in pure Tamil (as well as in Sanskrit). Thus, we find considerable variations in the style of *Maṇipravāḷa.*

It may also be pointed out that *Maṇipravāḷa* was generally written in Tamil script with *grantha* characters for those sounds which are not found in Tamil, or else, it was completely written in Telugu script with the addition of the Tamil characters for the two sounds peculiar to Tamil, *zh* and *ṛ*. When the Tamil script was used, often the direct Sanskrit quotations were completely written in *grantha* characters. The unique feature of Tamil *Maṇipravāḷa* is that the syntactical structure of the Tamil sentence is always preserved intact with its nominal and verbal terminations and post-positional particles and Sanskrit words, phrasals, however long, contained in lexical slots.

Unlike the Tamil *Maṇipravāḷa* sentence retaining the purely Tamil structure, Telugu and Malayalam use Sanskrit words with Sanskrit endings converting their sentence patterns into those of the language of cultural borrowings. The fact, that *Maṇipravāḷa* literature had a vogue in all the four south Indian languages in the medieval period, deserves to be recalled here. Defined as *bhāṣasaṁskr̥tayoryogam,* it served at that period as the medium of religious and other discourses.

I would like to conclude by saying that it is the need of the hour for all of us to direct all our efforts to do research in a direction where we can compare and contrast the contributions of the different authors in different languages. This would not only enrich the vast body of literature but also help us to appreciate the other cultures equally.

Contributors

Balasubramanian, R. (Ph.D and D.Litt, Madras University), was Professor and Head, Sri Aurobindo School of Eastern and Western Thought, and Chairman, Indian Council of Philosophical Research (ICPR), New Delhi. A specialist in Advaita, Phenomenology and Existentialism, he has a number of books and articles to his credit and has lectured in several universities in and outside India. He taught in Besant Theosophical College, Vivekananda College, and Annamalai University before joining the faculty of Radhakrishnan Institute for Advanced Study in Philosophy, University of Madras of which he was the Director for a number of years. He spent a year at Stanford University as a Fulbright and Smith-Mundt scholar for his post-doctoral studies. Some of his publications include *Personalistic Existentialism of Berdyaev* (1970); *The Taittirīyopaniṣad-bhāṣya-vārttika of Sureśvara* (1974, 1984); *Advaita Vedānta* (1976); *Some Problems in the Epistemology and Metaphysics of Rāmānuja* (1976); *A Study of the Brahmasiddhi of Maṇḍanamiśra* (1983); *Naiṣkarmyasiddhi of Sureśvara* (1988); and *Śivajñāna-saṁgrahabhāṣya of Śivāgrayogin* (Sanskrit, co-editor) (1992). address: old no. 5, New no. 16, Bhagirathi Street, Srinivasa Avenue, Chennai - 600 028, Tamil Nadu [*e-mail:* <balurajangam@gmail.com>].

Bilimoria, Purushottama, has taught and has had professorships and research fellowships at University of Melbourne (Australia), Oxford University, Harvard University, and Columbia University. His research areas of interest include South Asian Diaspora studies, comparative philosophy, philosophy of religion, ethics and law, and folk psychology. He is one of the Editors-in-Chief of *Sophia, International Journal in Philosophy and Traditions,* published by Springer. His work on Gandhi and African American Civil Rights began at Emory University and the King Center for Public Knowledge Program in

Atlanta, and he continues that today as a visiting professor/lecturer at UC Berkeley where he teaches in the Religious Studies and African American Studies departments. He is also an interdisciplinary visiting scholar with The Institute of International Studies and The South Asia Studies Collective at UC Berkeley. [*address*: Prof. Purushottama Bilimoria, Religious Studies Program, 4615, 239 Evans Hall No. 2922, University of Califorinia at Berkeley, BERKELEY, CA 94720 2923 (USA), *e-mail*: <p.bilimoria@unimelb.edu.au>].

Byrski, Maria Krzysztof, was born in Wilno (now Lithuania) in 1937. In 1955 he took up Indian studies. After completing them in 1960 he left for India to join the Banaras Hindu University. In 1966 he was awarded Ph.D in Ancient Indian History, Culture and Archaeology for a thesis entitled "Concept of Ancient Indian Theatre". Subsequently, he joined the Institute of Oriental Studies, Warsaw University to teach the Sanskrit literature and the Hindi language. In 1978 he was awarded the degree of doctor habilitatus (D.Litt) for the thesis entitled "Methodology of the Analysis of Sanskrit Drama". In 1993 he became the very first ambassador of sovereign Republic of Poland to India. In 1996 after the election of new President of Poland he relinquished his diplomatic post and rejoined the University, where he was elected director of the Institute of Oriental Studies. He was occupying this post for two continuous terms until 2002. Besides he was elected a member of the University Senate. Currently after his retirement, he is teaching at Collegium Civitas, Warsaw and also continues to teach Sanskrit at the Oriental Faculty of Warsaw University. He has to his credit over 100 publications in Polish, English and some in Hindi. He has been awarded several prestigious prizes in India, by different organizations and by the President and the Prime Minister of India [*address*: Smolna Street 8, Apt. 58, 00-375, WARSZAWA (Poland), *e-mail*: <m.k.byrski@uw.edu.pl>].

Chakrabarti, Kisor, is the Former Distinguished Professor of Philosophy and Religious Studies of Davis and Elkins College, Bethany College, Ferrum College, etc. Also he taught at University of Calcutta and University of California at Berkeley, and held Fellowships at Australian National University, Institute for Advanced Study, Princeton, etc. He has written seventy-eight papers and authored seven books including *Classical Indian Philosophy of Induction* (2010) and *Classical Indian Philosophy of Mind* (1999) [*address*: 1210 Jamestown Drive, ELON, NC 27244 (USA), *e-mail*: <kisorchak@gmail.com>].

Chandra, Lokesh, is presently the Director, International Academy of Indian Culture and a renowned scholar of Tibetan, Mongolian and Sino-Japanese Buddhism. He has to his credit over 400 works and text editions. Among them are classics like his *Tibetan-Sanskrit Dictionary, Materials for a History of Tibetan Literature; Buddhist Iconography of Tibet;* and the present *Dictionary of Buddhist Iconography* in 15 volumes. Dr Chandra was twice nominated by the President of India to the Rajya Sabha in 1974-80 and 1980-86. He had been the Vice-President of the Indian Council for Cultural Relations (ICCR) and Chairman of the Indian Council of Historical Research (ICHR) [*address*: J-22, Hauz Khas Enclave, NEW DELHI - 110 016, *e-mail*: <lokeshchandra 2011@gmail.com>].

Deshpande, Madhav M., was originally trained in Sanskrit studies in Pune, where he did his BA (1966) and MA (1968) in Sanskrit from the University of Pune. In 1972, he earned his Ph.D in Oriental Studies from the University of Pennsylvania, Philadelphia. In the same year he was appointed Professor of Sanskrit and Linguistics at the University of Michigan, Ann Arbor, Michigan, USA, where he continues to teach Sanskrit, Hinduism, and Buddhism, till date. His numerous research books and articles cover the areas of Sanskrit grammar, Indo-Aryan linguistics, and Indian religions and philosophies [*address*: Department of Asian Languages and Cultures, Suite 6111, Thayer Building , 202 South Thayer Street, The University of Michigan, ANN ARBOR, Michigan 48104-1508 (USA), *e-mail*: <mmdesh@umich.edu>].

Hirano, Katsunori, is a Part-time Lecturer at Aichi Gakuin University, Doho University, Gifu University, and Nagoya University, Japan. He did his Ph.D at Nagoya University in 2001. During 2007-12, he was an Assistant Professor at Nagoya University. In 2012, he published *Nyāya-Vaiśeṣika Philosophy and Text Science*. His papers have also appeared in *Nyāya-Vasiṣṭha: Felicitation Volume of Prof. V.N. Jha* (2006) and *Saṁskr̥ta-sādhutā: Studies in Honour of Professor Ashok N. Aklujkar* (2012) [*address*: 4-150-11 Ono-cho, Kasugai-shi,

AICHI, 486-0926 (Japan), *e-mail*: <katsunorih@hotmail.com>].

Kak, Subhash, is Regents Professor of Computer Science at Oklahoma State University in Stillwater. His research includes archaeo-astronomy and history of science and art. He has made the surprising discovery that the ancient Indians knew that the sun and the moon are approximately 108 times their respective diameters from the earth. This knowledge was coded into temple architecture, in the 108 poses of Indian classical dance, and the 108 prayer beads of the *japamālā* [*address*: 2605 W. Summerlin Ct., STILLWATER, OK 74074 (USA), *e-mail*: <subhashkak@gmail.com>].

Peralta, Miquel, is the founder and current director of the Devavāṇī: Center for Sanskirt Studies, located in Barcelona, a pioneer in its field in Spain. In 2008 he won the first Saraswati Award for essays written in Sanskrit, granted by ICCR. The prize-winning essay was subsequently published in the volume *Sanskrit Works of European Scholars*, edited by Satya Vrat Shastri. Miquel Peralta's current work centres on the aesthetic, hermeneutical, and soteriological implications of the oral paradigm in the Sanskrit tradition [*address*: Mariné 34-36 2-1, 08172 Sant Cugat, BARCELONA (Spain), *e-mail*: <miquelperalta@devavani.org>].

Phillips, Stephen, is Professor of Philosophy and Asian Studies at the University of Texas at Austin and has been Visiting Professor of Philosophy at the University of Hawaii, Manoa, and at Jadavpur University, Kolkata. He received his Ph.D from Harvard University after having attended Harvard College and for two years the Sri Aurobindo International Centre for Education in Pondicherry. He is the author of seven books, including (with N.S. Ramanuja Tatacharya) a 750-page translation of the perception chapter of Gaṅgeśa's "Tattvacintāmaṇi", entitled *Epistemology of Perception*, an overview of Yoga philosophy and defence of Yoga psychology and philosophy; *Yoga, Karma, and Rebirth: A Brief History and Philosophy*, which was named by *Choice* magazine an "Outstanding Academic Title" for 2010; and most recently, *Epistemology in Classical India: The Knowledge Sources of the Nyaya School*. He is also editor or co-editor of several anthologies and has published more than fifty papers, including many first-time translations of late classical

Sanskrit philosophic texts. Prof. Phillips teaches regularly an upper-division philosophy course on Yoga psychology and philosophies as well as upper-division and graduate-level courses on classical Indian philosophies [*address*: Department of Philosophy, University of Texas at Austin, 2210 Speedway, Stop C3500, AUSTIN, TX 78712-1737 (USA), *e-mail*: <phillips@mail.utexas.edu>].

Rajendran, C., former Professor of Sanskrit at University of Calicut, is a scholar of international repute. He has done work in Aesthetics, Theatre, Philosophy, Linguistics, Comparative Literature, Chess History, and Ancient Indian Management. His thesis, "A Study of Mahimabhatta's Vyaktiviveka" was acknowledged as a significant contribution to the studies in Sanskrit poetics. His other noted contributions include *Studies in Comparative Poetics; The Traditional Sanskrit Theatre of Kerala; Sign and Structure: Indological Essays; Abhinayadarpaṇa; Melputtur Narayana Bhatta; Kuntaka*, and *Understanding Tradition*. The prestigious works edited by him include *The Living Traditions of Nāṭyaśāstra; Contemporary Approaches to Indian Philosophy; Aspects of Pāṇinian Semantics; Current Readings in Arthaśāstra;* and *Narratology: Indian Perspectives*. He has also to his credit several books related to Indology in Malayalam. He has published about 200 learned articles in various national/ international journals. He is the recipient of Ramakrishna Sanskrit Award for outstanding contributions in Teaching and Research, instituted by Canadian World Education Foundation. He is the recipient of Kerala Sahitya Akademi G.N. Pillai Endowment Award, Professor M.S. Menon Endowment Award, Keralapanini Award, and I.C. Chacko Endowment Award. He has delivered lectures in various universities in Berlin, Helsinki, Milan, Cambridge, Leipzig, Cagliari, and Warsaw, and worked as visiting professor at Ecole des Hautes Etudes en Sciences Sociales (EHESS), Paris and Jageillonian University, Krakow, Poland. He is serving as a member of the editorial committee of *Pandanus*, an Indological journal published from Charles University, Prague. He was Dean, Faculty of Languages, University of Calicut and has also served as a member of the Advisory Board for Sanskrit and Malayalam of Sahitya Akademi, New Delhi [*address*: 28/1097, 'Rajadhani', T.P. Kumaran

Nair Road, Chevayur, CALICUT - 673 635, Kerala, *e-mail*: <crajenin@yahoo.com>].

Revathy, S., MA, M.Phil, Ph.D, Śiromaṇi (Vedānta), Madras University is presently Professor, Department of Sanskrit, University of Madras. She was awarded Ph.D degree of the University of Madras for her book *Three Little Known Advaitins* (*Anubhūtisvarūpācārya, Advaita-vidyācārya, Kavitārkika Cakravartī Nṛsiṁhabhaṭṭopādhyāya*). A specialist in Advaita and Navya-Nyāya, she has a number of research articles, three books and a monograph to her credit. She has critically edited *Upadeśa-sāharī* with Rāmatīrtha's commentary and *Śrīmadbhagavadgītā* with the commentary, and *Padayojanā* by Rāmacandrendra Sarasvati. She received "Ramakrishna Sanskrit Award" for her contribution to Sanskrit teaching and research in India from Sarasvati Visvas, Canada in the year 2002. She is also the recipient of "Academic Achivement Award 2002" from the University of Madras [*address*: Department of Sanskrit, University of Madras, Marina Campus, CHENNAI - 600 005], *e-mail*: <drsrevathy@gmail.com>].

Tripathi, Radhavallabh, has specialized in Nāṭyaśāstra and Sāhityaśāstra. His publications in these areas include *Nāṭyaśāstraviśvakośa* (an Encyclopaedic Dictionary of Nāṭyaśāstra); *Nāṭyalalitakalāsaṁgraha* (an Anthology of Texts on Performing and Plastic Arts); *Lectures on Nāṭyaśāstra*: *Aspects of Naṭyaśāstra*; *Bhāratīya Sāhityaśāstra kī Ācāryaparamparā*; and *Nayā Sahityaśāstra* [*address*: M-83, IInd Floor, South City I, GURGAON - 122 001 (Haryana), *e-mail*: <radhavallabh2002@gmail.com>].

Vaidya, Uma, Vice-Chancellor, Kavikulguru Kalidas Sanskrit University, Ramtek, Nagpur, is MA, Ph.D in Sanskrit from University of Bombay and an expert in Pāli. Formerly, she was R.G. Professor and head of the Department of Sanskrit, University of Bombay, and head, GTCCL, University of Mumbai. On the post-doctoral research front, she has done five projects so far. Under her guidance, five students have been awarded their Ph.D and two are pursuing their research. She has written or edited six books and has written eighty research articles for journals of international repute. She is a recipient of many awards, among them are Pradnyavanta Puraskara: Sesquicentennial Best Performance Incentive Award; Rashtriya Gaurava Award; Ideal Teacher Award of Government of Maharashtra; Rashtriya Prabhodan Puraskar; Kalidas Sanskrit Sadhana Puraskar; Sanskrit Seva Samman; and Shaitya Saraswati. She is a visiting professor to many universities in Australia, Italy, Japan, Mauritius, and the US. Dr Vaidya's contributions in the academic front are manifold. She wrote entries for a Sahitya Akademi project, was a catalyst in preparing syllabus of Sanskrit in Chinese universities, and worked on thirty-eight administrative committees of various universities [*address:* Vice-Chancellor, Kavikulguru Kalidas Sanskrit University, Prashaskiya Bhavan, Mouda Road, RAMTEK - 441 106, Dist. Nagpur, Maharashtra, *e-mail*: <umacvaidya@yahoo.co.in>].

Wada, Toshihiro, is Professor of Indian Studies at Nagoya University. He obtained his Ph.D from the University of Pune in 1988 and D.Litt from Nagoya University in 2002. He published three books: *Invariable Concomitance in Navya-Nyāya; The Analytical Method of Navya-Nyāya*; and *A Navya-Nyāya Discussion on the Meaning of the Negative Particle NaÑ* (co-authored). In addition, he has published thirty-eight papers in reputed international journals and twenty-two papers in Japanese journals [*address*: Head, Department of Indian Studies, Graduate School of Letters, Nagoya University, Furo-cho, Chikusa-ku, NAGOYA 464-8601 (Japan), *e-mail*: <twada@lit.nagoya-u.ac.jp>].

Index